IMAGES
of America

EDGAR ALLAN POE IN RICHMOND

ON THE COVER: On April 26, 1922, the founders of the Poe Museum pose in front of the recently constructed shrine made from bricks and granite salvaged from the *Southern Literary Messenger* building. It was at the *Southern Literary Messenger* that Poe began his career in journalism and first achieved literary fame. The tall gentleman to the left is probably Granville Valentine, the Richmond preservationist responsible for saving the Poe Museum's Old Stone House from destruction. Seventy-three years earlier, his brother Edward Valentine had met Edgar Allan Poe on the poet's last visit to Richmond. (Courtesy of the Poe Museum.)

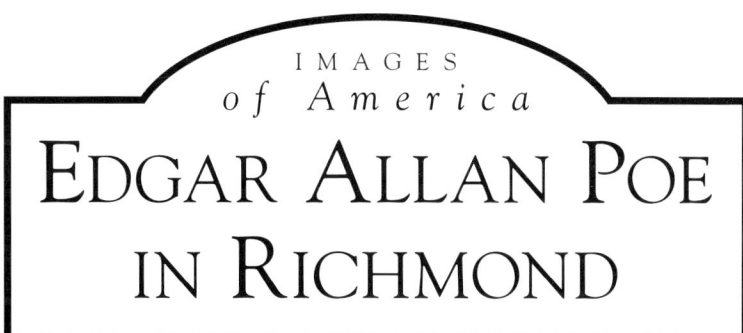

IMAGES
of America

EDGAR ALLAN POE
IN RICHMOND

Keshia A. Case and
Christopher P. Semtner on
behalf of the Poe Museum

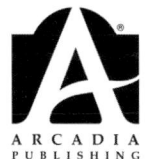

ARCADIA
PUBLISHING

ISBN 978-0-7385-6714-3

Published by Arcadia Publishing
Charleston SC, Chicago IL, Portsmouth NH, San Francisco CA

Printed in the United States of America

Library of Congress Catalog Card Number: 2008933053

For all general information contact Arcadia Publishing at:
Telephone 843-853-2070
Fax 843-853-0044
E-mail sales@arcadiapublishing.com
For customer service and orders:
Toll-Free 1-888-313-2665

Visit us on the Internet at www.arcadiapublishing.com

Keshia Case would like to dedicate this book to John, Alex, and Ben Case. Christopher Semtner would like to dedicate this book to Jessie Yeager.

CONTENTS

ACKNOWLEDGMENTS

The authors are honored to have the opportunity to share with the public many previously unpublished images that may otherwise have never been seen. For any fan of Poe's work, there is simply no substitute for seeing these images, which help bring Poe's story to life.

This book would not have been possible without the assistance of the Edgar Allan Poe Museum, which provided access to the images as well as to its reference library. For over 86 years, Richmond's Edgar Allan Poe Museum has collected the artifacts and memorabilia that document the world of "America's Shakespeare." Unless otherwise noted, all images in this book appear courtesy of the Edgar Allan Poe Museum. The authors are especially grateful for the Poe scholars who have uncovered the details of Poe's life and work. Arthur Hobson Quinn's landmark study of Poe's life remains unsurpassed. Agnes Bondurant's thesis, *Poe's Richmond*, was an especially valuable source of information. The works of Richmond historians Samuel Mordecai, Virginius Dabney, and Mary Wingfield Scott have also been important resources.

Keshia Case would like to thank Dr. Charles Brownell, Katarina Spears, Chris Semtner, and Linda Harris. Christopher Semtner would like thank Katelyn Kelly and the Historic Richmond Foundation for allowing him access to the Elmira Shelton House and Monumental Church. The authors would like to thank their Arcadia editor, Brooksi Hudson.

INTRODUCTION

Edgar Allan Poe (January 19, 1809–October 7, 1849) shaped world literature by exploring the darkest recesses of the human mind in his fiction and poetry. The forces that shaped his own life and inspired his imagination can be traced to the many years he spent in Richmond, Virginia. First arriving in the city when he was only a year old, Poe maintained a lifelong association with the city. Over the course of his 40-year life, he spent 13 years in Richmond—longer than he lived in any other city. Poe grew up, fell in love, married, wrote his first poems, and began his literary career in Richmond. Even when he moved to New York and Philadelphia, Poe boasted of his Richmond roots and challenged the Northern literary establishment. This is why he famously wrote in an 1841 letter, "I am a Virginian—at least I call myself one, for I have resided all my life, until within the last few years, in Richmond."

The earliest memories of Poe's hometown were overshadowed by the tragedy that would later influence his melancholy verse. By the time Poe was two years old, his father had abandoned him, his brother, William Henry, and his sister, Rosalie. Their actress mother, Elizabeth Arnold Poe, died of tuberculosis on December 8, 1811. A few weeks after her death, the theater in which she had last performed burned, claiming the lives of 72 prominent Richmond citizens. Owing both to the fire and to a preexisting prejudice against the acting profession, theatrical performances were temporarily banned in the city, and Poe grew up being looked down upon in some circles for having been the son of an actress.

He was raised in the home of tobacco merchant John Allan and his wife, Francis Keeling Valentine Allan, who gave Poe his middle name. The young boy was never entirely accepted by his new family, and he was often reminded by John Allan that he only lived in their house out of charity. For the rest of his life, Poe would carry with him the manners and prejudices he learned growing up in the home of a Southern gentleman. The mansions like Moldavia in which he lived as a child would provide him the vivid descriptions of grand manor houses in such works as "The Fall of the House of Usher."

Richmond's population in the early 19th century was roughly 10,000 people. About half of the population was white, and about the same number was African American, the majority of whom were enslaved. As was common among wealthy Southerners of Poe's time, his foster parents owned slaves, and as a child, Poe is said to have enjoyed listening to them tell ghost stories. Richmond was a center of the domestic slave trade. In fact, one of Poe's boyhood homes was located only a few blocks from the notorious slave market Lumpkin's Jail, known as the "Devil's Half Acre." As an adult, Poe was too poor to own slaves, but they do appear as characters in his tales "The Gold Bug" and "The Predicament."

The author's earliest poems were written to Richmond schoolgirls. His first "purely ideal love" was the mother of one of his classmates, Robert Stanard. To Jane Stanard, he dedicated his haunting poem "To Helen." Once again, tragedy struck when she died young. Poe soon fell in love again, this time to Elmira Royster, whose father vehemently opposed the match. After a secret engagement, Poe left Richmond to attend the University of Virginia. While at school, Elmira's father intercepted Poe's letters to her in order to convince Elmira that she had been forgotten. Returning home after his first term, Poe discovered that Elmira was engaged to another man. Meanwhile, Allan, who refused to pay the many debts Poe had accumulated at the university, put Poe to work in his warehouse. After one of many heated arguments with Allan, Poe stormed out of the Allan home in a quixotic quest to become a famous poet.

Poe's journey brought him to Boston in 1827, where he published his first book, *Tamerlane and Other Poems*. At this time, he also enlisted in the U.S. Army and was stationed in Boston and Charleston before returning to Virginia, where he served as an artificer at Fortress Monroe. While at Fortress Monroe, he learned of his foster mother's illness. Frances Allan was dying from tuberculosis and had requested Edgar see her one last time before her death. He reached Richmond the night after her funeral. United in their grief, Poe and John Allan briefly reconciled. Allan agreed to aid Poe in attaining an appointment to the U.S. Military Academy at West Point, where Poe stayed for about eight months before being expelled.

Always stormy, their relationship never recovered after Poe's expulsion from the academy. Poe did, however, make one last attempt at reconciliation. Shortly before Allan's death, Poe visited the Allan home only to be told by Allan to leave and never come back.

After John Allan's death, Poe returned to Richmond in 1835 to accept an editorial position at the *Southern Literary Messenger*. Within months, the circulation had increased by seven times, and the journal was attracting national attention. At this time, Poe turned from poetry to journalism. Although he continued to spark controversy with his gruesome tales, it was his scathing literary reviews and inventive magazine articles that finally brought him fame.

During Poe's tenure at the *Messenger*, he brought his widowed aunt Maria Poe Clemm and her daughter, Virginia, from Baltimore to Richmond. The three lived in a small boardinghouse overlooking the Virginia State Capitol. In the parlor of the boardinghouse, Poe and Virginia were married on May 16, 1836. The groom was 27, and his bride was 13. After 17 months with the *Messenger*, Poe had helped make it one of the leading journals in the South, but his salary remained only $15 a week. He received an additional income of $300 a year selling his stories to the magazine, but this was not enough to provide a comfortable lifestyle for his new bride and mother-in-law. As he would throughout his life, Poe borrowed money, spending $200 on furniture and asking for $100 more to help pay off the first debt, but in many cases, he would never be able to repay these debts. Years later, when he filed for bankruptcy, Poe still owed his Richmond friend Robert Stanard $200, which was approximately what Poe would have paid for two years' rent for a modest home.

In the face of growing debts and increasing conflicts with his employer, Poe finally left the *Messenger* in January 1837. He hoped to find more lucrative employment in the significantly larger city of New York. While Richmond's population had only grown to about 15,000, New York City was home to approximately 500,000 and was becoming the center of the American publishing industry. Just as Poe moved north, the American economy was devastated by the crisis known as the Panic of 1837. At that time, many magazines closed, and Poe moved from New York to Philadelphia after one year. Between magazine jobs, he attempted to become the first American author to support himself entirely from his writing. This was especially difficult in Poe's time, because the lack of effective copyright laws meant that he was not always paid for his published works. Compounding the matter, publishers were unwilling to pay well for writing, which could easily be reprinted for free from other magazines. In the years to come, Poe's works were printed throughout the United States and Europe without him receiving compensation.

When Poe returned to Richmond in July 1848, he was the internationally famous author of "The Raven." His tale "The Gold Bug" had been reprinted so often that Poe estimated its circulation at 100,000. The story had also been adapted into a stage play. In spite of Poe's popularity, he was broke and alone. His wife, Virginia, had died the previous year, and he had received only $14 for his last book, *Eureka*. In hopes of earning more money to support his mother-in-law, Poe delivered lectures, one of which attracted an audience of 1,800. In Richmond, he also intended to sell subscriptions to *The Stylus*, a literary magazine he hoped to publish under his sole editorial control. While in the city, Poe became acquainted with John R. Thompson, the new editor of the *Southern Literary Messenger*, who agreed to pay Poe to provide some articles for the journal. Poe also visited the offices of the *Semi-Weekly Examiner* and challenged the editor, John Moncure Daniels, to a duel. Daniels offered to have a drink with Poe instead, and the two men became friends. By September, Poe announced his plan to embark on a lecture tour of the South to support *The Stylus*, but he unexpectedly decided to travel north instead to pursue the Rhode Island poetess Sarah Helen Whitman. After rejecting his first proposal to her, she accepted his second, only to break off their engagement after one month.

Poe returned to Richmond for the final time in July 1849. His plans for starting *The Stylus* had been revitalized when the Illinois publisher Edward H. N. Patterson offered to place Poe in control of a new national literary magazine. As he had the previous summer, Poe intended to sell subscriptions during a lecture tour of the Southern states. His first lecture of the tour was delivered in Richmond's Exchange Hotel on August 17, 1849. The *Semi-Weekly Examiner* reported that the hotel's "concert room was completely filled."

The sculptor Edward Valentine recalled that, as boys in the summer of 1849, he and his brother "rushed out into the street, passed him and stood by the sidewalk as he went by." Valentine continues, "I then stared at him with all the eyes I had." Other children followed Poe down the street, croaking "Nevermore" in imitation of the raven from his most popular poem, and he responded by flapping his arms like a raven.

Poe wrote to his mother-in-law that he "never was received with so much enthusiasm" as he renewed acquaintances with his Richmond friends and family. He spent much of his time with his sister, Rosalie Poe, at the home of her foster family, the Mackenzies. During this visit, Poe proposed to Elmira Shelton, his first fiancée, who had been widowed in 1843. Although she initially laughed at him, she eventually accepted his proposal. At his next Richmond lecture on September 24, Shelton sat directly in front of the stage while Poe read. He concluded the evening with a recitation of "The Raven." This would be Poe's final public reading. Two days later, he would call on Elmira for the last time on the evening of September 26.

He was planning to travel to Philadelphia to edit a volume of poetry and to continue to New York City to bring his mother-in-law Maria Clemm to Richmond. Citing that Poe seemed ill, Shelton urged him not to make the trip. Possibly to find medicine for his illness, Poe left Shelton's house to visit his friend Dr. John Carter. Early the following morning, Poe left Richmond by steamer and disappeared for five days. He was found semi-conscious in a Baltimore public house. On his deathbed, Poe spoke deliriously of his desire to return to Richmond to see his wife, but he had not yet married Elmira Shelton. He died 10 days before the wedding was to have taken place. His latest poem, a mournful ballad of undying love, had been intended for publication with his wedding announcement, but this poem, "Annabel Lee," first appeared in print at the end of the poet's obituary instead. Poe died at Washington College Hospital of unknown causes.

Elmira Shelton learned of his death in the newspaper. She never remarried and seldom granted interviews to Poe's many biographers. Poe's sister and mother-in-law fought over the ownership of Poe's trunk of possessions but were less interested in retaining the rights to Poe's literary estate. Maria Clemm signed over the rights to Poe's works to one of Poe's enemies, Rufus W. Griswold, an editor and anthologist who immediately attacked Poe in print with a defamatory obituary and controversial biography in an effort to destroy Poe's character. In spite of (or because of) Griswold's portrayal of Poe as a madman, Poe's works sold even better after his death. Neither his sister nor his mother-in-law benefited from the sales, and both died in charity homes.

In the century and a half since his death, the City of Richmond alternately embraced and slighted its most famous author. His homes in the city were demolished. An effort to erect a statue of the author was unsuccessful in finding public support after an editorial in the 1906 Richmond *News Leader* stated Poe was unworthy of such a monument. The effort to save the offices of the *Southern Literary Messenger* from demolition also failed. Seventy-two years after Poe's death, in 1922, a small group of his admirers united to build the Poe Shrine in his memory. Among those responsible for establishing the shrine was Edward Valentine, who as a boy had watched Poe walk past him on the street. Also present at the opening was William Stanard, a descendant of Jane Stith Craig Stanard, the woman Poe considered his first "purely ideal love." Now known as the Poe Museum, this shrine to Poe still draws thousands of visitors every year from around the globe. The museum boasts the world's finest collection of Edgar Allan Poe artifacts and memorabilia. Among the museum's holdings are the author's boyhood bed, a lock of his hair, and his vest. A particularly important collection is the photography archive consisting of historic images of Poe as well as the people and places he knew. This book, compiled with the assistance of the Poe Museum, will reveal these rarely seen images in an effort to offer a glimpse into Poe's Richmond and his continuing presence in the city.

One
POE'S EARLY YEARS

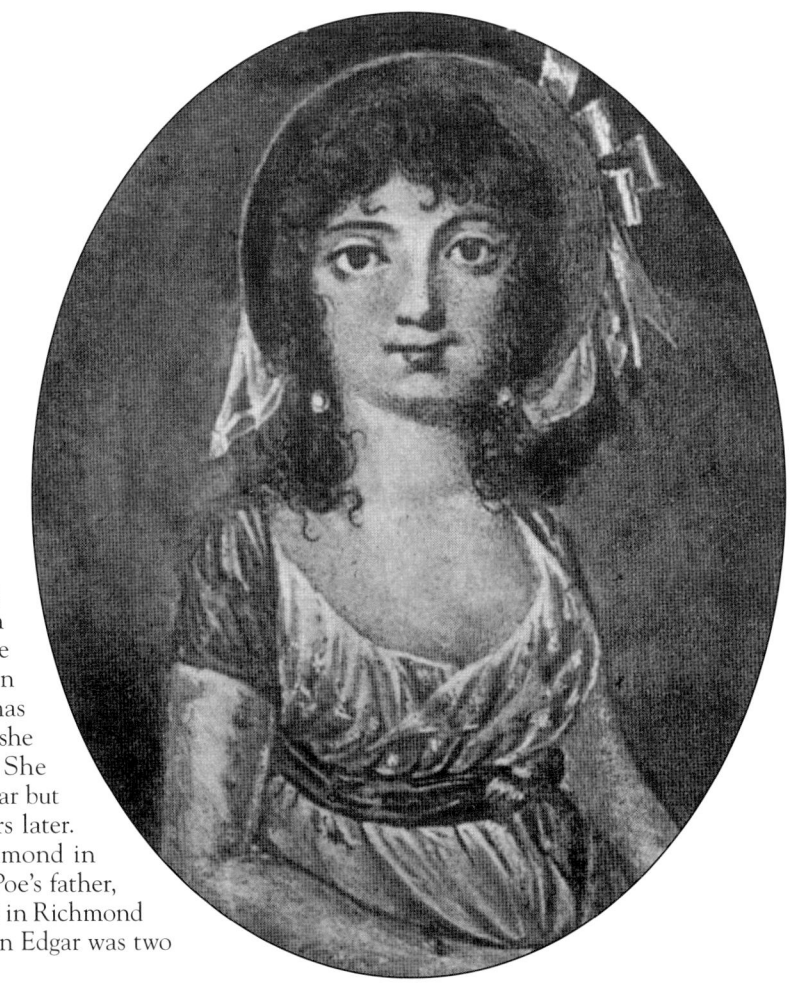

This is a miniature of Edgar Allan Poe's mother, the traveling actress Elizabeth Arnold Poe. The image was painted in Richmond by Thomas Sully in 1802 when she was 15 years old. She was married that year but widowed three years later. On a visit to Richmond in 1806, she married Poe's father, David Poe. She died in Richmond five years later, when Edgar was two years old.

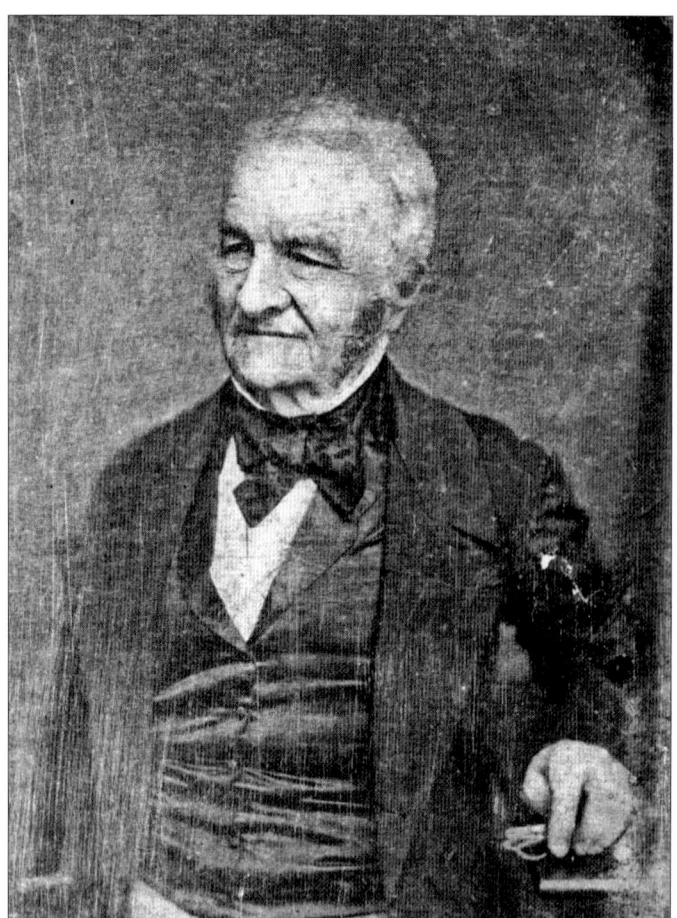

The Richmond historian Samuel Mordecai appears in this daguerreotype taken about 1850. What little is known about the fate of Poe's father David Poe comes from a letter Mordecai wrote to his sister in 1811. In this letter, he mentions that Edgar Poe's parents had quarreled and parted ways. When or where Poe's father died remains unknown.

> ☞ *TO THE HUMANE HEART.*
> On this night, *Mrs. Poe*, lingering on the bed of disease and surrounded by her children, asks your assistance; and *asks it perhaps for the last time.*— The generosity of a Richmond Audience can need no other appeal.
> For particulars, see the Bills of the day.

This brief notice appeared in the *Richmond Inquirer* while Poe's mother, Elizabeth Arnold Poe, lay dying in a boardinghouse, entirely dependent on charity of strangers. Samuel Mordecai noted it was "a singular fashion" for the wealthy ladies of the city to bring Elizabeth meals. Two of these society ladies, Frances Allan and Jane Mackenzie, would take care of Edgar and his sister after their mother's death.

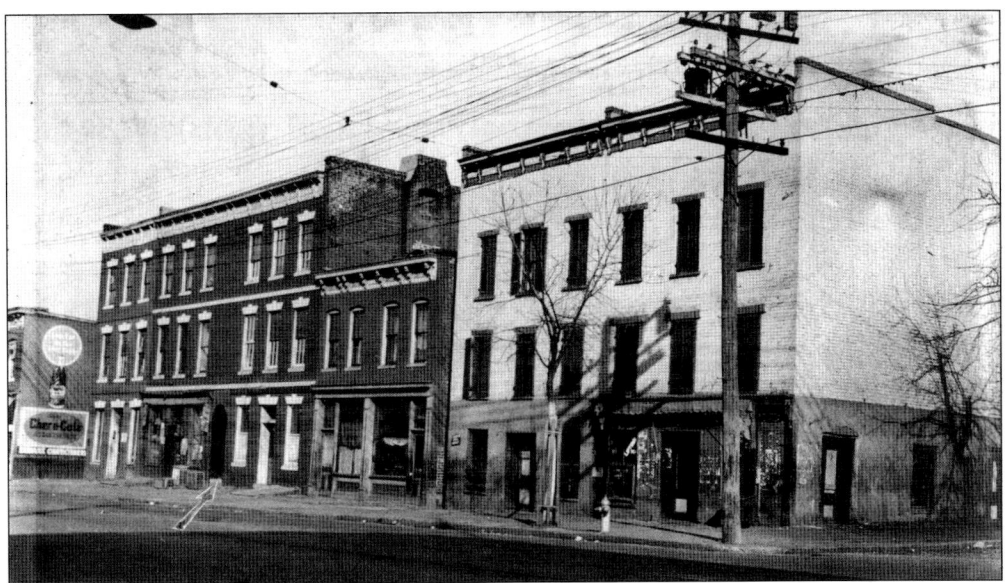

These houses on East Main Street were photographed around 1920 by Poe scholar James Whitty, who was convinced Poe's mother had died in one of them. In 1927, the newly founded Poe Shrine constructed a replica of the structure adjoining its garden. By 1940, Elizabeth Valentine Huntley and Louise F. Catterall proved that the buildings seen here were not standing at the time of Elizabeth Poe's death.

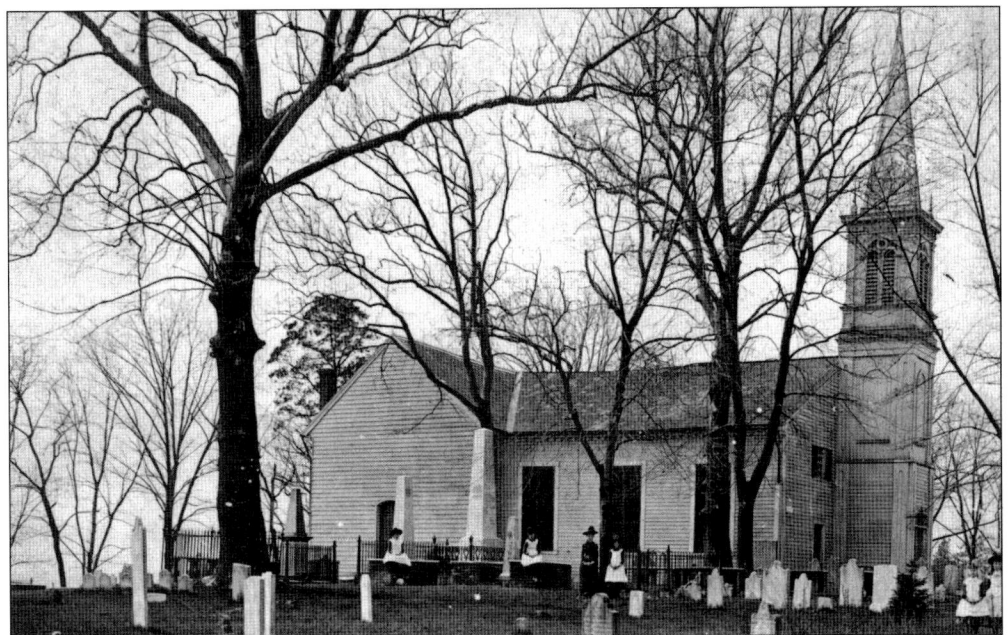

St. John's Church is Richmond's oldest church, built in 1741. Best known as the site of Patrick Henry's 1775 "Liberty or Death" speech, the church is surrounded by the city's oldest burying ground. Although some members of the congregation objected to having an actress buried on hallowed ground, Poe's mother was buried in an unmarked grave along the eastern edge of the courtyard. At the time this 1890 photograph was taken, the location of her burial had long since been forgotten, and the exact location remains a mystery.

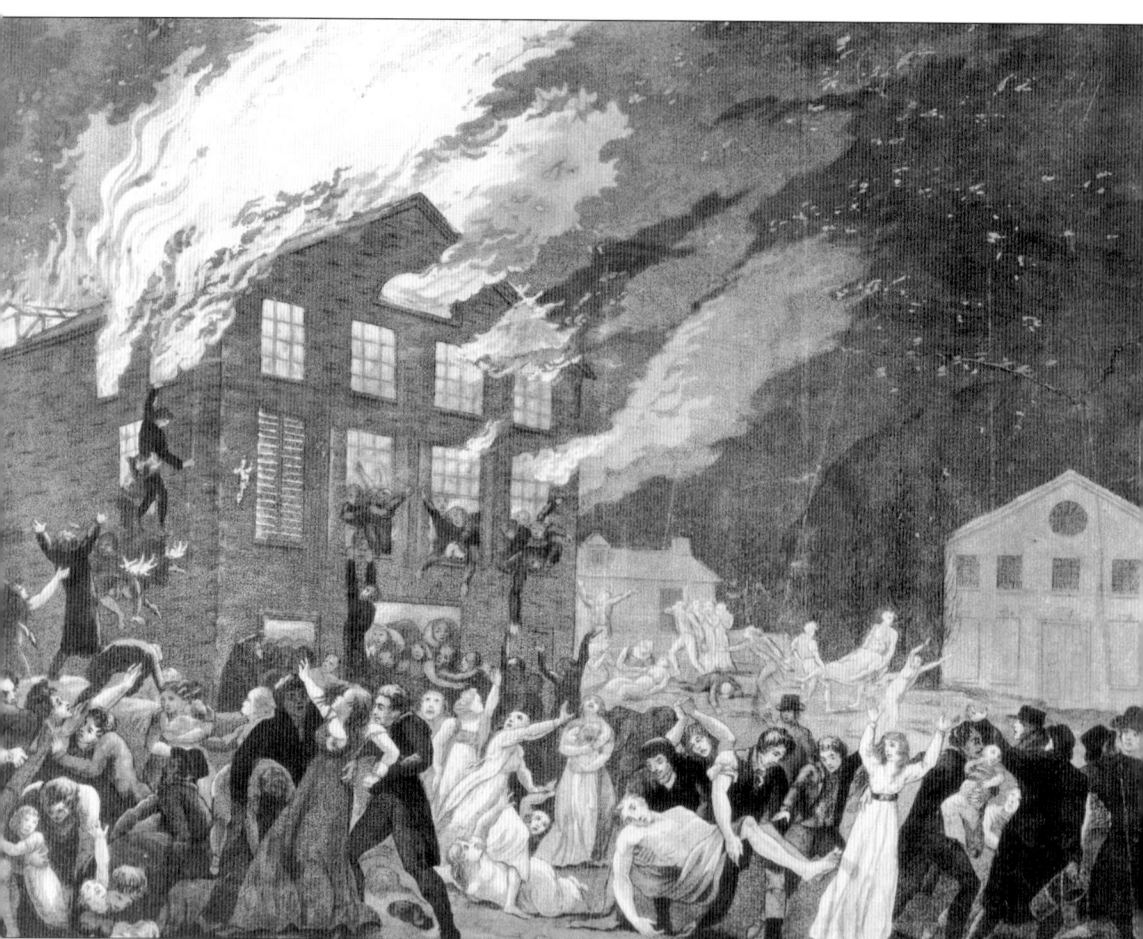

Poe's mother, Elizabeth Arnold Poe, gave her final performance in the Richmond Theatre in October 1811. Elizabeth died on December 8, and on December 26, the theater burned during a well-attended performance of *Raymond and Agnes*. Trapped inside, 72 of Richmond's most prominent citizens perished in the fire. This print produced in Philadelphia shortly after the event is evidence of the national attention the story provoked.

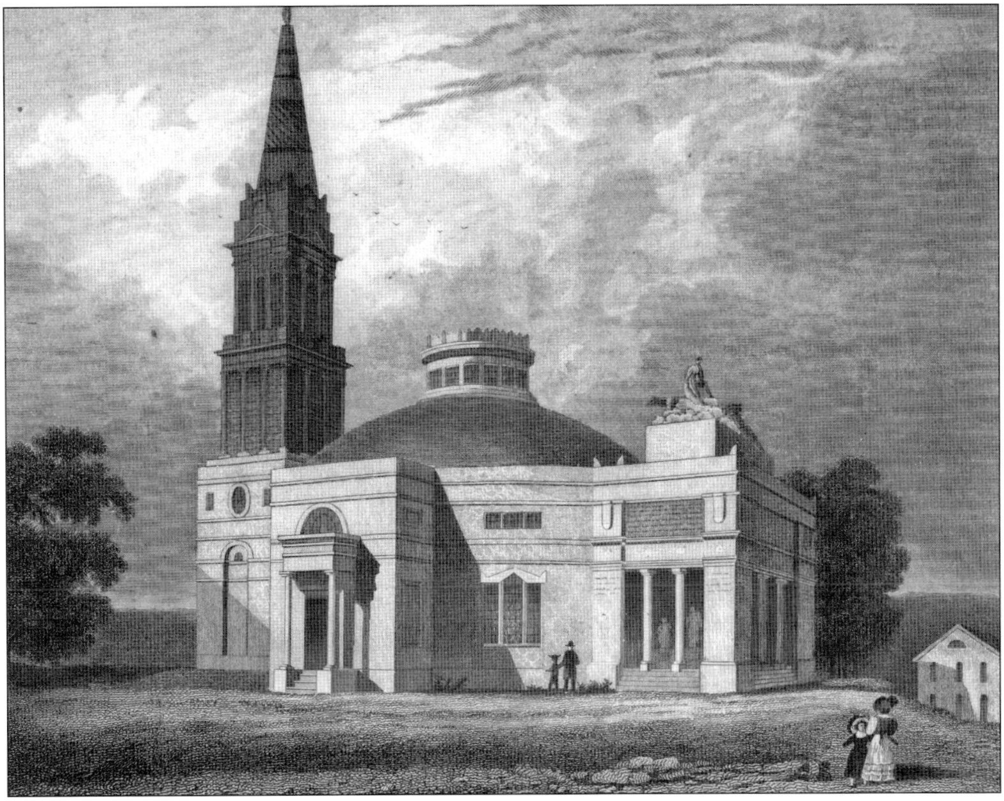

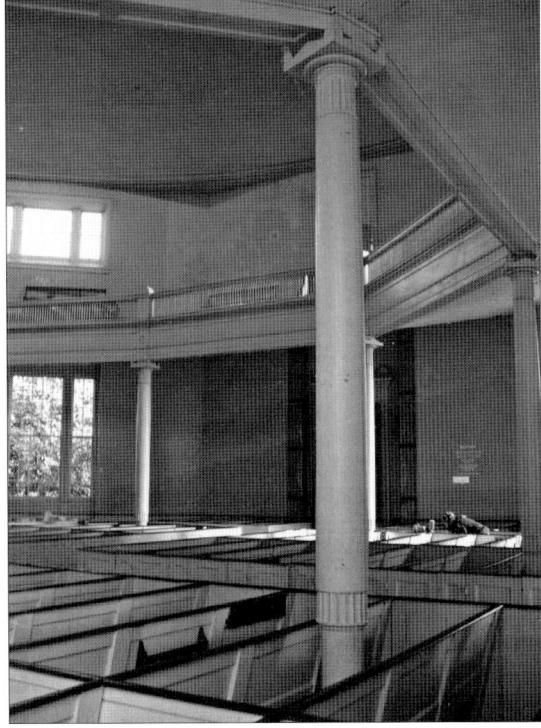

This 1814 print depicts Monumental Church, designed by Robert Mills in 1812. The young Edgar Allan Poe worshipped in this church. The name Monumental Church derives from its construction as a memorial to the victims of the Richmond Theatre fire. The deceased are entombed beneath the church portico. In addition to the Poes' foster parents, several other prominent Richmonders owned pews at the church, including Chief Justice John Marshall.

The designer of Monumental Church, Robert Mills, was an apprentice of Thomas Jefferson. Jefferson's influence can be seen in the octagonal design of the structure. In the 1960s, the church was deconsecrated and fell into disrepair. Recently the Historic Richmond Foundation restored the building and opened the church for tours. Many people visit the church to learn about its history and the building's connections to historical characters like Edgar Allan Poe.

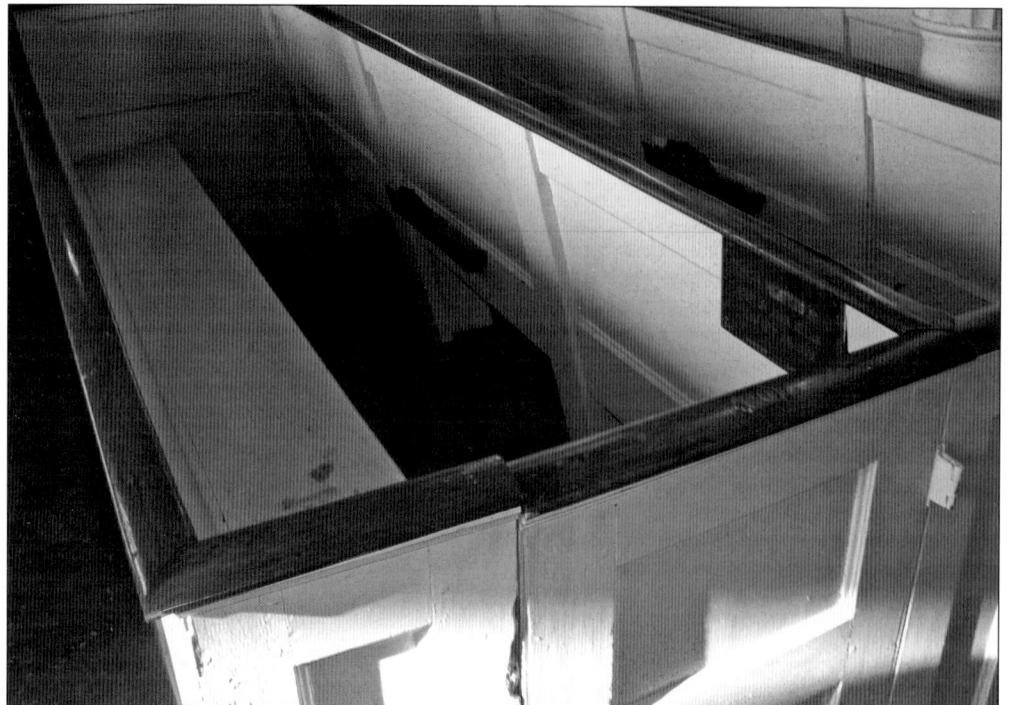

As a child, Poe worshipped in this pew at Monumental Church. The pew belonged to his foster father, John Allan. Poe and his foster mother, Frances Allan, are said to have attended church together every Sunday. However, John Allan was an atheist and did not attend with his family. Mary Brockenbrough, who sat in front of the Allan pew, described the young Poe as "a pretty little boy with big eyes and curly hair."

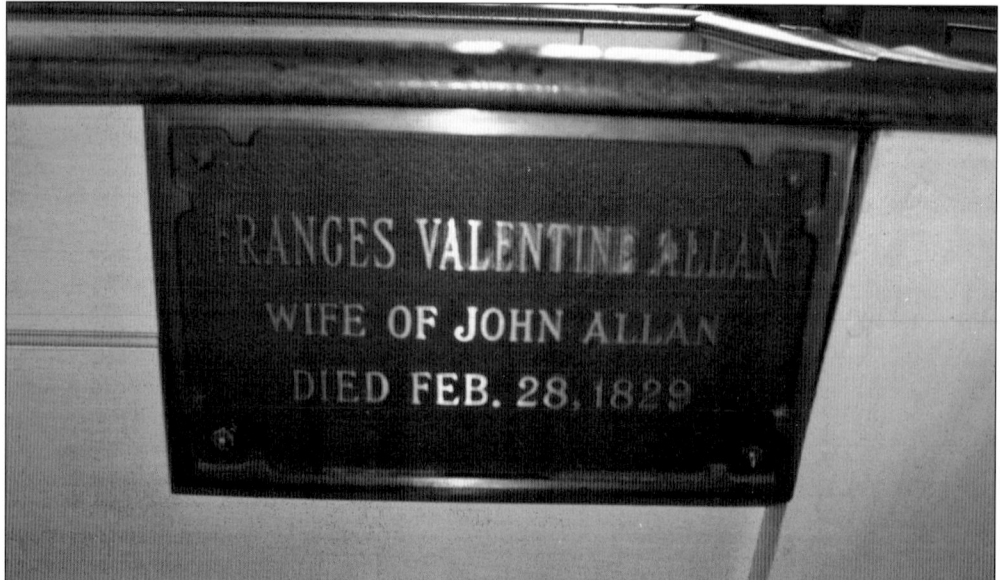

This plaque was placed in the Allan family pew, number 80, at Monumental Church after the death of Poe's foster mother, Frances Valentine Allan, in 1829. When Frances Allan died, Poe was stationed at Fortress Monroe and returned to Richmond the night after her funeral.

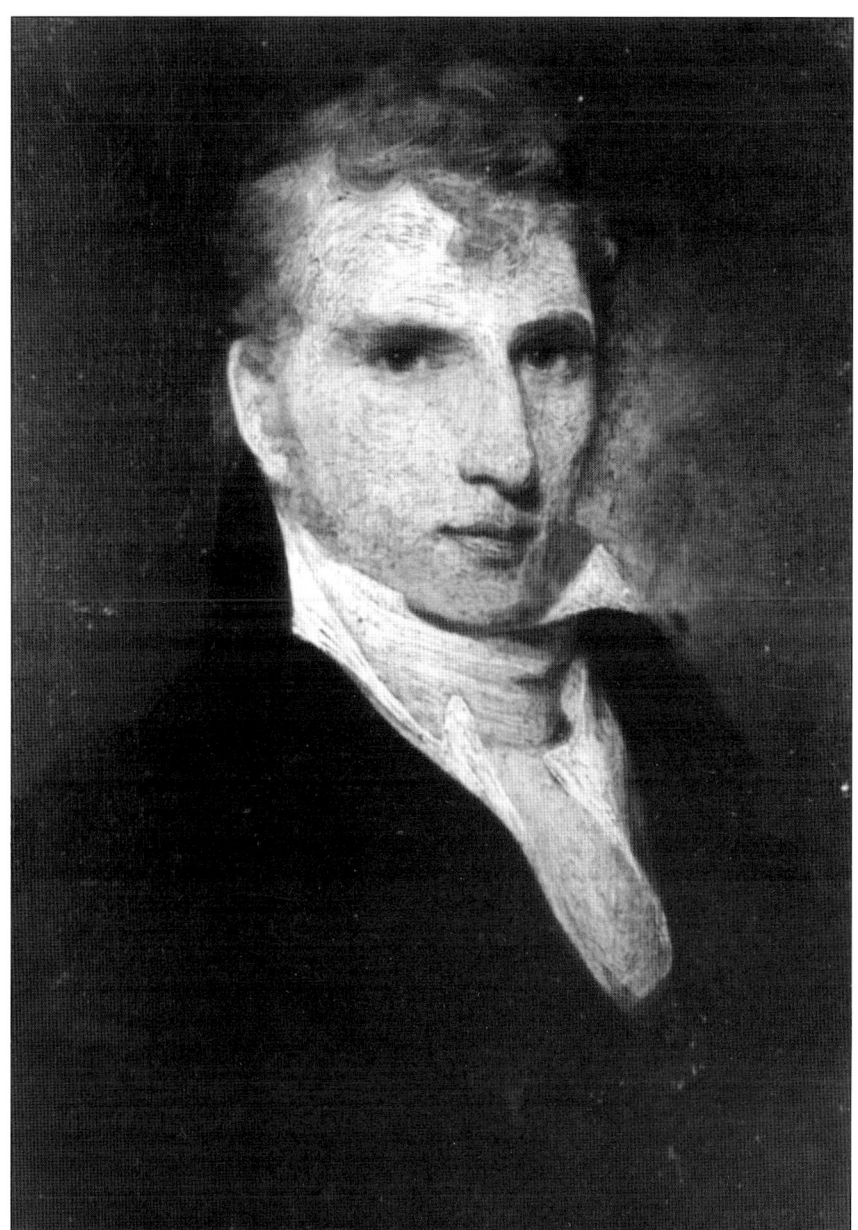

Poe's foster father, John Allan, appears here in a portrait painted around 1804 by Thomas Sully. Although this wealthy Scottish-born tobacco merchant agreed to take the young orphan Edgar Poe into his home, Allan refused to pay for Poe's university education and left Poe out of his will. Allan's will did, however, provide for two illegitimate children Allan admitted he had never seen. One of Poe's Richmond friends, John Hamilton Mackenzie, described John Allan as "a good man in his own way," but "often when angry with Edgar he would threaten to turn him adrift, and [Allan] never allowed him to lose sight of his dependence on his charity." In a letter, Allan once wrote that Poe was "quite miserable, sulky & ill-tempered. . . . How we have acted to produce this is beyond my conception—why I have put up so long with his conduct is little less wonderful. The boy possesses not a spark of affection for us nor a particle of gratitude for all my kindness towards him."

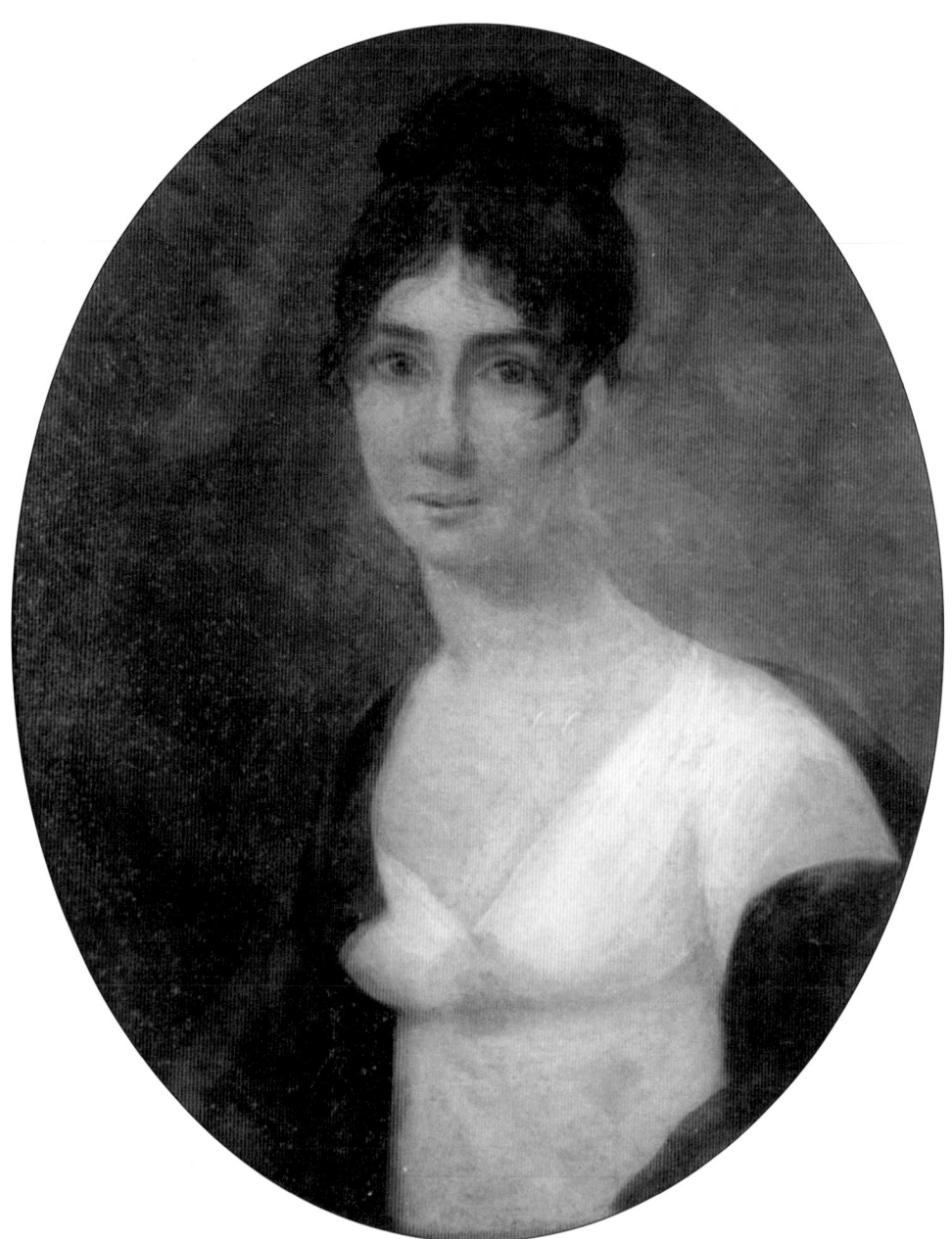

Poe's foster mother, Frances Keeling Valentine Allan, sat for this portrait by Robert Sully around 1828. Allan was among the Richmond society ladies who cared for Poe's mother during her final illness. Unable to have children of her own, Allan welcomed the opportunity to care for the two-year-old Edgar Poe after he was orphaned, but she apparently had some difficulty convincing her husband, who was already paying for an illegitimate son's education, to take in the orphan. Poe was devoted to his foster mother and is said to have been deeply hurt by her husband's extramarital affairs. Often in fragile health, Frances frequently complained of illness and took retreats to natural springs in hopes of improving her condition. In 1829, tuberculosis claimed Frances just as it had Poe's mother years earlier. The portrait was donated to the Poe Museum by one of Allan's relatives, Edward Valentine, the director of the Valentine Museum.

Edgar Poe's younger sister, Rosalie Poe, was taken into the home of William and Jane Scott Mackenzie, who appears in this 1850 portrait by Robert Sully. Jane Mackenzie's sister-in-law operated a girls' school, which Rosalie attended. Rosalie was never legally adopted by the Mackenzies. She took on their last name as her middle name and continued to live with Jane Mackenzie from 1811 until Mackenzie's death in 1865.

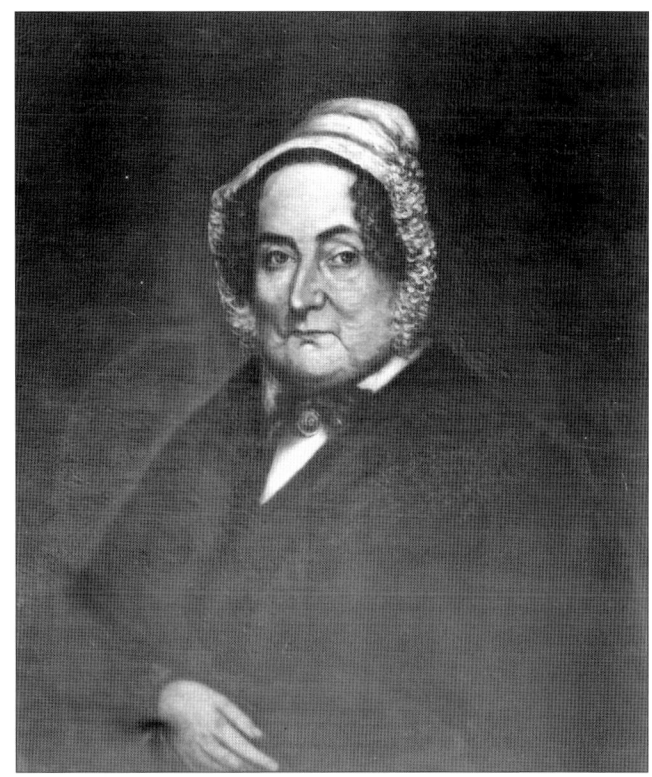

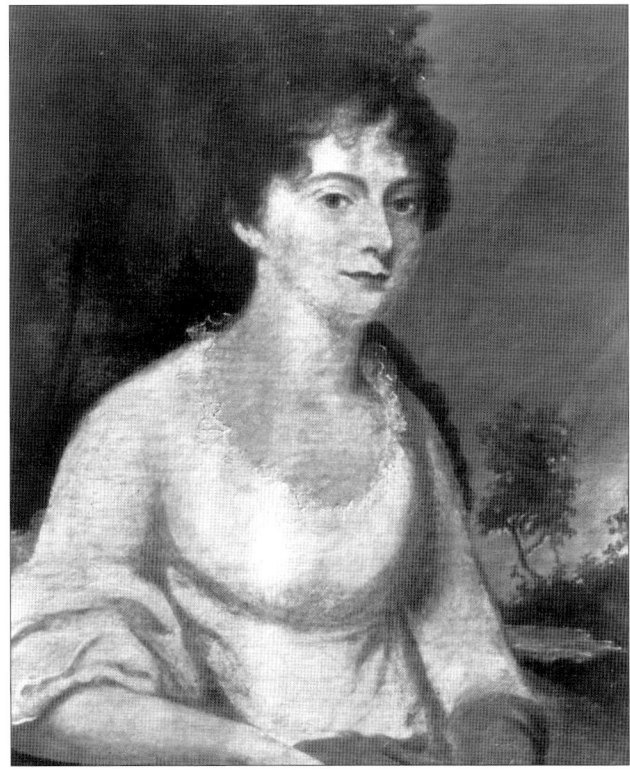

This Thomas Sully portrait of Jane Scott Mackenzie's sister Sally Scott Gray hung in the Mackenzie home Duncan Lodge. A lifelong friend of the Mackenzies, Poe would often visit their home on his visits to Richmond. He likely would have seen this portrait on these visits. It was among the pieces sold to the Poe Museum by the Mackenzie family in the 1920s.

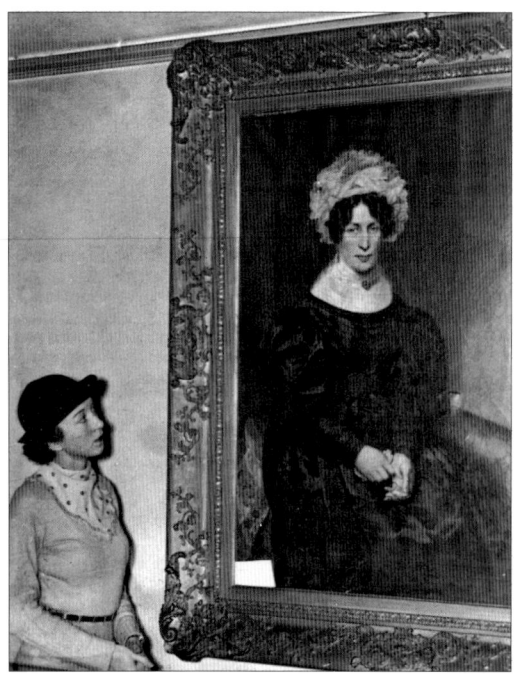

An 1805 portrait by James Tannock of John Allan's sister Mary Allan appears in the background of this undated 20th-century photograph taken at the Poe Museum. While John Allan left Scotland to seek his fortune in the New World, Mary Allan remained in Irvine, Scotland. A six-year-old Edgar Poe visited her with his foster parents in 1816, and John Allan reputedly offered to leave Poe there.

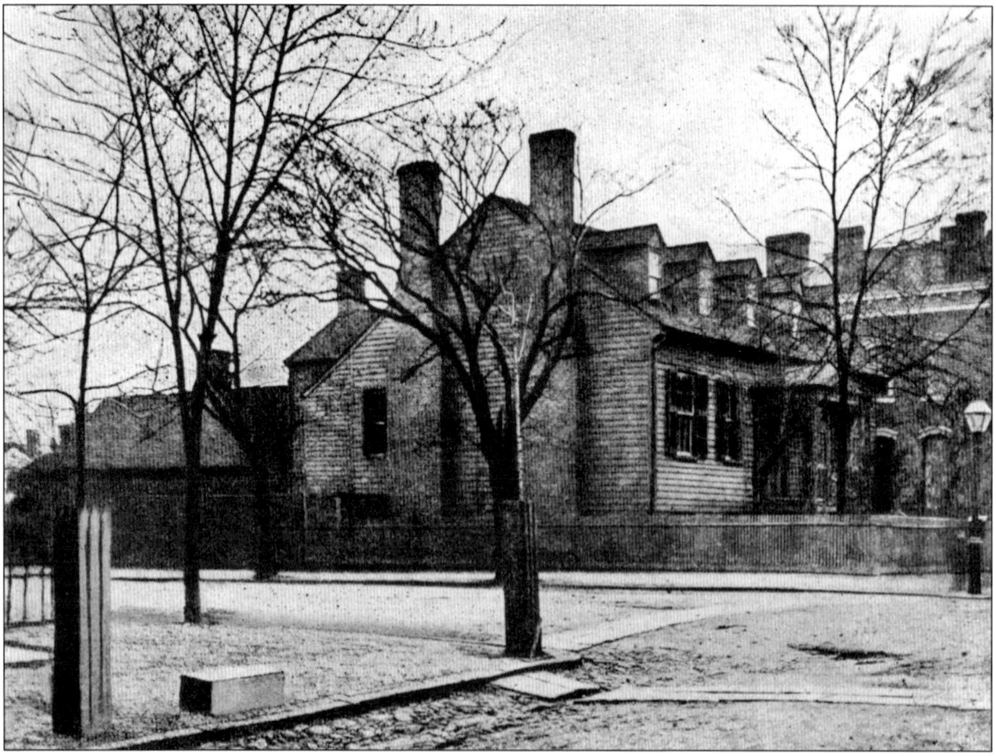

Poe lived in the Ellis home at the corner of Second and Franklin Streets in 1820. This was their home when his foster parents returned to Richmond after having lived in London for five years. The photograph was taken in 1877, and the building was demolished six years later. This is now the site of the Main Branch of the Richmond Public Library.

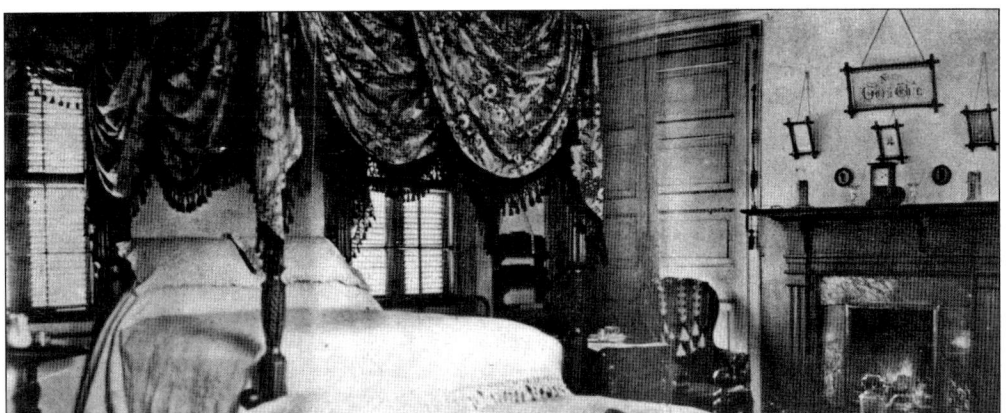

This 1877 photograph shows the bedroom Poe's foster mother, Frances Allan, slept in while the Allan family was living in the Ellis house. The bed visible here is said to be the one she used while living in the house. In Poe's time, it was not uncommon for husbands and wives to sleep in separate rooms.

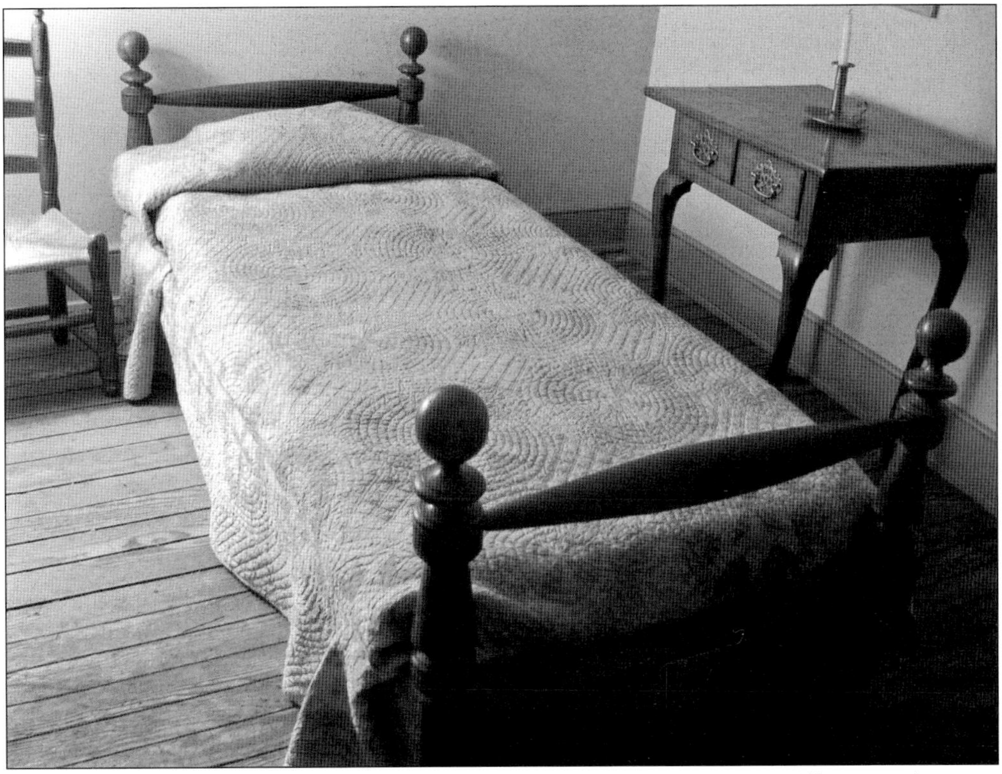

This is the bed Poe used as a boy in the Allan home. After Poe outgrew it, Allan gave the piece to his business partner Charles Ellis, whose daughter used it. The bed stayed in that family until it was donated to the Raven Society, which, in turn, gave the bed to the Poe Museum.

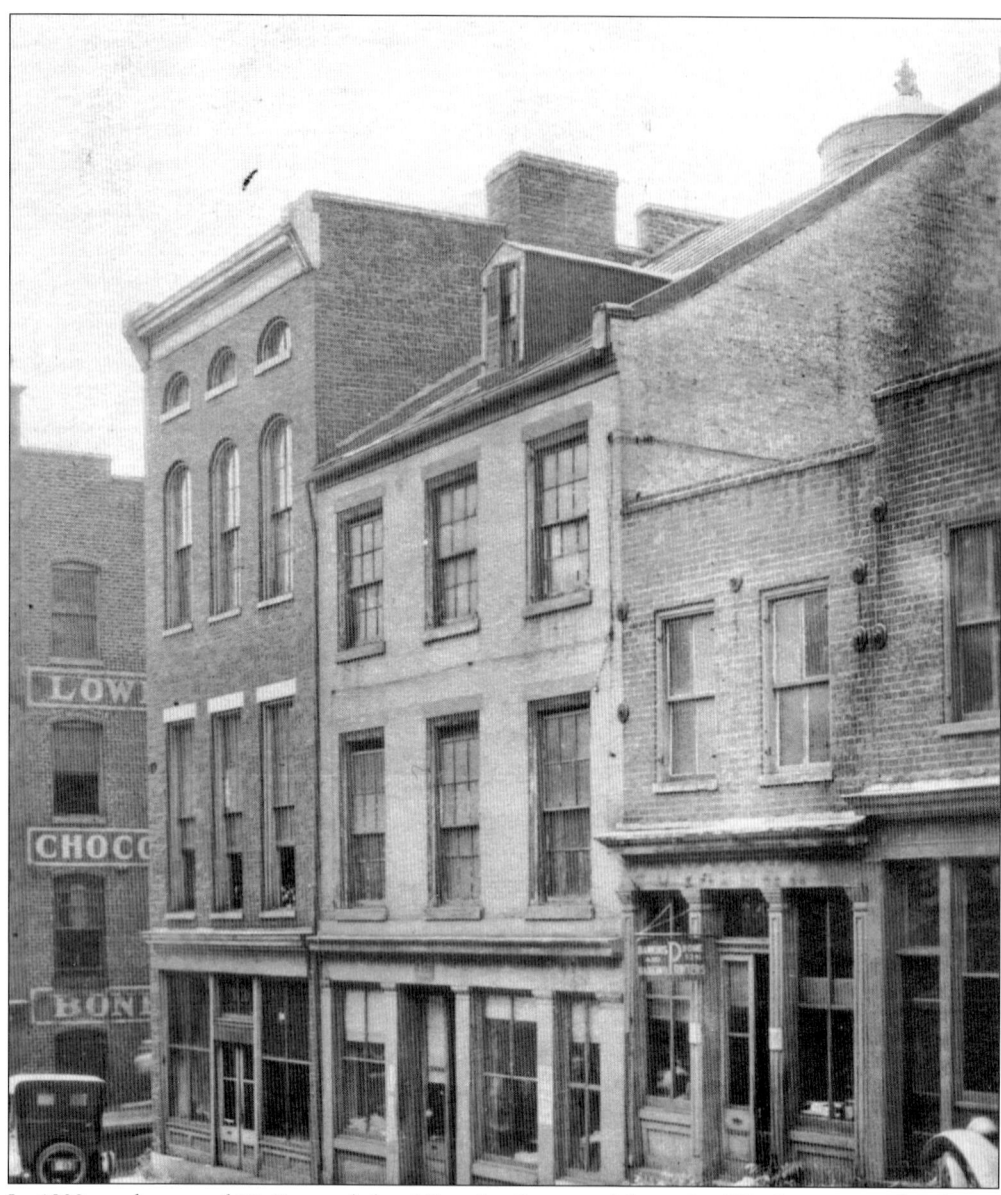

In 1822, at the age of 13, Poe and the Allan family moved from the Ellis house into this home at Fourteenth Street and Tobacco Alley. It was at this time that Poe collected his poetry into a book he asked Allan to have printed for him. Poe's headmaster advised Allan against publishing the volume because he thought Poe already had too much pride. Poe found a more receptive audience for his poetry among his sister's classmates at the Mackenzie School for Girls. After Poe had dedicated poems to several different young ladies, it was revealed he had merely dedicated the same poem to every girl. Unfortunately, little of Poe's early poetry survives. Perhaps the earliest surviving poem by Poe was discovered on an undated sheet in John Allan's files. The couplet reads, "Last night with many cares and toils oppress'd / Weary, I laid me on a couch to rest."

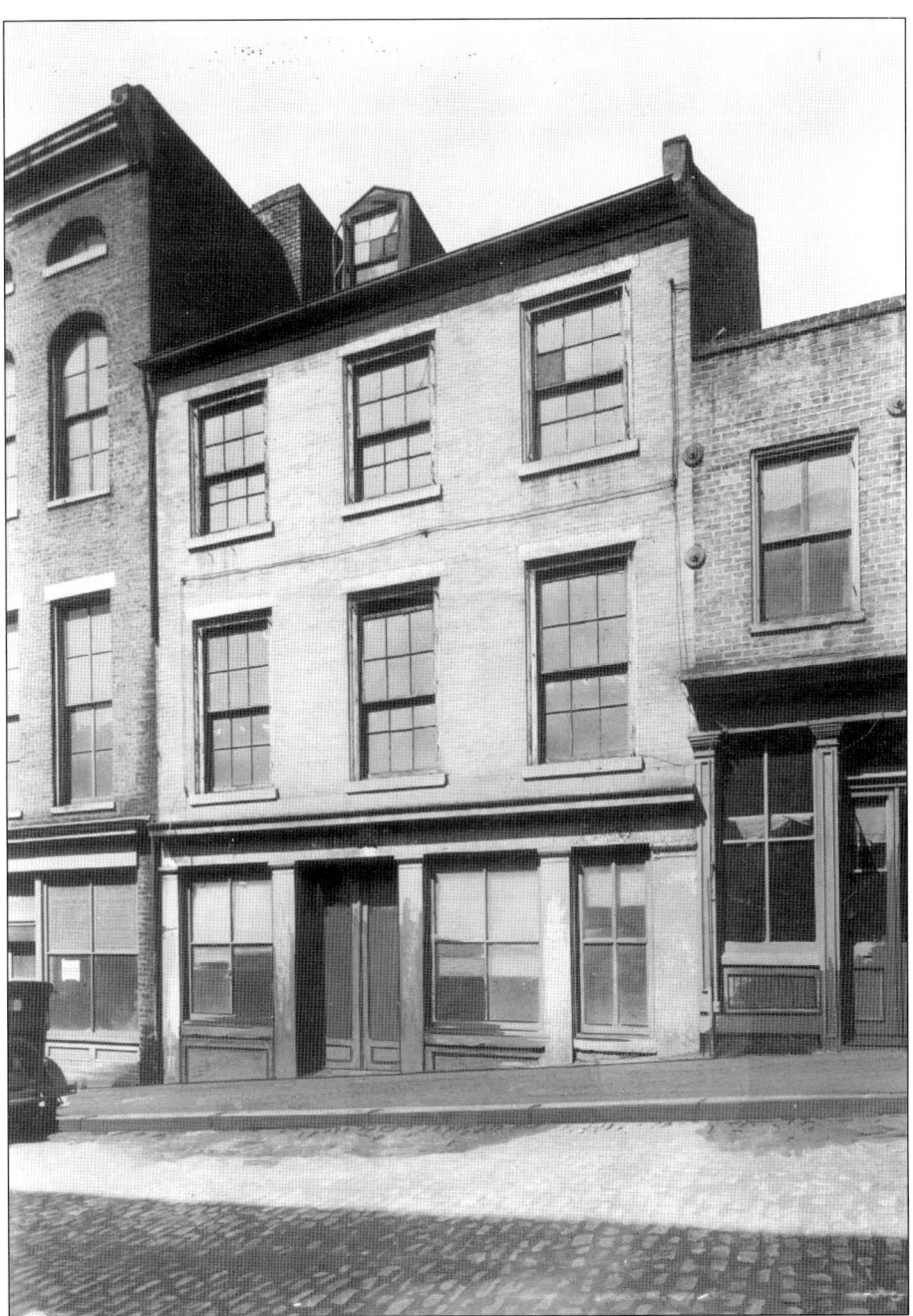

The Allan house at Fourteenth Street and Tobacco Alley appears in the center of this 1924 image. Both this building and the taller structure on the left were built by John Allan's business partner Charles Ellis. This photograph gives few clues as to the nature of the neighborhood as Poe would have known it. During his time, the Allan home was located near the state capitol and the fashionable Court End neighborhood. The house was also near the farmer's market and a slave market through which passed thousands of slaves each year. A few blocks south of the Allan home, the James River became a favorite haunt of the young Poe, who at age 15 swam a record-setting six miles against the current.

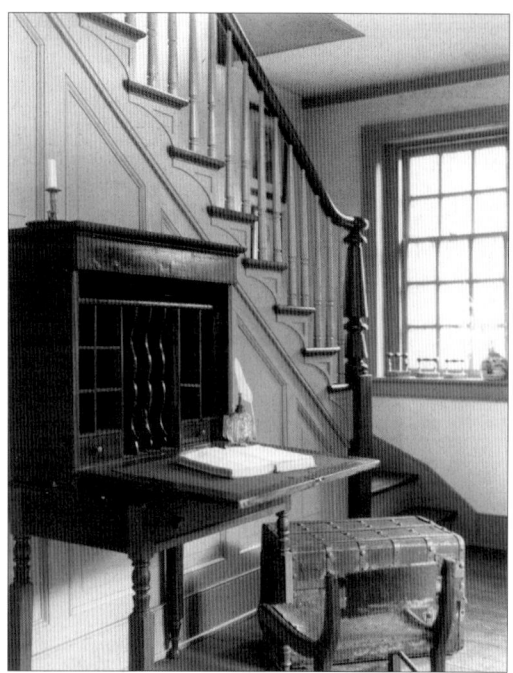

A familiar sight to the young Poe was the staircase from the Allan family's Fourteenth Street home. Before the building was demolished, the founders of the Poe Museum asked the owner to send it to the museum. The staircase was incorporated into the Elizabeth Arnold Poe Memorial Building and can be seen there today.

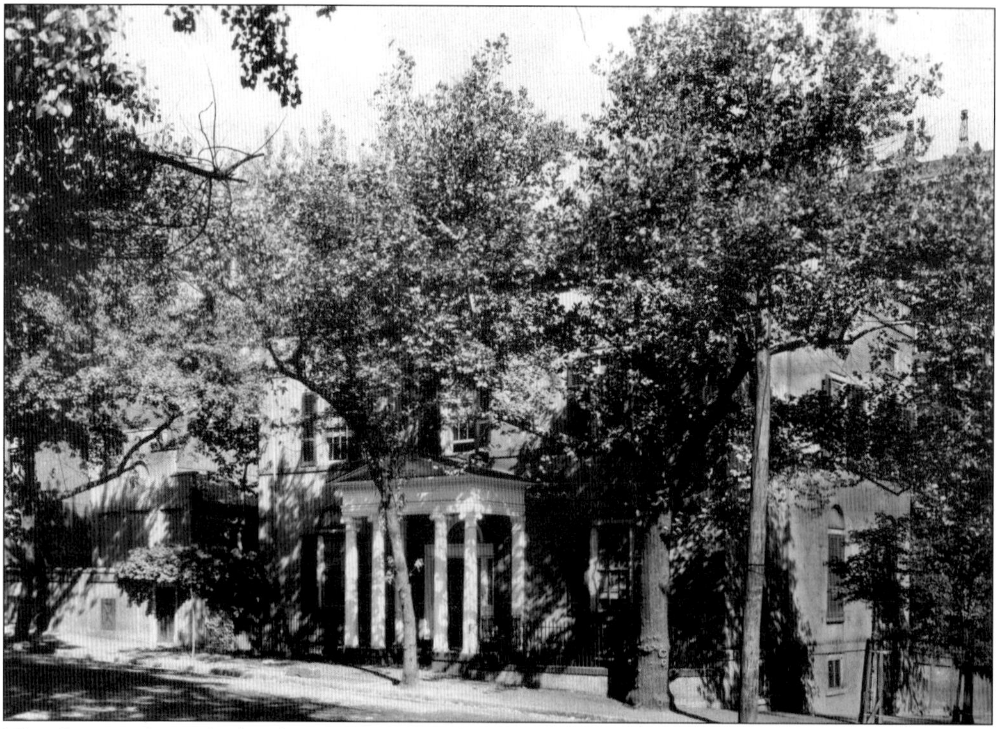

The Cunningham-Archer house once stood at the corner of Sixth and Franklin Streets. John Allan's uncle William Galt lived in the house for several weeks in 1817 while recovering from an illness. A successful tobacco merchant, Galt was one of the wealthiest men in Virginia. When he died eight years later in 1825, he left a considerable amount of his fortune to John Allan. This photograph was taken around 1920.

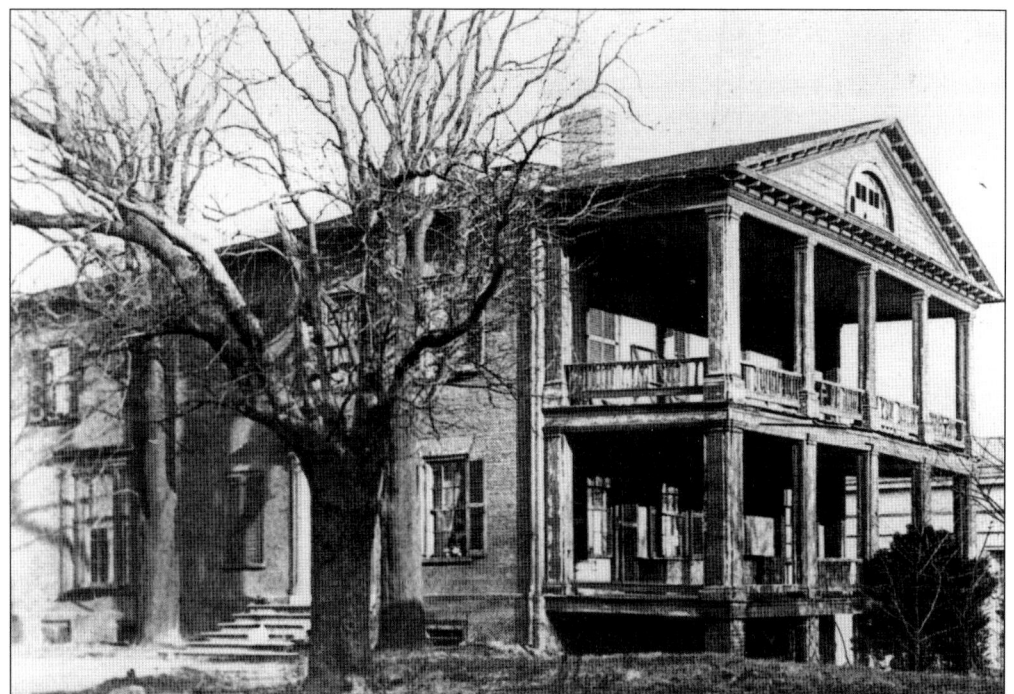

This photograph taken in 1890 depicts Moldavia, the mansion John Allan bought in 1825 after inheriting a fortune estimated at over $750,000 from his uncle William Galt. Poe and his foster parents soon moved into the house. Poe lived at Moldavia until he left to attend the University of Virginia in 1826.

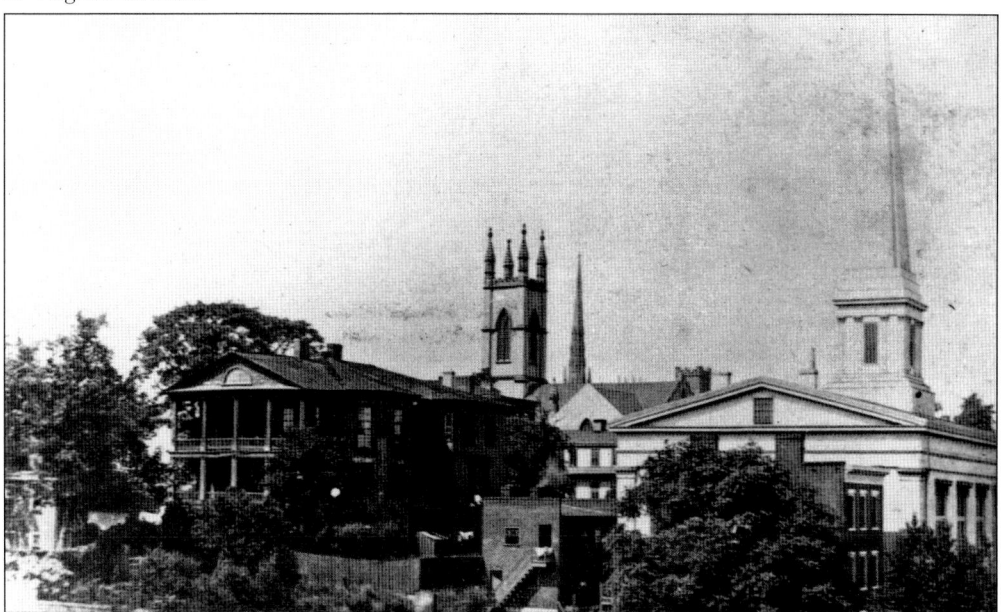

Moldavia is seen from the south on the left side of this 1890 picture. The mansion sat atop a large hill overlooking the James River. Poe's bedroom opened onto the second floor of the portico. He owned a telescope, which he used to view the stars from there. Astronomy became a lifelong fascination for Poe, whose last book, *Eureka*, is a long essay about the universe.

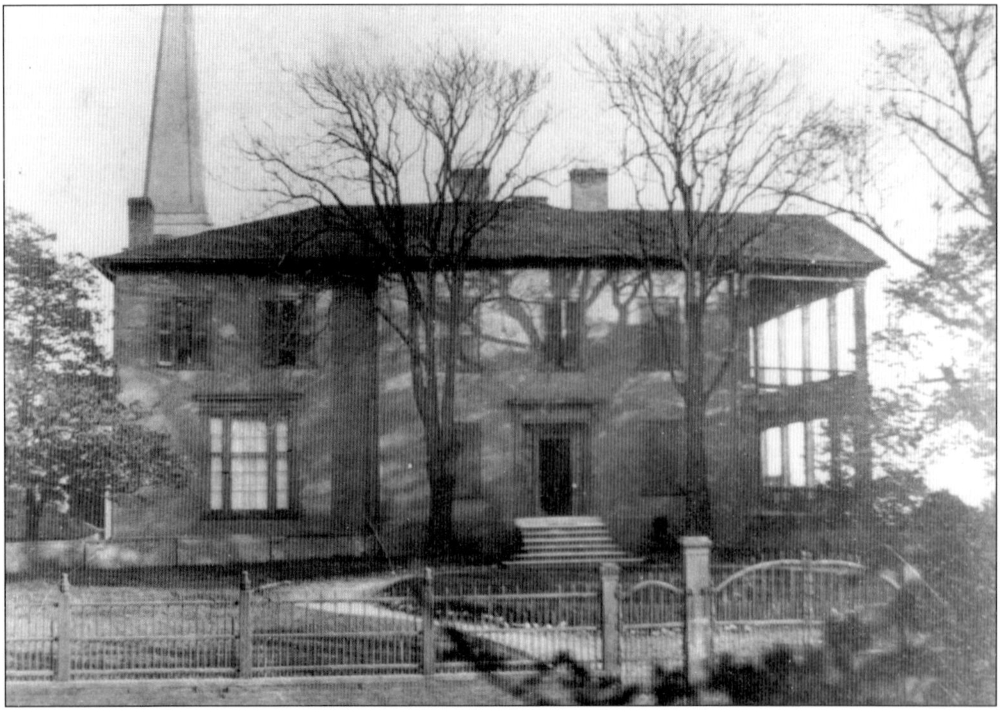

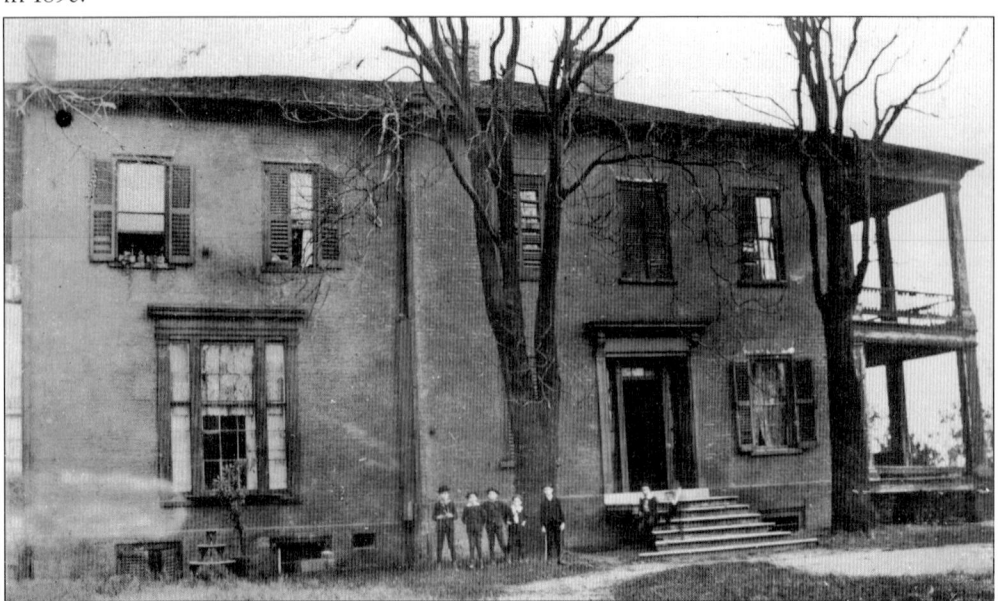

The west side of the Allan mansion, Moldavia, is visible in these 19th-century photographs. Built in 1800, the house is named for its first owners, Molly and David Randolph. It was later home to Joseph and Mary Gallego. The latter perished in the Richmond Theatre fire. When Allan purchased the house, it was already partially furnished with pieces left by the Gallegos. Allan added to these bronze sculptures, antique furniture, and oil paintings. An 1881 advertisement for an auction of the mansion's contents listed a set of rosewood chairs from an 800-year-old German castle among the "extensive and valuable" household furniture. The mansion was demolished in 1890.

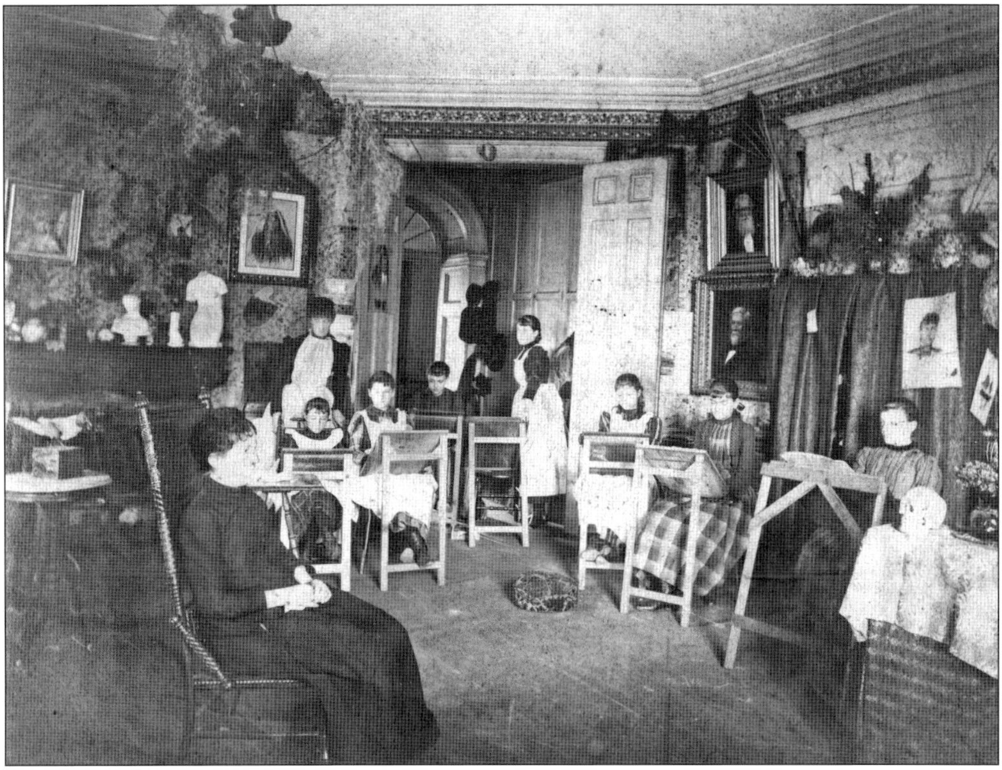

This image taken in the 1880s is the only surviving photograph of the interior of the Allan mansion, Moldavia. It serves as a rare glimpse into one of Poe's boyhood homes. The last of the Allan family members had moved out of the mansion in 1881, and by the time this photograph was taken a few years later, Lillie Logan was holding art classes there.

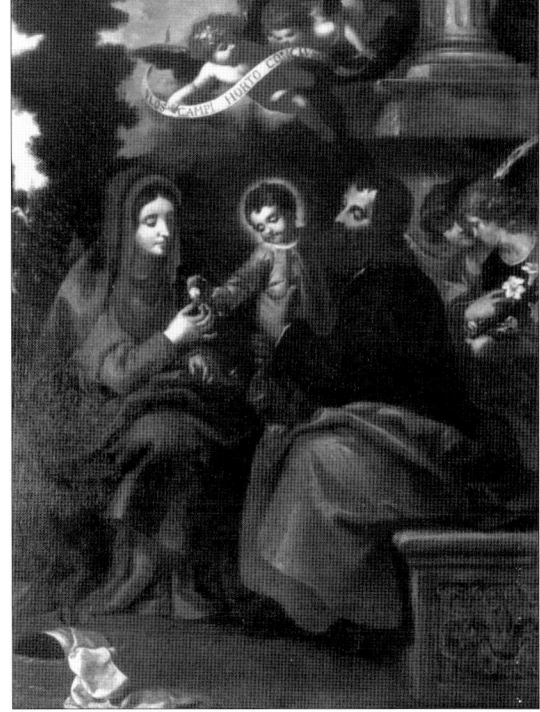

This painting, which once hung in the Allan mansion, serves as further evidence of the wealth and luxury in which Poe spent his childhood. It was painted in 1647 by the Austrian artist Tobias Pock. For the rest of his life, Poe was interested in fine art and displayed knowledge of great paintings in his tales and essays.

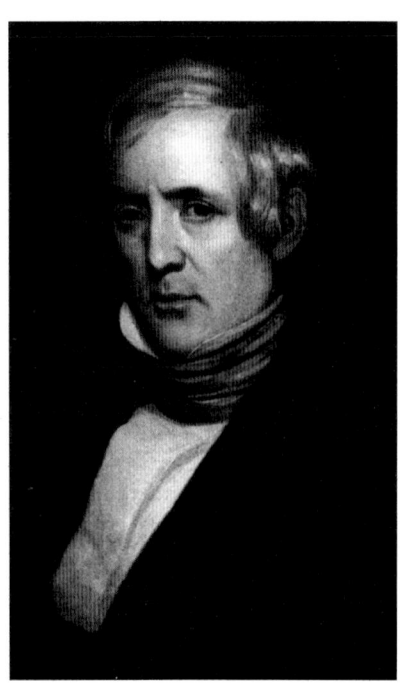

Poe's headmaster Joseph Clarke appears in this portrait by Rembrandt Peale. Poe entered Clarke's academy in 1820 at the age of 11 and stayed until 1823. During this time, Poe studied English, French, Greek, and Latin. He excelled in languages throughout his academic career. Poe was also a gifted athlete who distinguished himself in running, swimming, and boxing.

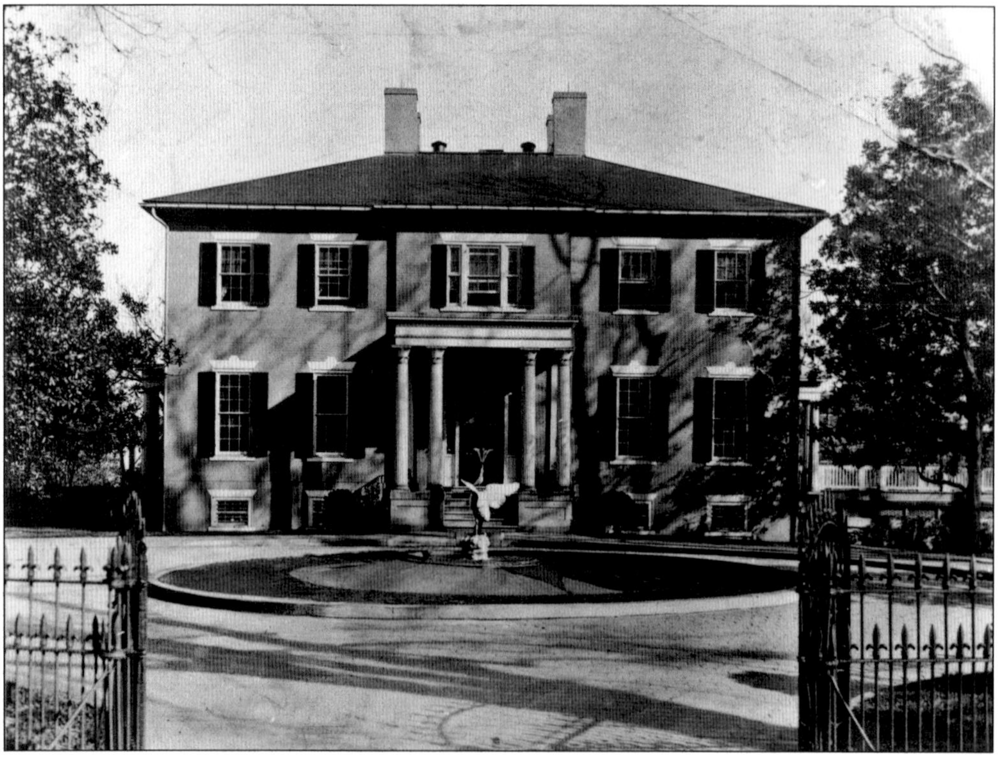

The Virginia Executive Mansion was built in 1811 by the Boston architect Alexander Parris. This building would have been familiar to Poe as a child but has been renovated several times since its construction. The Virginia Executive Mansion is the oldest occupied governor's residence in the United States.

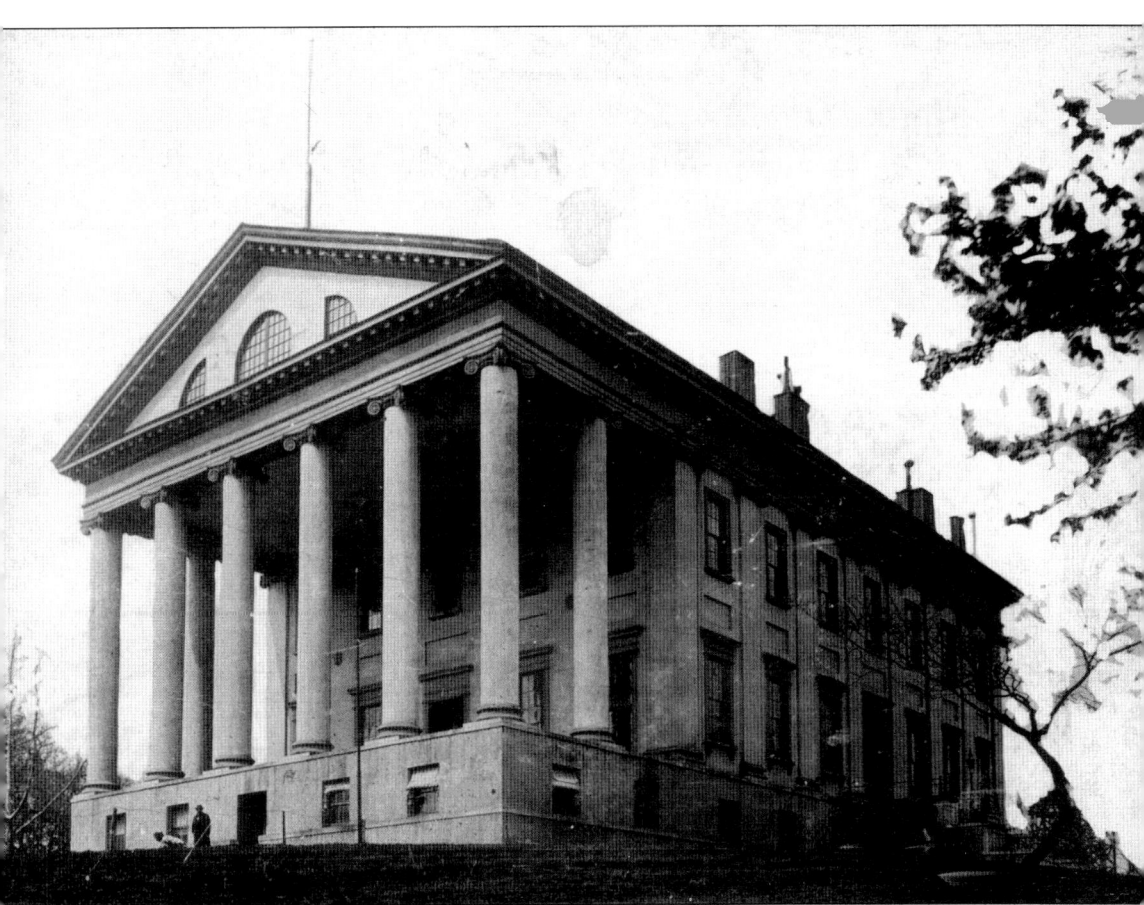

The Virginia State Capitol was designed by Thomas Jefferson in 1785, and upon its construction, it became the first neoclassical public building in the New World. This imposing structure was a constant presence throughout Poe's life, since he grew up in its shadow and was married in a boardinghouse overlooking it. He visited his first love, Jane Stanard, in a house bordering Capitol Square, and "To Helen," the poem he dedicated to her, may make reference to this neoclassical edifice in the line, "To the glory that was Greece, and the grandeur that was Rome." This photograph was taken in 1890 by Foster Studios, which was located in the Stanard house once occupied by Jane Stith Craig Stanard.

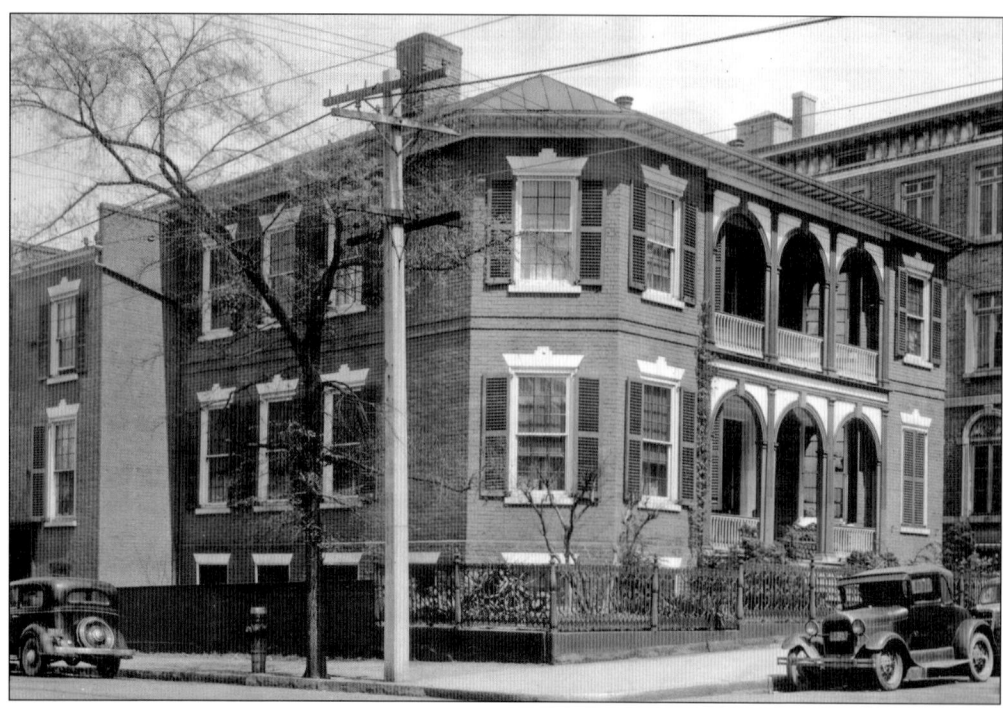

The Wirt-Caskie House, seen in this 1936 photograph by W. Harry Bagby, stood on the opposite corner of Fifth and Main Streets from the Allan mansion. The most famous occupant, William Wirt, was an attorney general of the United States as well as an accomplished writer. It was Wirt who first recorded Patrick Henry's "Liberty or Death" speech decades after the fact.

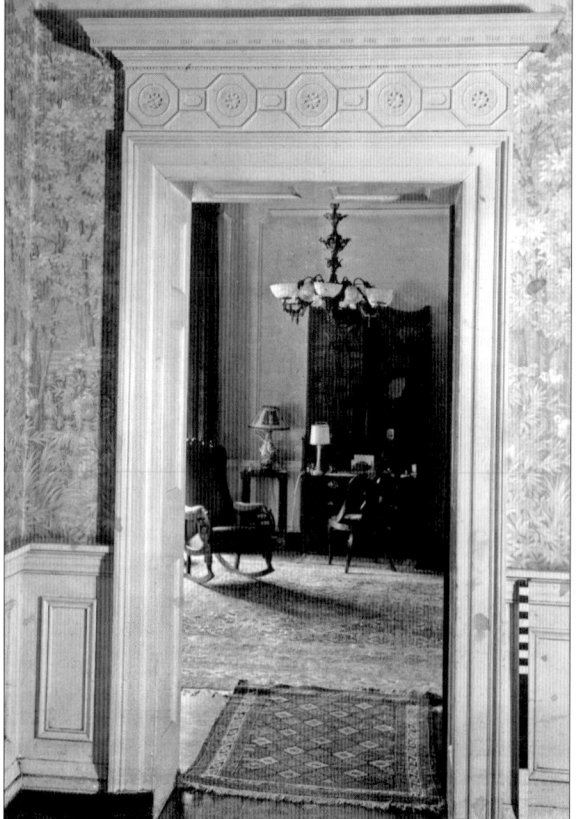

This 1936 image by W. Harry Bagby depicts the interior of the Wirt-Caskie House. One of the residents, William Wirt, offered Poe encouragement as the latter began his literary career. After Poe showed Wirt his poem "Al Aaraaf," Wirt admitted to being confused by the poem and wrote that it would probably be appreciated by those with more "modern" tastes.

Two unidentified men stand on the front steps of the Masonic lodge in this undated photograph by Cook Studios. During Poe's time, many prominent members of Richmond society were members, including his sister Rosalie Poe's foster father, William Mackenzie. Poe is known to have visited it while serving on Revolutionary War hero Lafayette's junior honor guard, which escorted the latter through the city in 1824.

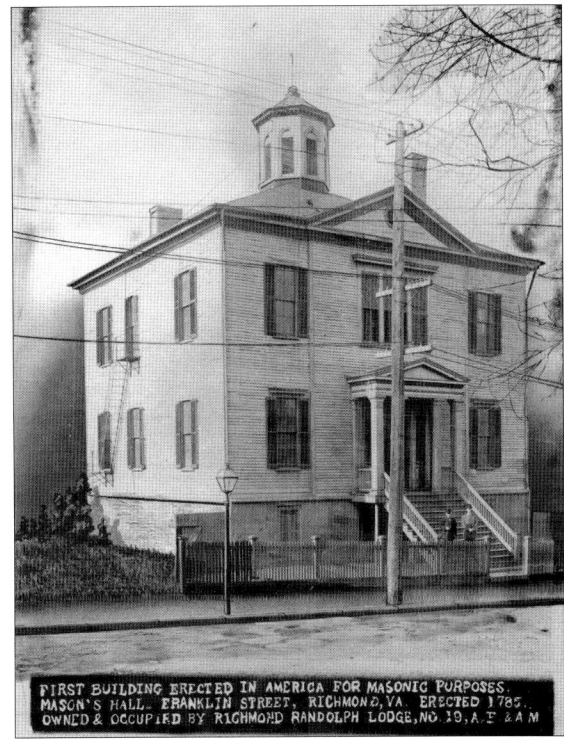

FIRST BUILDING ERECTED IN AMERICA FOR MASONIC PURPOSES.
MASON'S HALL. FRANKLIN STREET, RICHMOND, VA. ERECTED 1785.
OWNED & OCCUPIED BY RICHMOND RANDOLPH LODGE, NO. 19, A. F. & A M

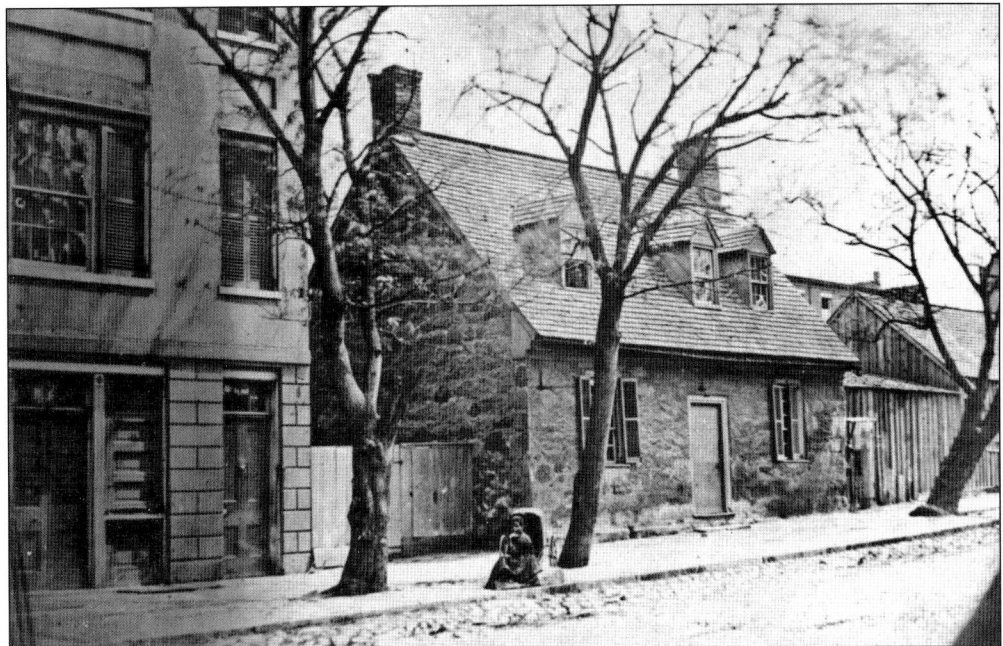

Photographed in 1865, the 1754 Old Stone House was already a city landmark during Poe's time. He visited the house while serving on the honor guard charged with escorting Lafayette around the city. The 15-year-old Poe stood guard outside the building while Lafayette was entertained inside by the owners, the Ege family. Poe's time with the honor guard may have inspired him to join the military as an adult.

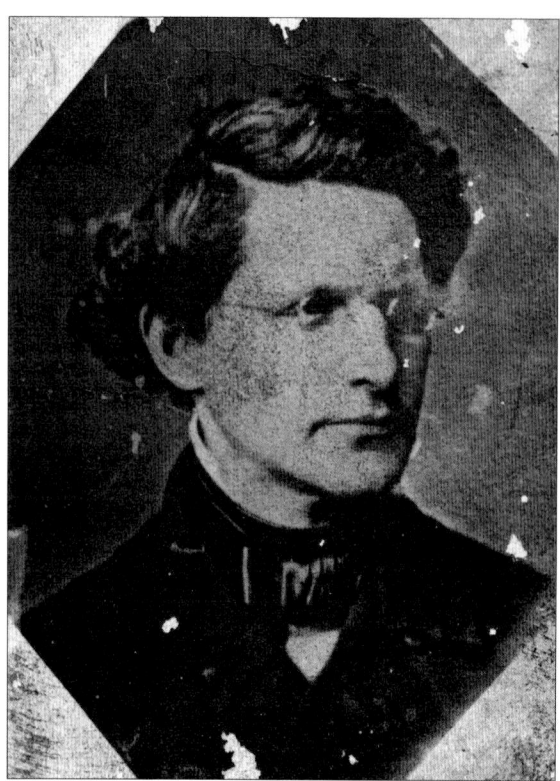

Poe's childhood friend Robert Craig Stanard appears in this ambrotype taken around 1857. At the age of 14, Poe became enamored with Stanard's mother, Jane Stith Craig Stanard. Unfortunately, not long after he met her, Jane Stanard went insane and died. After her death, Poe and Robert Stanard held frequent vigils at her grave. Years later, Poe dedicated his poem "To Helen" to her.

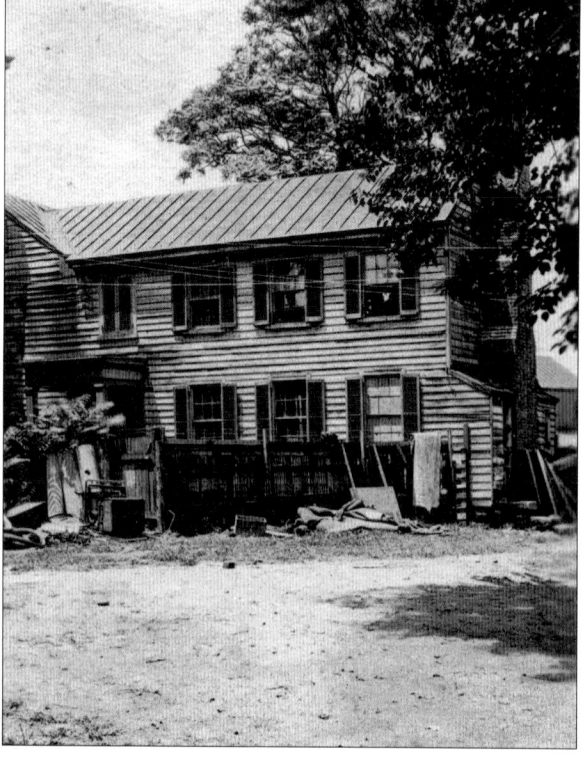

In spite of the dilapidated condition of the Craig House in this early-20th-century photograph, this building still stands today, fully restored as the oldest frame house still standing in Richmond. Built by 1787 for Adam Craig, the house is best known as the birthplace of his daughter Jane Stith Craig Stanard, whom Poe considered "the first, purely ideal love of my soul."

The Stanard House is partially obscured in this 19th-century photograph by a statue of Henry Clay. As a boy, Poe was a frequent visitor to this house, in which his friend Robert Craig Stanard lived. It was here that Poe met Jane Stanard. He later recounted that when he first heard her voice, he was left speechless and nearly lost consciousness.

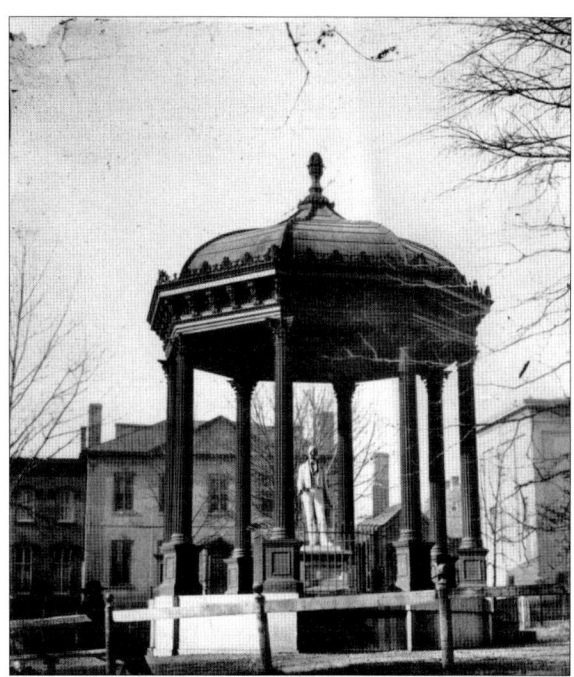

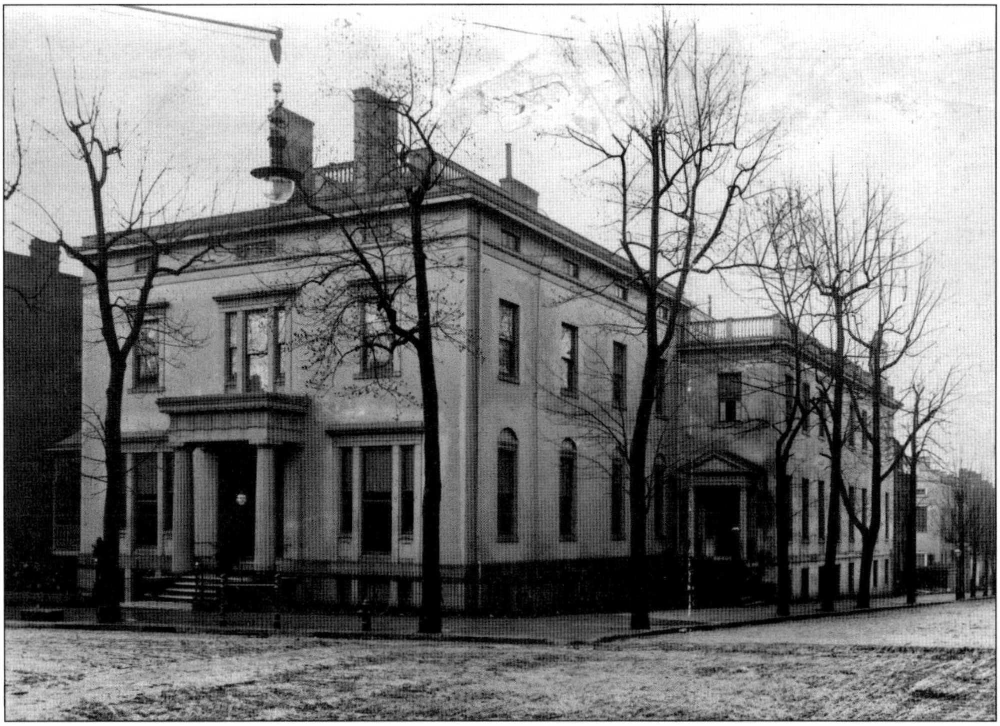

Fifteen years after the death of Jane Stanard, her husband, Robert Stanard, a successful lawyer, moved into this mansion on East Grace Street in 1839. After his death in 1846, his son, Robert Craig Stanard, the boyhood friend of Edgar Poe, lived there until his own death in 1857. During the younger Stanard's occupancy, the house hosted such visiting dignitaries as novelist William M. Thackery and Vice Pres. Alexander Stephens.

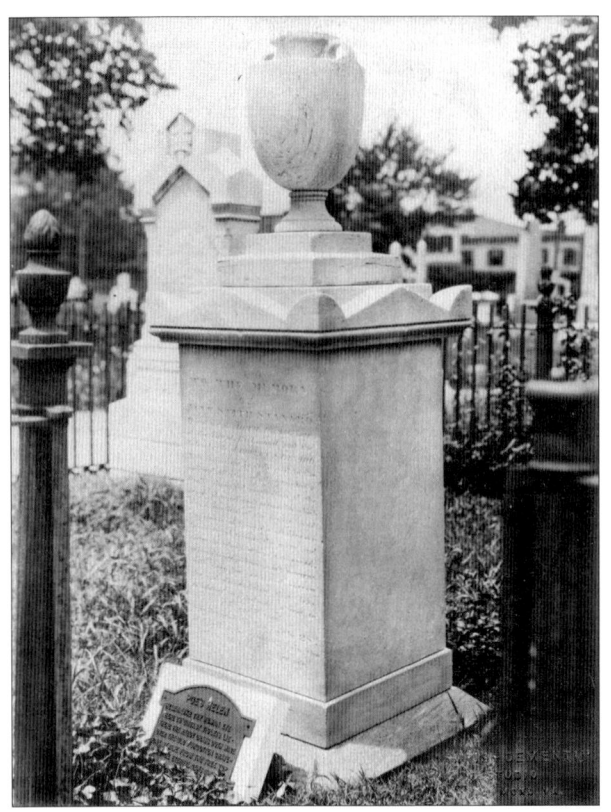

Shortly after Poe met Jane Stanard, he began bringing her his poetry, to which she responded with motherly advice and encouragement. For unknown reasons, Stanard quickly descended into madness and died from what doctors of the time termed "exhaustion from mania." Poe was devastated and held vigil at her Shockoe Cemetery grave, pictured here in a 1923 photograph by Dementi Studios.

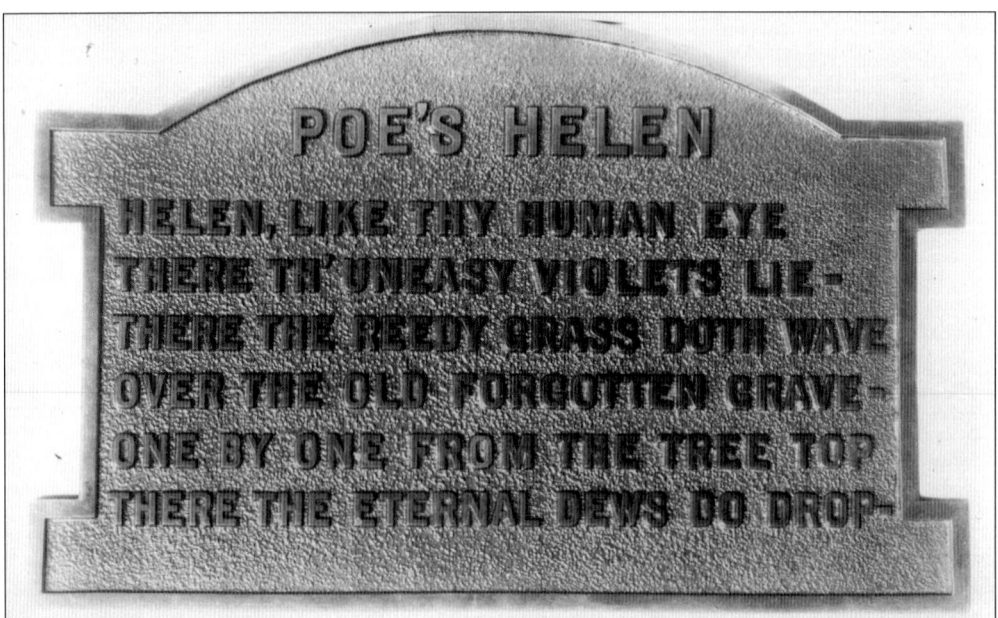

POE'S HELEN

HELEN, LIKE THY HUMAN EYE
THERE TH' UNEASY VIOLETS LIE -
THERE THE REEDY GRASS DOTH WAVE
OVER THE OLD FORGOTTEN GRAVE -
ONE BY ONE FROM THE TREE TOP
THERE THE ETERNAL DEWS DO DROP-

Poe admirer John Robertson placed this plaque on Jane Stanard's grave. Although the 1831 poem "To Helen" is one of Poe's most critically acclaimed compositions, one that Thomas Ollive Mabbott regarded as "the finest of Poe's lyrics," the well-intentioned Robertson inscribed this plaque with lines from a different poem, "The Valley Nis."

As the inscription states, this drawing by Nora Huston was copied from one said to have been drawn by a teenaged Poe of his fiancée Elmira Royster. A gifted artist, Poe frequently provided young ladies with sketches as presents. He drew Royster's portrait at least twice, giving one to her and saving the other for himself.

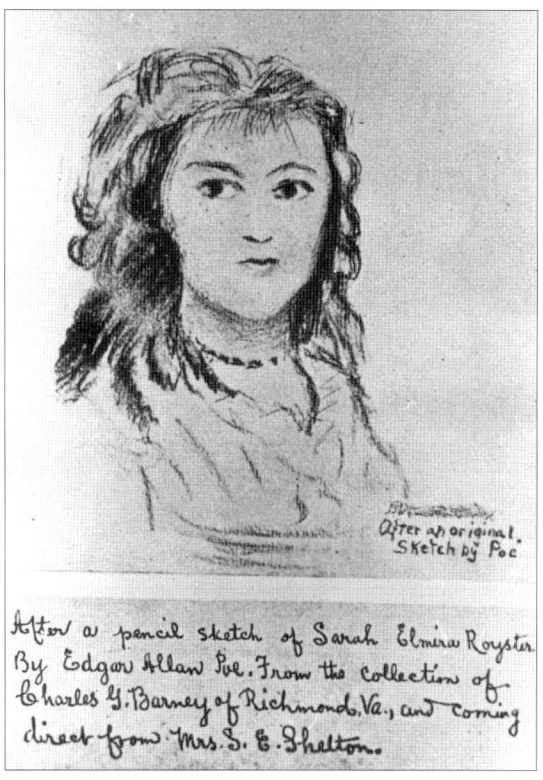

After an original
Sketch by Poe

After a pencil sketch of Sarah Elmira Royster
By Edgar Allan Poe. From the collection of
Charles G. Barney of Richmond. Va., and coming
direct from Mrs. S. E. Shelton.

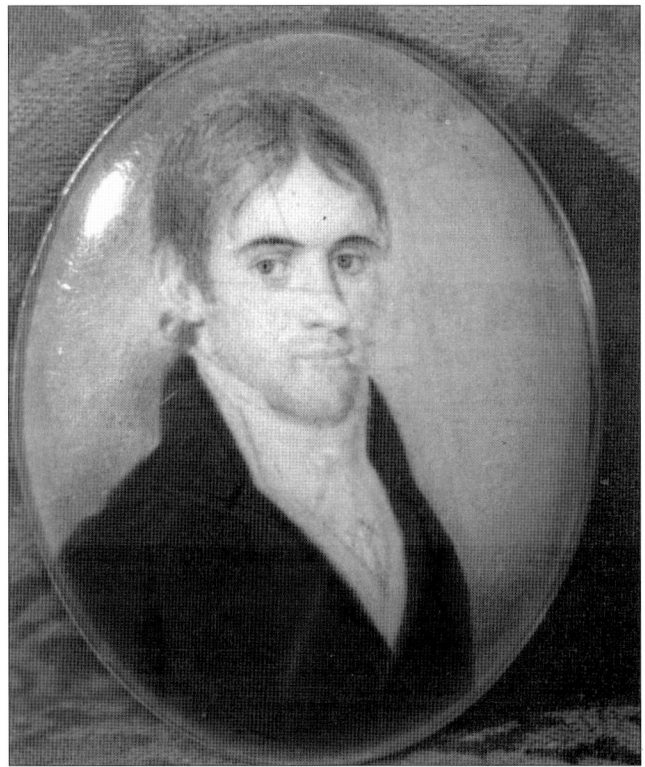

James Royster was the father of Poe's fiancée Elmira Royster. Considering Poe too young, Royster disapproved of the relationship. In spite of Royster's objections, Poe and Elmira became secretly engaged before Poe left to attend the University of Virginia in 1826.

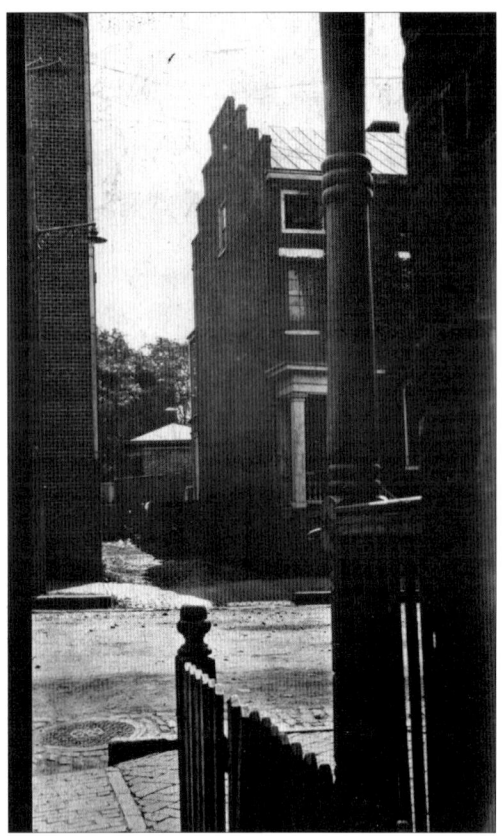

This house, once located a short distance from the Ellis garden where Poe and Elmira Royster met, was believed to have been Elmira Royster's home while she was engaged to Poe. There is, however, no evidence to support these claims. In fact, the house was probably built after Poe's death. Unfortunately, the home was one of many demolished to make way for a public library.

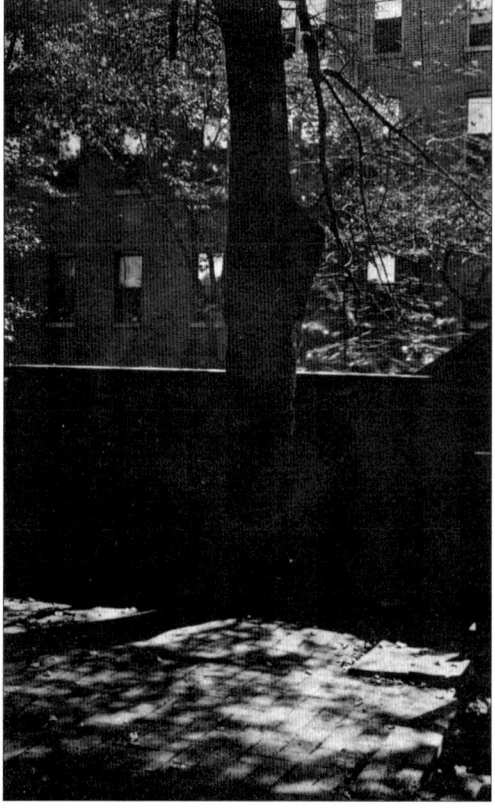

Poe and Elmira Royster are said to have rendezvoused in this garden Allan's business partner Charles Ellis owned on Franklin Street. By the time of this early-20th-century photograph, most of the garden had been replaced with a row of houses built between 1848 and 1853. The block was named Linden Row after the linden trees that once grew in abundance in the garden.

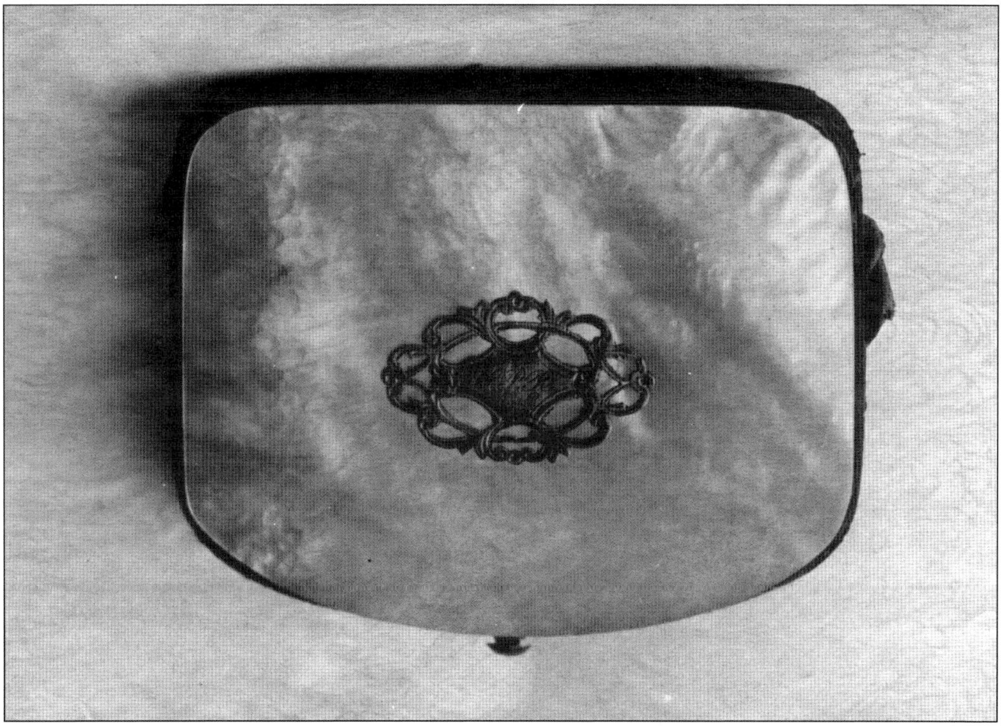

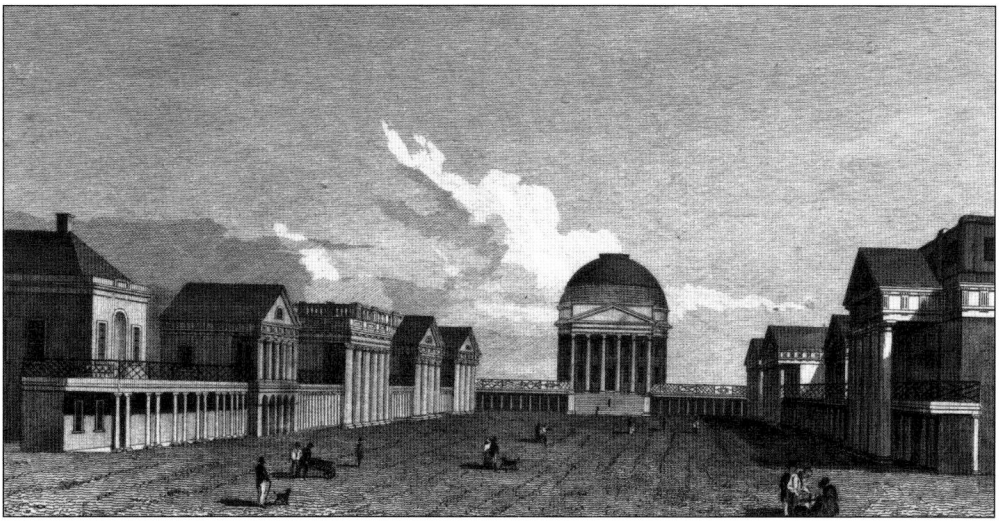

This photograph, taken about 1920, shows the mother-of-pearl purse Poe gave to his fiancée Elmira Royster around 1826. Although they considered themselves engaged by the time Poe left Richmond to attend the University of Virginia in February 1826, her father intercepted Poe's letters to her and convinced her Poe had lost interest in her. When Poe returned to Richmond in December, she was engaged to another man.

Poe was in the second class to attend the University of Virginia. He entered Thomas Jefferson's academic village in 1826, in the last year of Jefferson's life. This 1831 print shows the newly founded university as Poe would have known it. At $350 per year, it was the most expensive school in the country. Poe excelled academically but accumulated about $2,000 in gambling debts while attempting to pay his way through school.

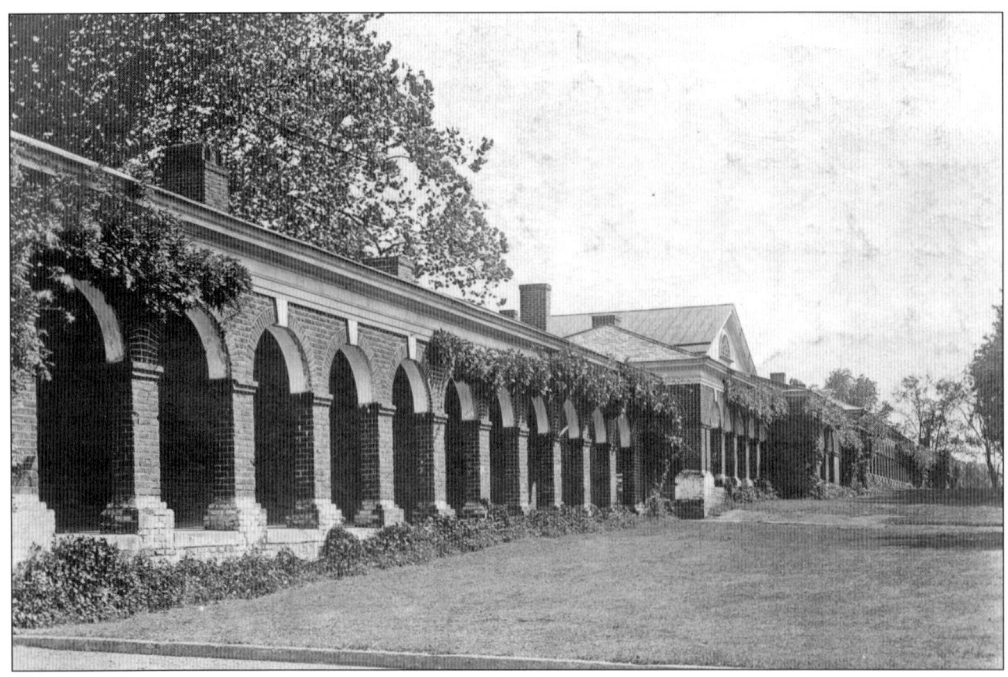

This 1926 view depicts the West Range, where Poe stayed while attending the University of Virginia. During Poe's time there, the university had become so lawless that, in one of his letters to his foster parents, Poe described a violent fight that took place immediately outside his room. One student bit the other multiple times on the arm from the shoulder to the elbow.

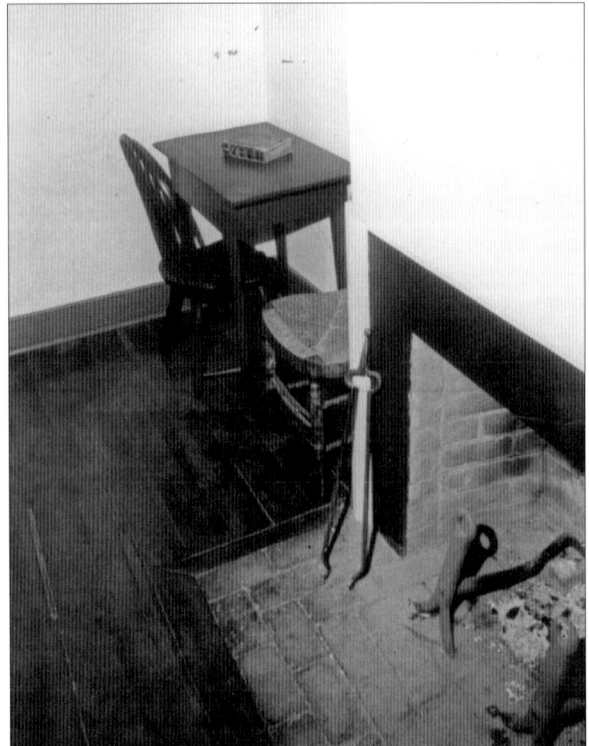

Poe's room, 13 West Range, at the University of Virginia is preserved as a shrine to the author. Though the room is decorated with period furnishings, Poe's actual furniture does not survive because he burned it to keep warm after he ran out of money for firewood. During his residence, the walls of the room would have been covered with murals of dragons and monsters he had drawn in charcoal.

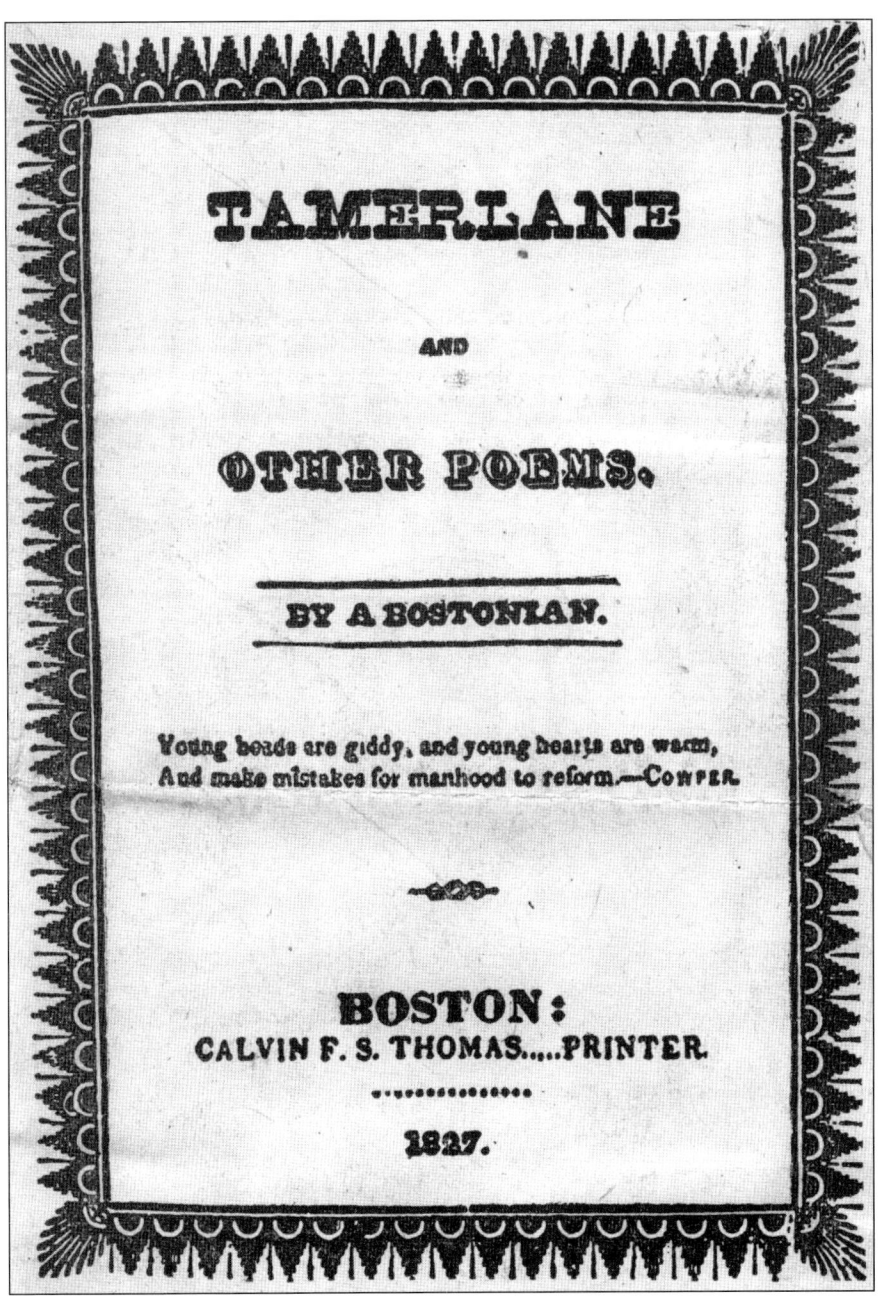

One of the most valuable pieces in American literature, *Tamerlane* is Poe's first book and was published in 1827 when the author was just 18 years old, but he claimed the work had been completed by the time he was 14. The title poem tells of the hero Tamerlane who has returned from conquering the world only to find that his beloved Ada has died in his absence. This is believed to reflect Poe's sense of loss after having returned from the University of Virginia to Richmond to discover his own fiancée Elmira Royster engaged to another man. A few months after this discovery, Poe took a coal ship to Boston, where he published this book. About 50 copies were printed, and no more than 12 of these are known to exist today. Poe complained that the publication of the book was "suppressed," so it was most likely never distributed.

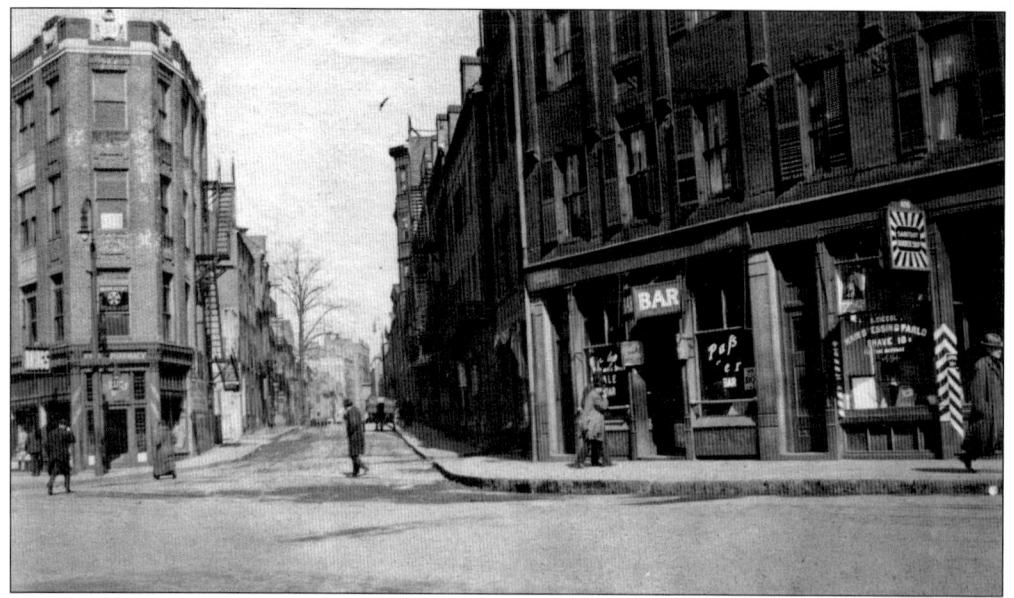

The inscription on the back of this 1924 photograph taken in Boston by E. G. Buttrick states, "Poe was born at No. 62 Carver Street (right-hand side) in block half way up street." As an infant, Poe had lived briefly in the city before moving with his parents to New York. When the 18-year-old Poe left the Allan home, he returned to Boston to begin his literary career.

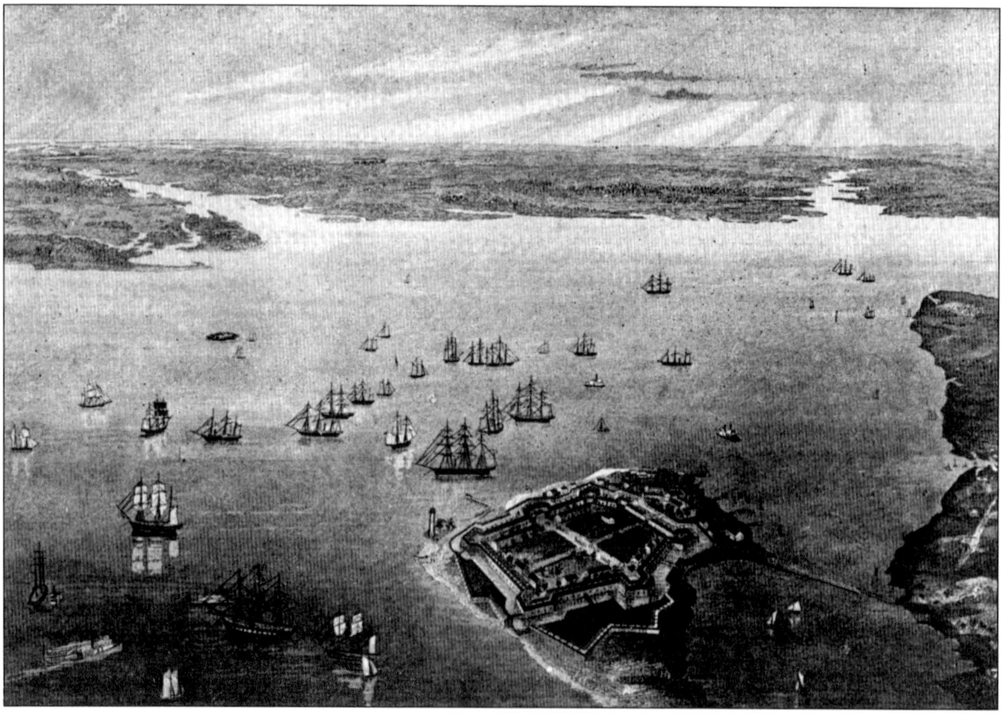

Poe was stationed at Fortress Monroe, Virginia, during the latter part of his enlistment in the U.S. Army. After two years in the army, he achieved the rank of sergeant major, an accomplishment that usually took over a decade to achieve, and hired a substitute to serve in his place the duration of his term. This allowed Poe to apply to the U.S. Military Academy at West Point.

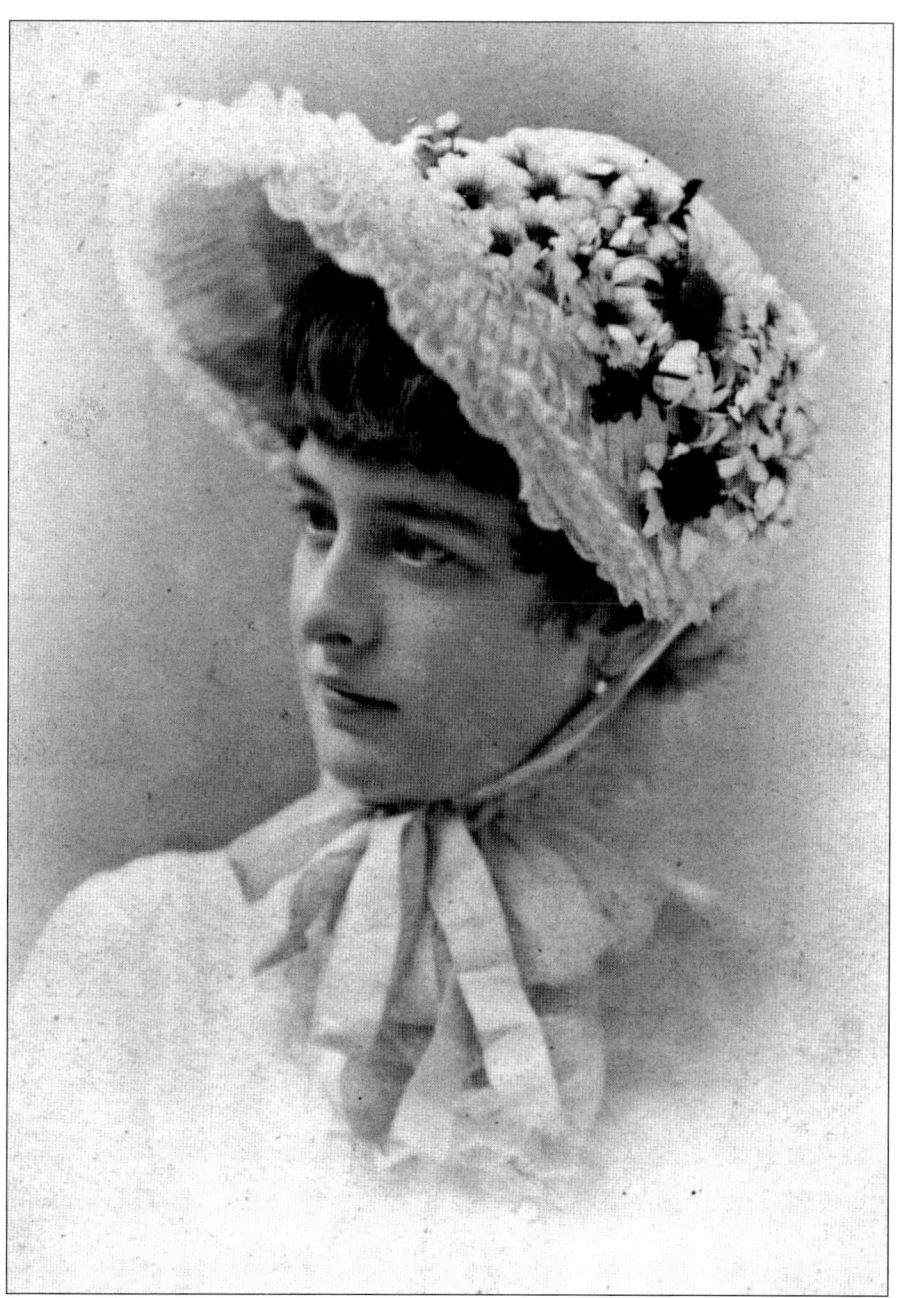

Louise Allan, who appears in this undated albumen print by George Cook of Richmond, was the granddaughter of John Allan and his second wife, Louisa Gabriella Patterson. Louisa had married Allan in 1830 while Poe was attending West Point. When the second Mrs. Allan bore Allan children the following year, they became the legitimate heirs to Allan's fortune, and Poe lost all hope of inheriting a portion of the estate. Allan died just four years later in 1834 while sitting at home in his armchair. Louisa heard her children screaming in his chamber and hurried to the room, where she made the grim discovery. After her husband's death, Louisa lived at Moldavia until 1881 and became a popular hostess of extravagant parties. Louise Allan later recounted that her grandmother, Louisa Allan, disdained Poe's "ingratitude, fraud, and deceit."

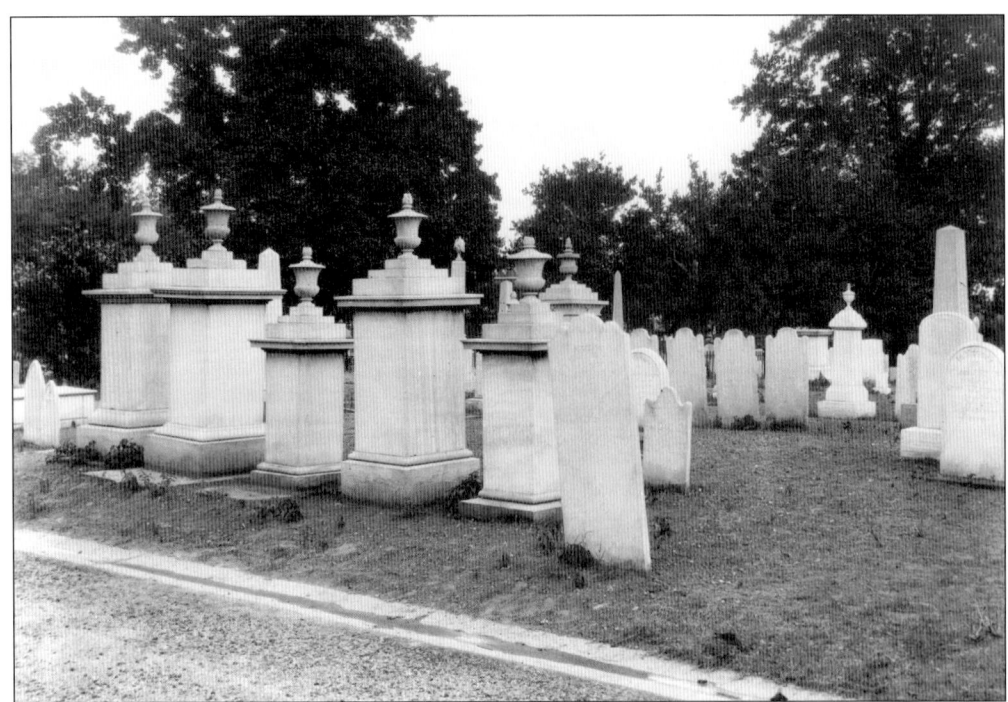

These 20th-century images depict the graves of Poe's foster parents in Shockoe Cemetery in Richmond. The grave of John Allan's second wife, Louisa, is on the left of the photograph. John Allan's monument stands to the right of Louisa's, and Frances Allan's marker is to the right of John Allan's. When Frances Allan died in 1829, Poe was stationed at Fortress Monroe and returned to Richmond the night after her funeral. According to Poe biographer Mary Phillips, "Poe's homecoming to see her was most harrowing, as was also the keen sorrow he could not control at her grave." Poe was already familiar with this section of the cemetery because, five years earlier, he had kept vigil at the grave of Jane Stanard, located only a few meters from the Allan family plot.

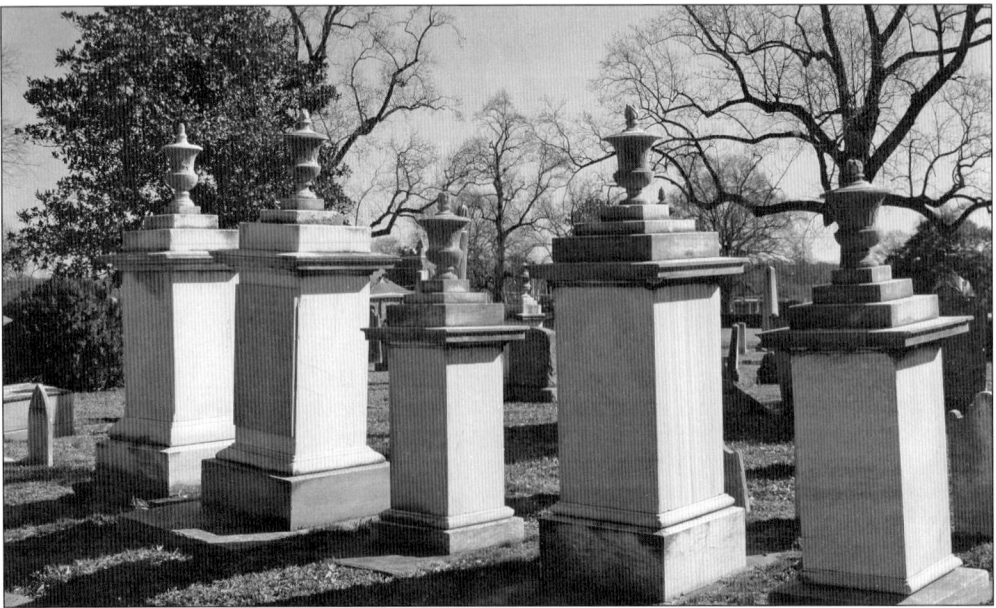

Two

POE AT THE *SOUTHERN* *LITERARY MESSENGER*

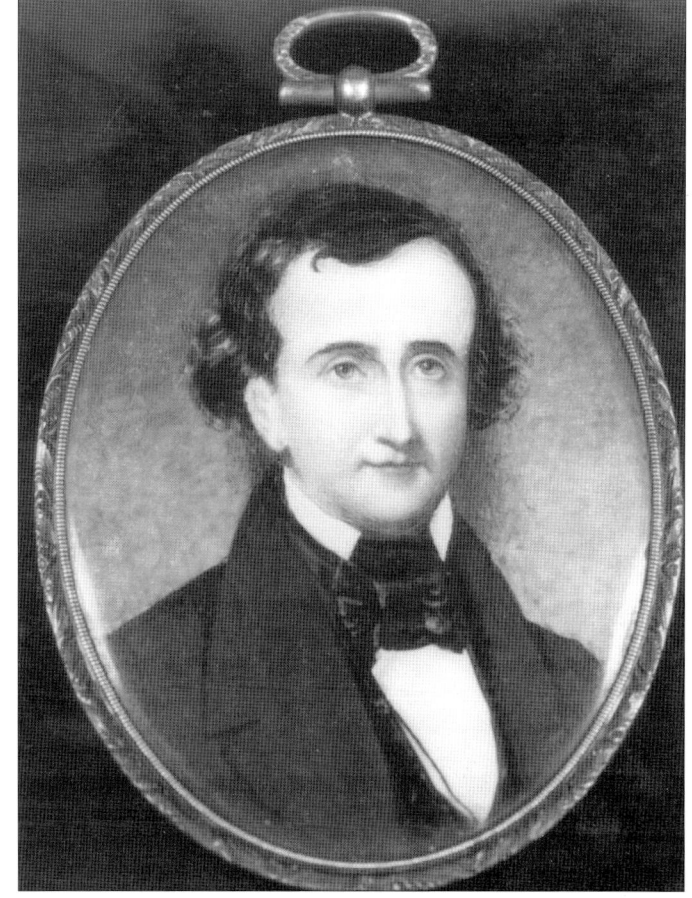

Poe appears as a young man in this miniature by an unidentified artist. Once considered the earliest known portrait of Poe, this piece is now considered a forgery painted around 1900. Since it was based on other portraits of the poet, this miniature provides a good impression of Poe's appearance about the time he returned to Richmond at the age of 26 to work for the *Southern Literary Messenger.*

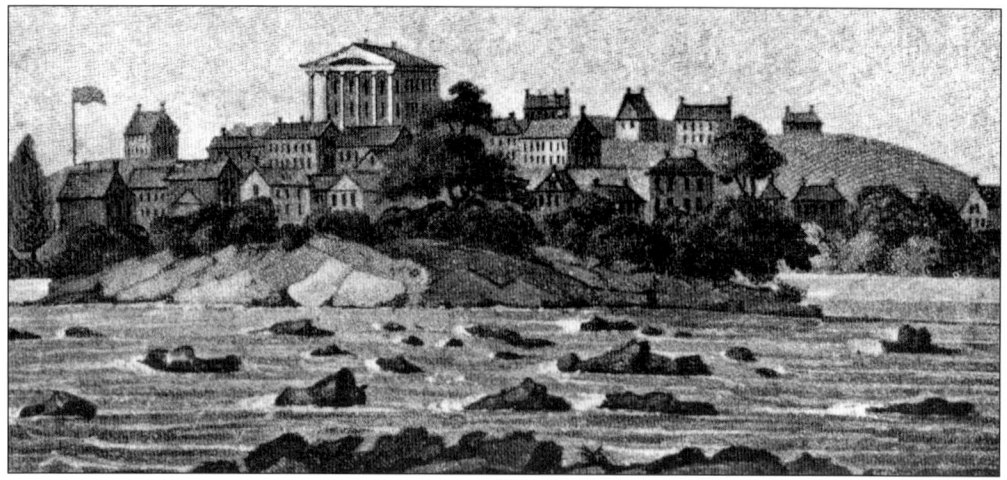

This 1830 engraving of Richmond shows the city much as it would have appeared when Poe returned in 1835. Poe took up residence in a boardinghouse facing the Virginia State Capitol, the largest building on the skyline. As an adult in the city of his childhood, Poe lived within blocks of his boyhood home Moldavia but was no longer welcomed there because Allan's second wife disliked him.

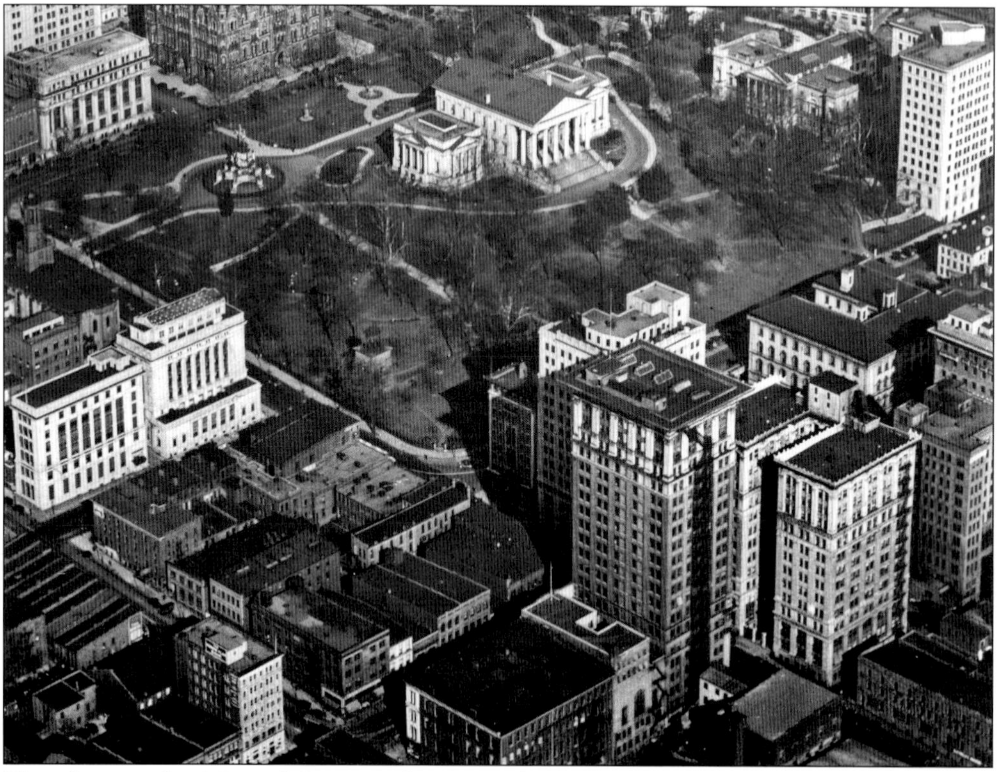

This photograph of Capitol Square, taken around 1930, shows the Jefferson-designed Virginia State Capitol. This landmark was familiar to all Richmonders of Poe's time, when it was still one of the largest buildings in the city. While working as the editor of the *Southern Literary Messenger*, Poe lived in Poore's Boarding House and Mrs. Yarrington's Boarding House, both of which stood on Bank Street, which ran in front of the Capitol.

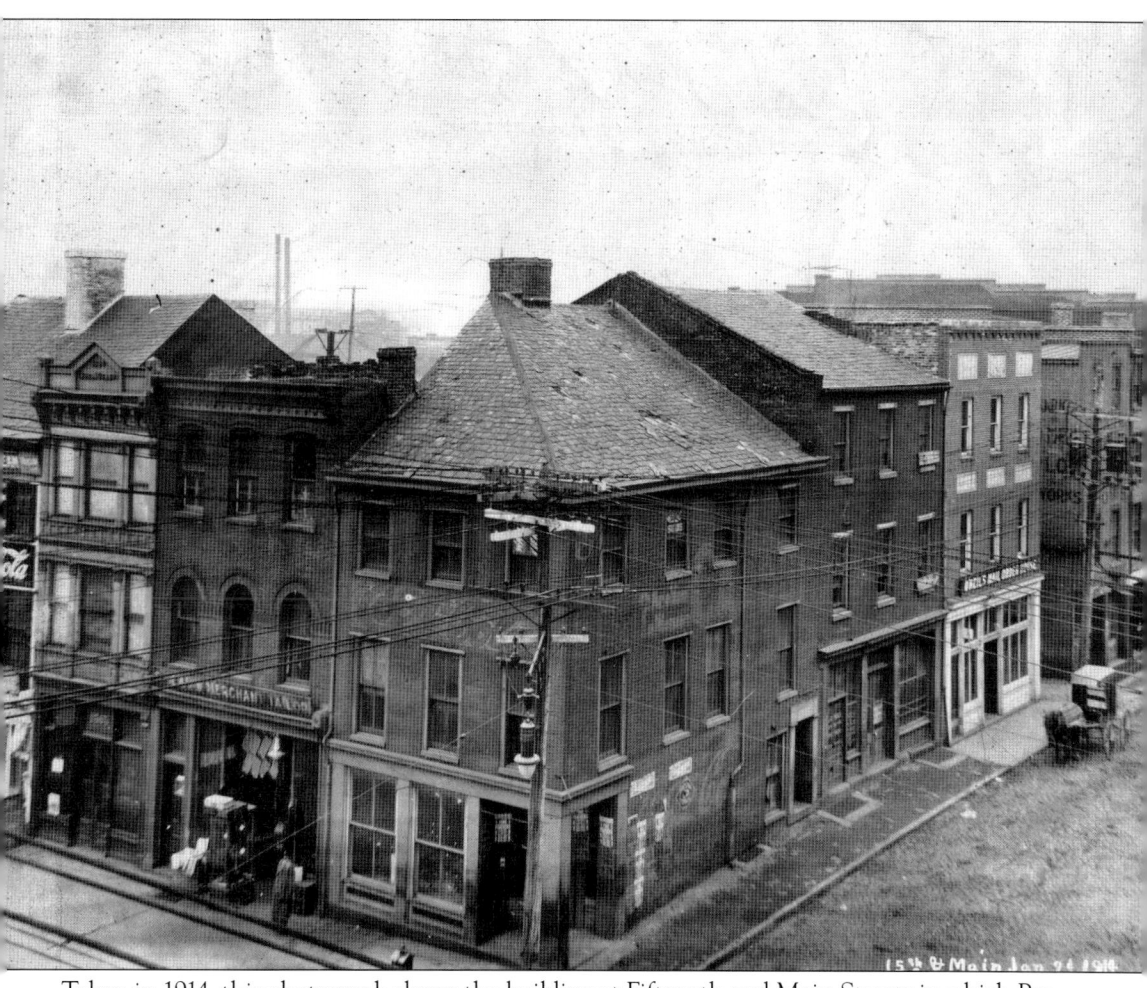

Taken in 1914, this photograph shows the building at Fifteenth and Main Streets in which Poe worked as editor of the *Southern Literary Messenger*. The *Messenger* office was located on the second floor while Poe was employed there. When the magazine was started in 1834, the owner, Thomas White, sought to champion the cause of Southern literature, which was being ignored by the Northern literary establishment in New York and Boston. Poe's first contribution was the short story "Berenice," a tale of an obsessed man who steals into his wife's grave to tear out her teeth. White published the tale but later objected to the subject matter, so Poe responded that this was exactly the kind of story the public wanted to read. That Poe was correct was proven when the magazine's circulation increased seven times in the next 17 months. Two years after this picture was taken, the building was demolished to allow the city to widen Fifteenth Street, but the city decided to widen Fourteenth Street instead.

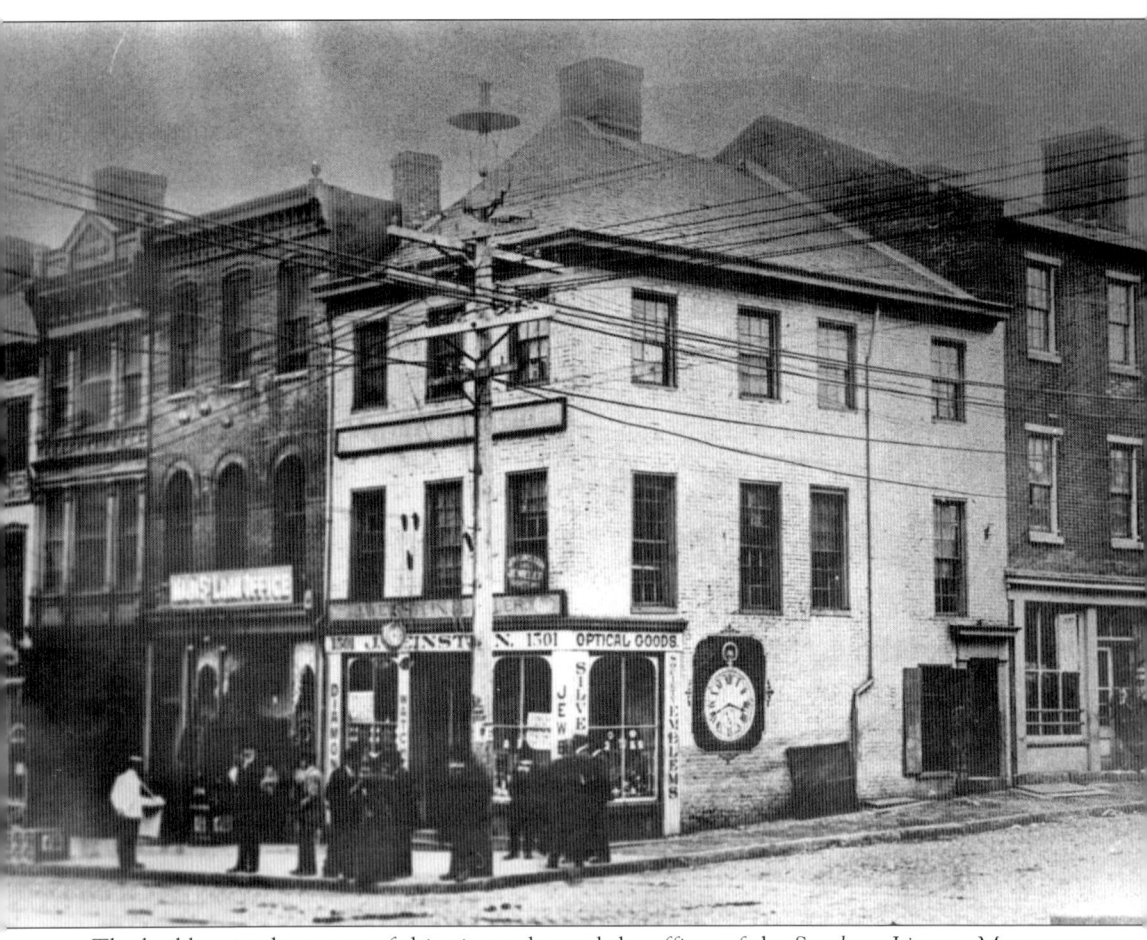

The building in the center of this picture housed the offices of the *Southern Literary Messenger*, in which Poe worked from 1835 until 1837, during which time Poe first established a national reputation. Although he is now best known as a writer of poems and tales, it was as an editor and literary critic that he first achieved literary infamy. In an April 1835 review of the book *Confessions of a Poet*, Poe began his review by stating that the best thing about the book is the bad paper on which it is printed and concluded by advising the author of the best way to shoot himself. The building on the right of the *Southern Literary Messenger* building was the warehouse of the Ellis and Allan Firm, co-owned by Poe's foster father, John Allan. Poe worked there briefly as an unpaid bookkeeper in 1827.

This is the cover of the February 1837 issue of the *Southern Literary Messenger*. Poe stopped working at the *Messenger* in 1837 because he wanted higher pay and greater editorial control. During his tenure, the circulation had increased by seven times, and the magazine had gained national prominence.

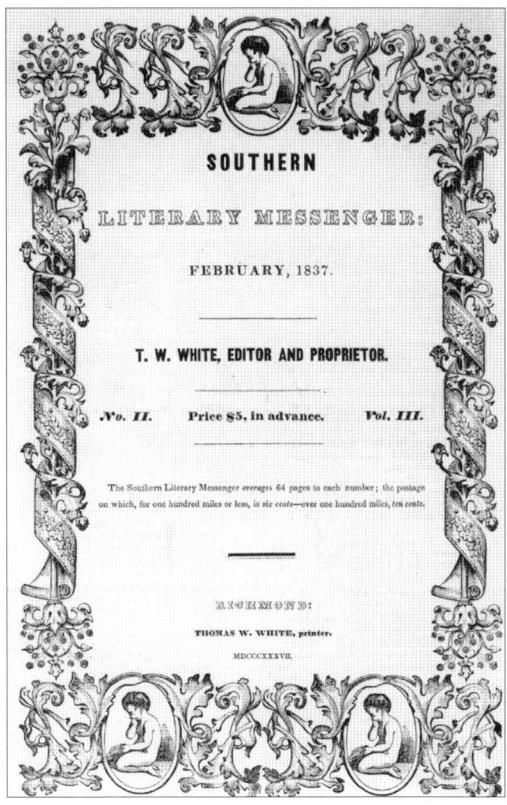

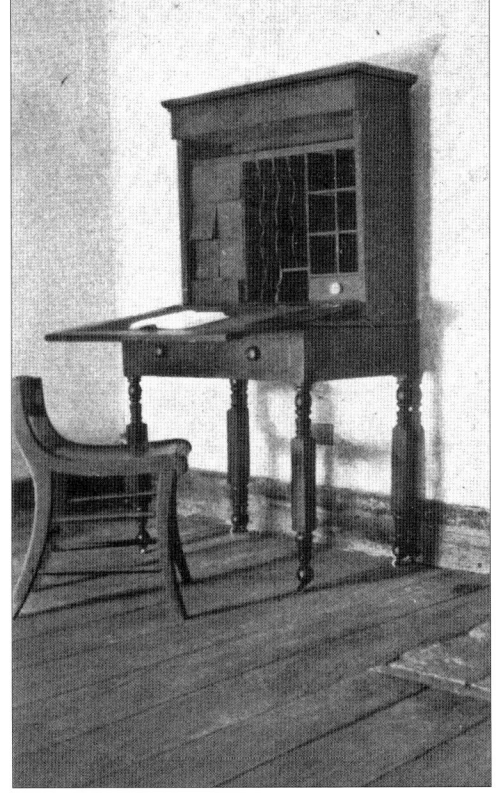

This 1922 photograph depicts the desk and chair Poe used in the offices of the *Southern Literary Messenger*. Supposedly Poe's employer T. W. White cut down the back of Poe's chair to prevent Poe from leaning back. The desk was discovered in the 20th century by Poe collector James H. Whitty, who also found some of Poe's manuscripts in a secret compartment.

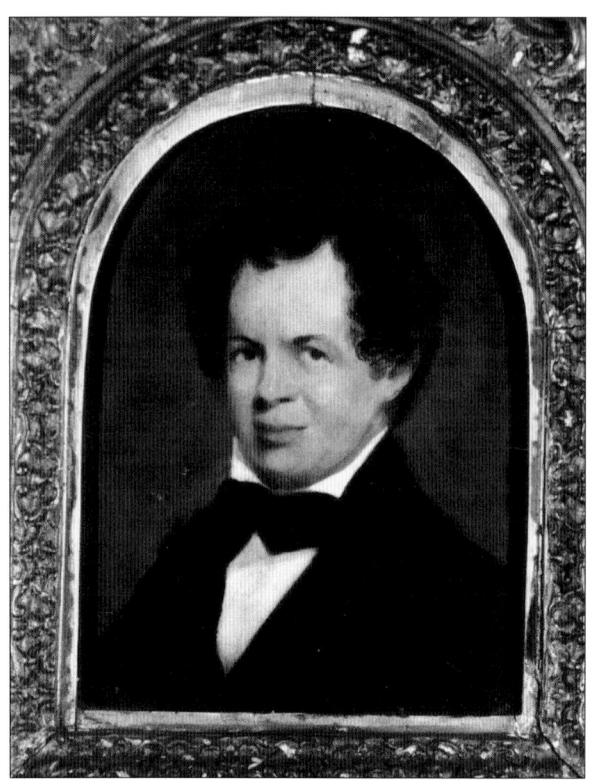

Thomas Willis White, depicted here in an undated portrait given to the Poe Museum by the subject's great granddaughter, was the owner of the *Southern Literary Messenger* and gave Poe his first job in journalism. Although White praised Poe's "fine talents," he was troubled by Poe's drinking and advised him that "no man is safe who drinks before breakfast."

This image of the automaton Maelzel's Chess Player accompanied an 1836 article by Poe in the *Southern Literary Messenger.* Poe had played chess with the robot and lost. He later became so fascinated by the mechanism that he wrote this article to explain how it worked. In the process, he determined it was not a robot but a puppet operated by a man hiding inside a box.

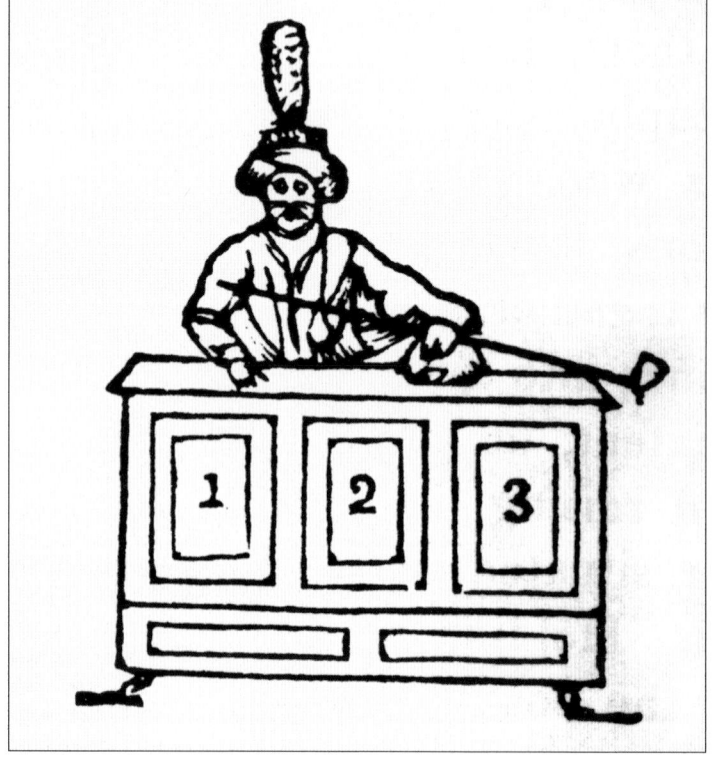

This 1849 daguerreotype depicts Poe's widowed aunt and mother-in-law, Maria Clemm. The sister of Poe's biological father, Clemm had taken Poe into her Baltimore home after his expulsion from West Point, when he was no longer welcomed in John Allan's home. When Poe had established himself as an editor at the *Southern Literary Messenger*, he brought his aunt and her daughter, Virginia, to Richmond to live with him.

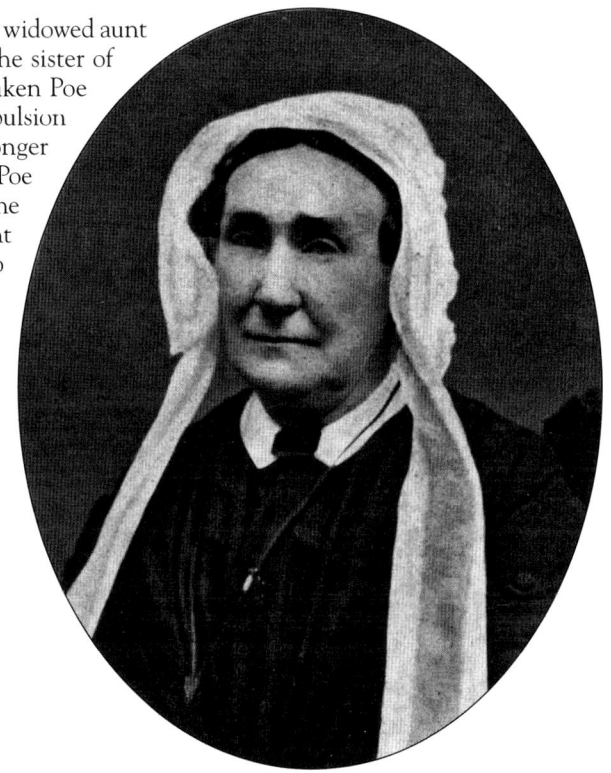

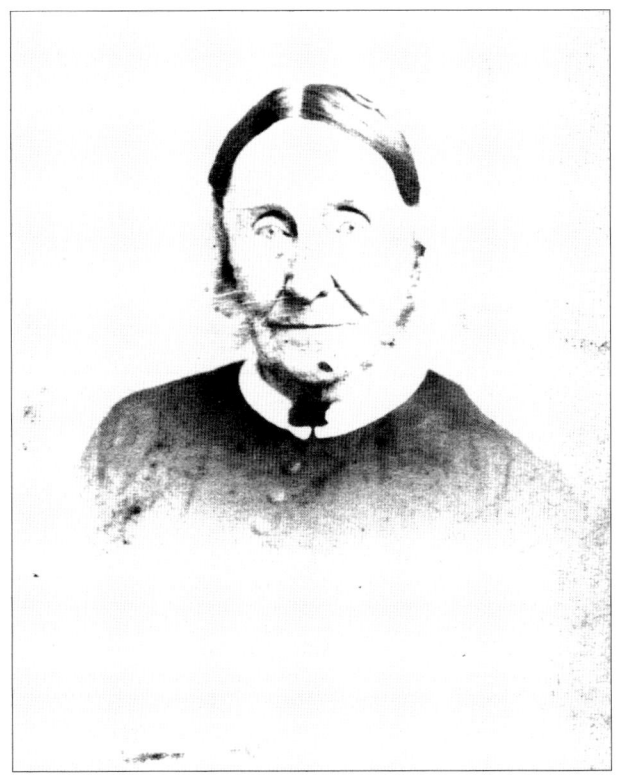

This is a previously unpublished 1868 albumen print photograph of Maria Clemm, who Poe called "Muddy." He dedicated his poem "To My Mother" to her. She, in turn, was devoted to Poe and helped earn money for the family by selling his stories and by taking on sewing jobs.

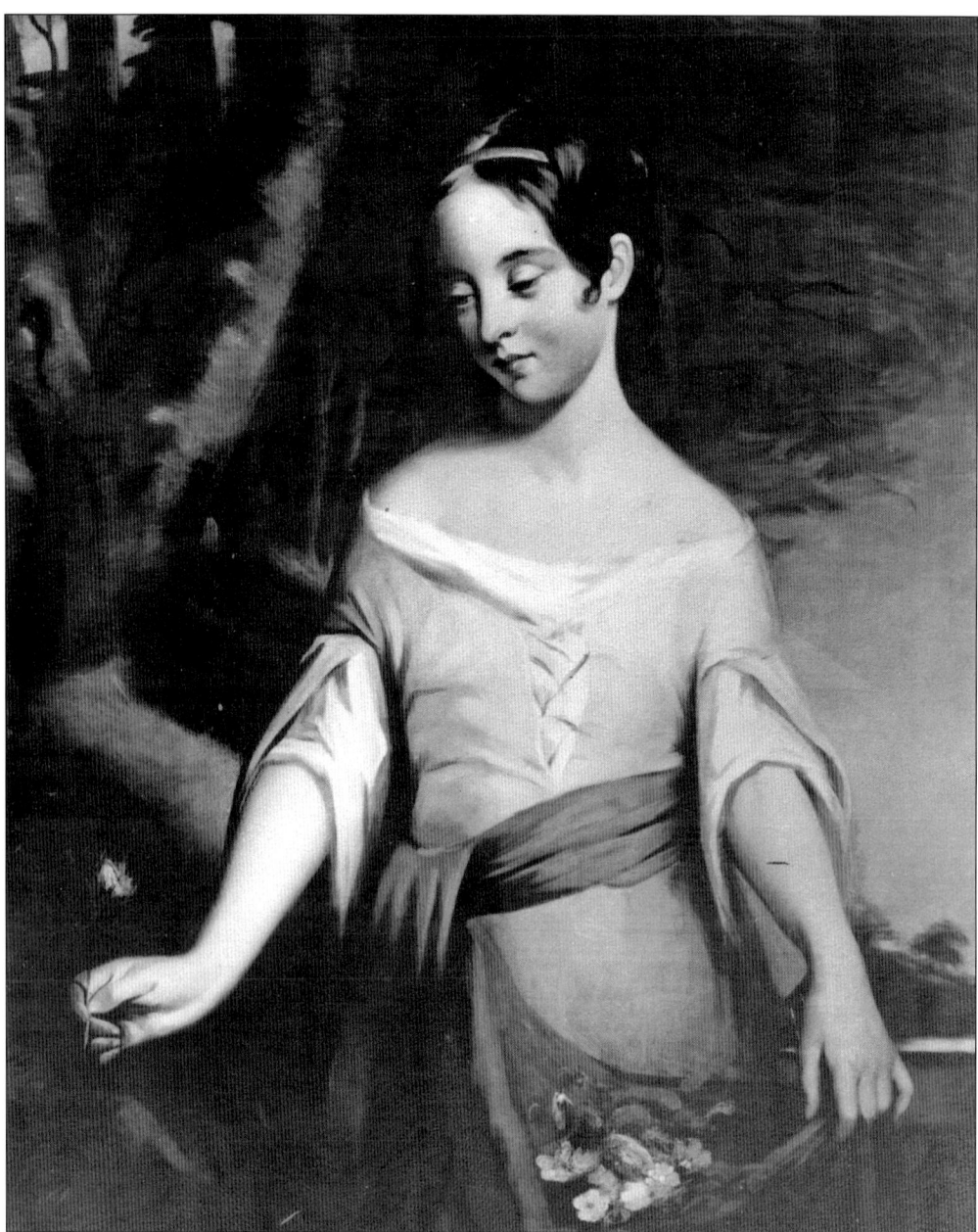

Poe's cousin Virginia Clemm was nine years old when he first moved into her mother's home in Baltimore. By some accounts, Poe used her to carry love letters to ladies in the neighborhood. When he moved to Richmond, he left Virginia Clemm and her mother in Baltimore with his grandmother. After the death of Poe's grandmother Elizabeth Cairnes Poe, who had been receiving a government pension, Maria and Virginia Clemm had no source of support, so a relative, Neilson Poe, offered to take them into his home. Hearing the news, Edgar Poe pleaded with the Clemms to move to Richmond with him instead. Although this portrait said to represent Virginia Poe does bear a striking resemblance to authentic portraits, the attribution of the subject remains dubious. The portrait was offered for sale to the Poe Museum in the 1930s, but the museum declined to purchase the piece because it could not be authenticated.

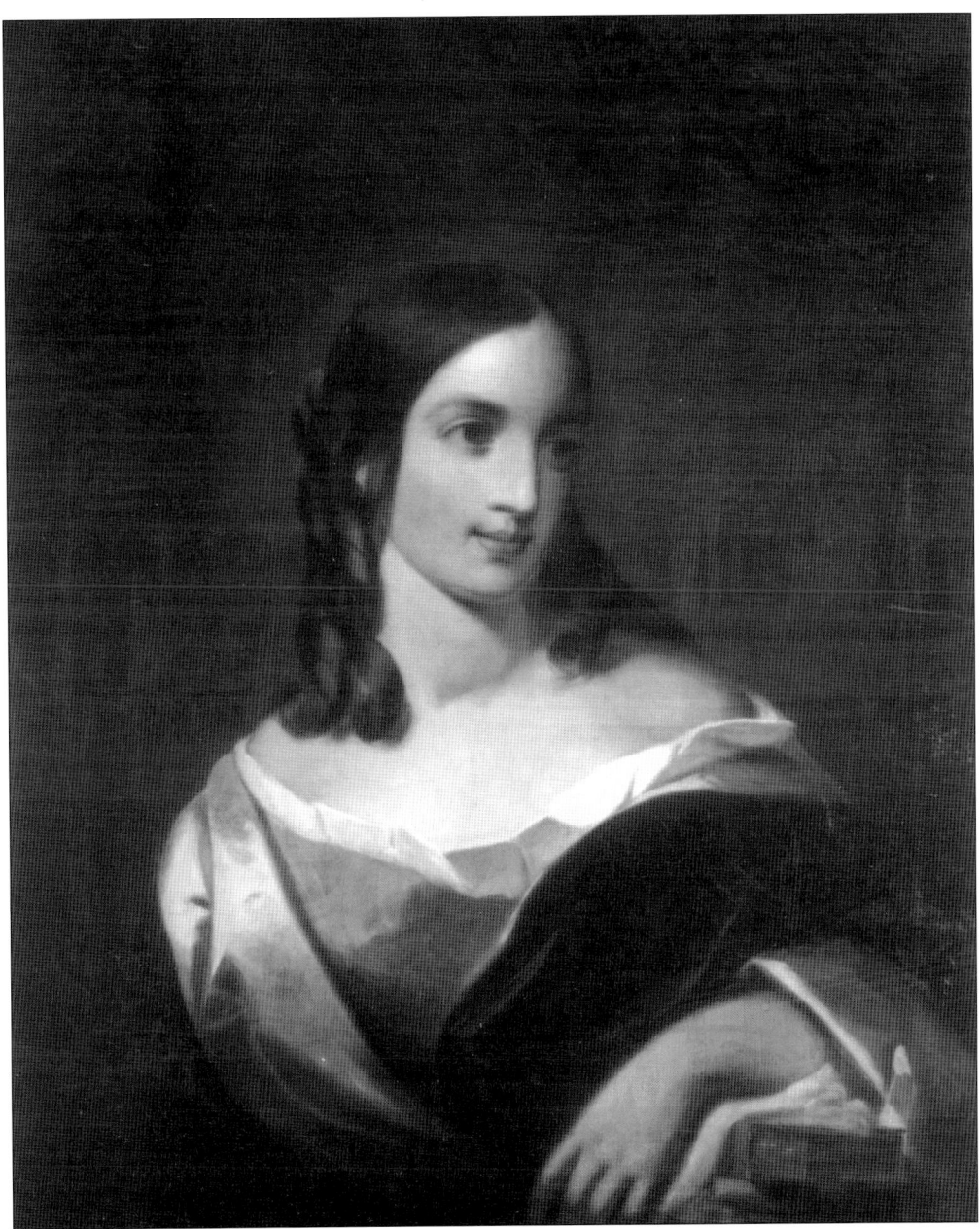

This portrait of Edgar Allan Poe's cousin and wife, Virginia Clemm, was painted by his friend Robert Matthew Sully around the time of Poe's marriage in 1836. Virginia was 13 and Poe was 27. Apparently thinking of her as a little sister, Poe called her "Sissy" while he called her mother "Muddy" or "Mother." By all accounts, Poe and Virginia had a happy marriage. He provided her with a piano and harp so the couple could sing together at night. A friend of the Poes, Francis Osgood, described Virginia as Edgar Poe's "young, gentle, and idolized wife" and stated, "I believe she is the only woman he ever truly loved." Another friend, Mary Grove, wrote of Virginia, "Her pale face, her brilliant eyes, and her raven hair gave her an unearthly look." After 11 years of marriage, Virginia Poe died of tuberculosis on January 30, 1847. (Courtesy of Antoinette Suiter.)

KNOW ALL MEN BY THESE PRESENTS, That we *Edgar A*
Poe *and* *Thomas W. Cleland*
and acting as governor
are held and firmly bound unto *Wyndham Robertson, Lieutenant* Governor of the
Commonwealth of Virginia, in the just and full sum of ONE HUNDRED AND FIFTY DOLLARS, to the
acting
payment whereof, well and truly to be made to the said Governor, or his successors, for the use of
the said Commonwealth, we bind ourselves and each of us, our and each of our heirs, executors
and administrators, jointly and severally, firmly by these presents. Sealed with our seals, and
dated this *16th* day of *May* — 183*6*.

  THE CONDITION OF THE ABOVE OBLIGATION IS SUCH, That whereas a
marriage is shortly intended to be had and solemnized between the above bound *Edgar*
A. Poe and *Virginia E. Clemm*
of the City of Richmond. Now if there is no lawful cause to obstruct said marriage, then the
above obligation to be void, else to remain in full force and virtue.

Signed, sealed and delivered }
  in the presence of }

Cho. Howard

Edgar A Poe [SEAL.]

Tho. W. Cleland [SEAL.]

CITY OF RICHMOND, To wit :
  This day *Thomas W. Cleland* above named, made oath
before me, as *Deputy* Clerk of the Court of Hustings for the said City, that
Virginia E. Clemm is of the full age of twenty-one years, and a
resident of the said City. Given under my hand, this *16.* day of *May* 183*6*

Chs Howard

This is Poe's marriage bond, dated May 16, 1836. The document is signed by the lieutenant
governor of Virginia and verifies that Poe's wife, Virginia Clemm, is 21 years of age, but she was
actually 13. At 27, Poe was more than twice her age.

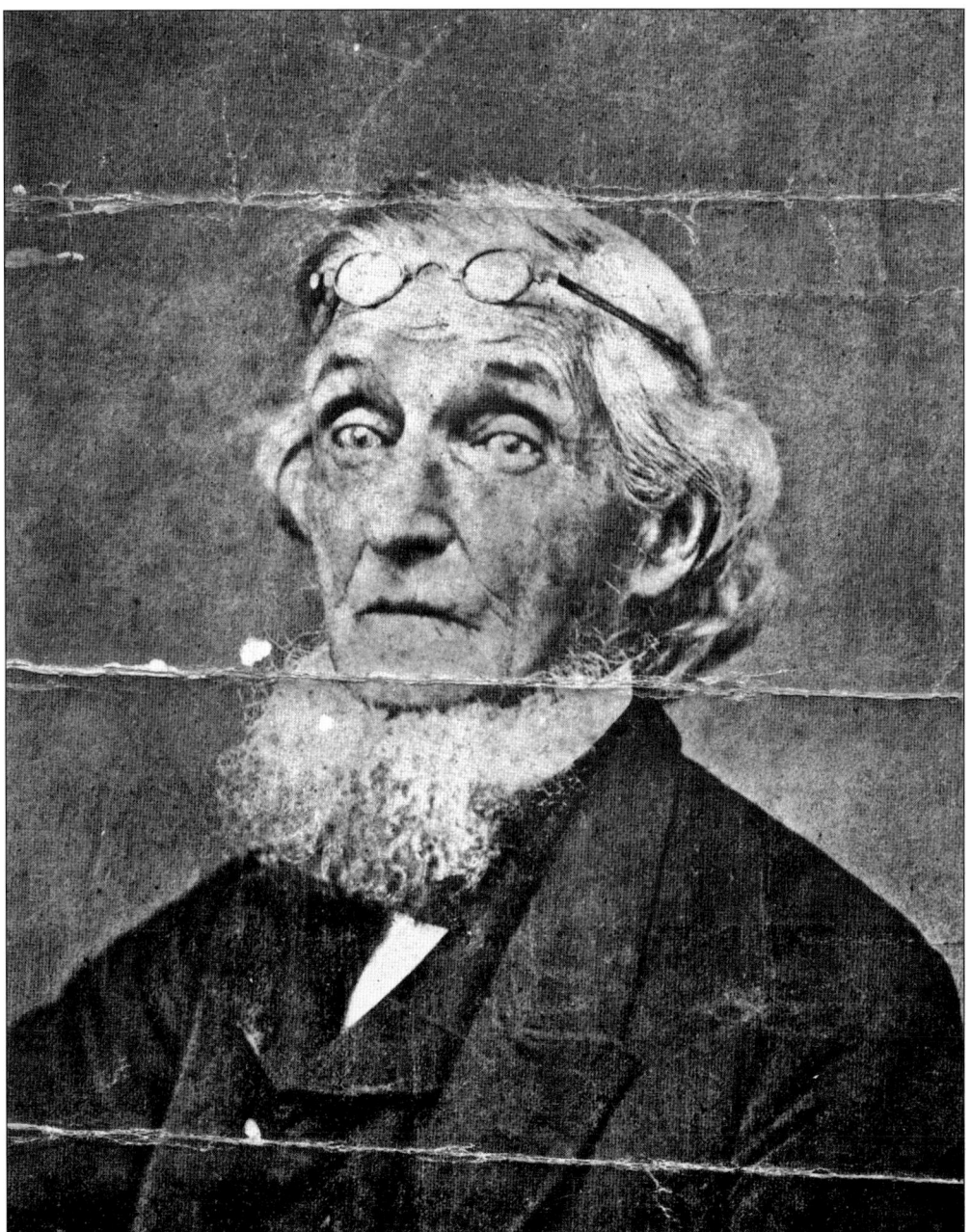

Seen here in his later years, Amasa Converse was the minister who performed Poe's wedding ceremony, which took place in Mrs. Yarrington's Boarding House on Bank Street, directly in front of the Virginia State Capitol. In attendance were Poe's employer Thomas White, White's daughter Eliza White, Mr. and Mrs. Thomas W. Cleland, William McFarlane, John W. Ferguson, Martha Yarrington, and Jane Foster. The bride's mother baked the wedding cake. One of Virginia's playmates who witnessed the wedding told Poe researcher James Whitty she "was full of thrills with thoughts of seeing so young a girl, like her own self, getting married" but was surprised when, after the ceremony, Virginia was not "suddenly transported into matured womanhood." In addition to being a Presbyterian minister, Converse was the editor of the *Southern Religious Telegraph*.

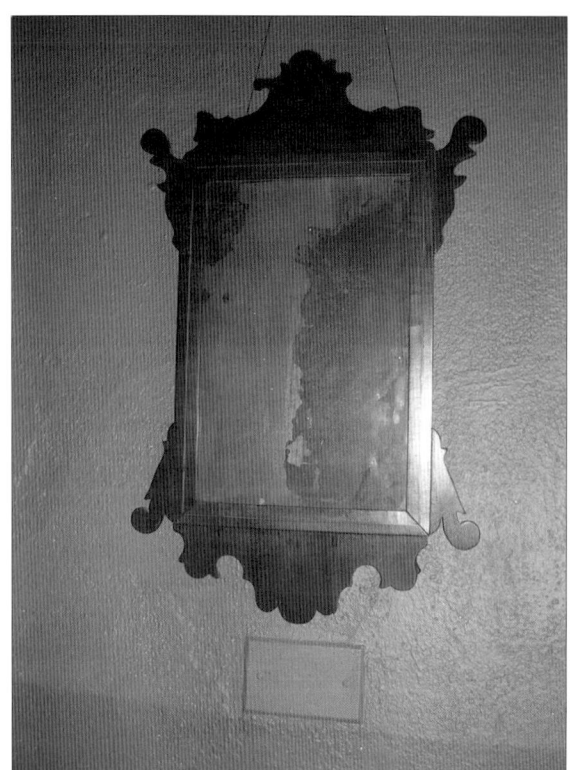

This mirror was among the belongings found in Poe's trunk after his death and is believed to be his wife's mirror. The reflective mercury backing has largely darkened and detached from the glass, but Poe and Virginia would have seen their reflections in this mirror over 160 years ago.

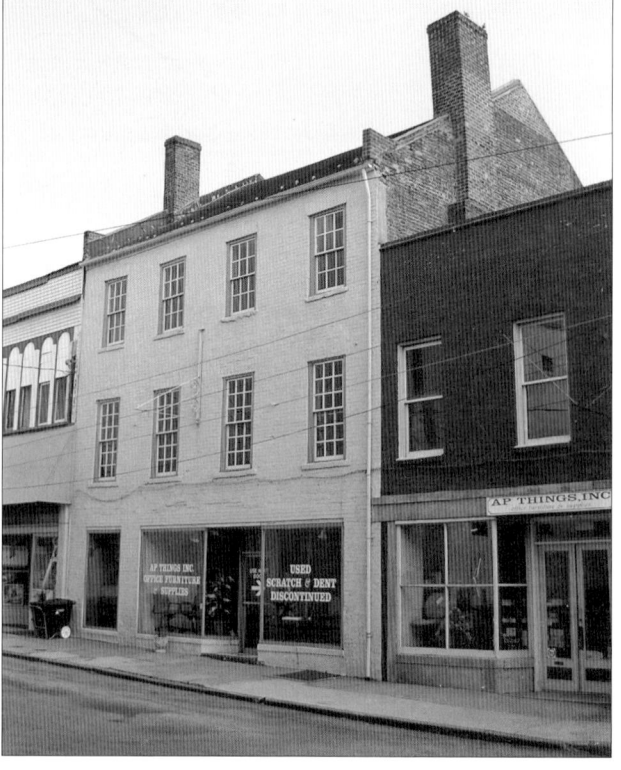

The Hiriam Haines House is located about 30 miles south of Richmond in the city of Petersburg. Haines was a friend and supporter of Poe's, and it is rumored Poe spent his honeymoon in this building. By the time of this photograph, the building had long since fallen into disrepair, and as the sign indicates, it had been used as an office furniture store.

Three

POE'S FINAL VISITS

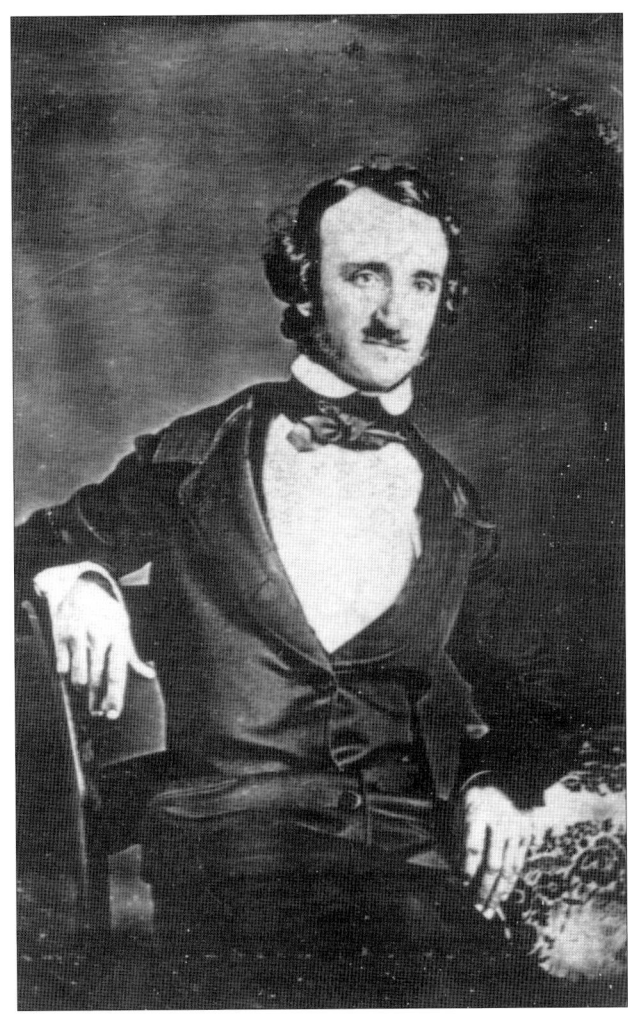

Poe looks every bit the polished Virginia gentleman in this daguerreotype taken about 1846. Of Poe's appearance, his friend John R. Thompson recalled, "He was unmistakably a gentleman of education and refinement. . . . He was dressed with perfect neatness; but one could see signs of poverty in the well-worn clothes, though his manner betrayed no consciousness of the fact."

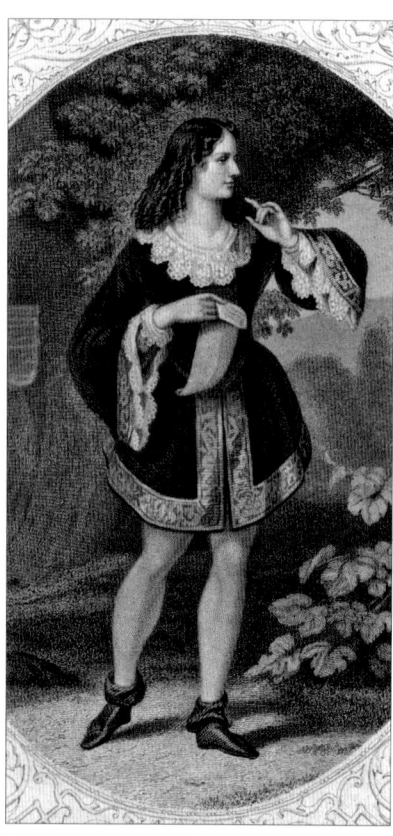

Poe took a keen interest in the theater. Among his favorite actresses was Anna Cora Odgen Mowatt, pictured here in one of her roles, about whom Poe wrote glowing reviews. Although acting was still not considered a respectable profession for a lady, Poe boasted in an 1845 *Broadway Journal* review of Mowatt that he was the son of an actress.

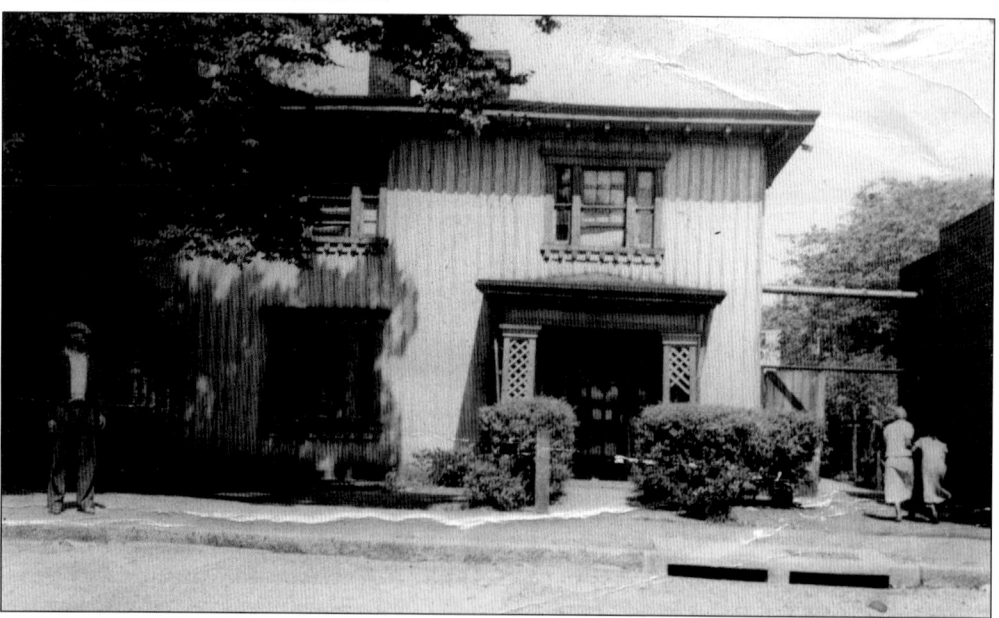

Built in 1853, the Ritchie Cottage at 616 North Ninth Street was the home of the author and actress Anna Cora Odgen Mowatt, who had married W. F. Ritchie, the son of *Richmond Enquirer* editor Thomas Ritchie. Poe and Mowatt lived in New York in the 1840s. Shortly after the death of her first husband in 1851, she married Ritchie and moved to Richmond.

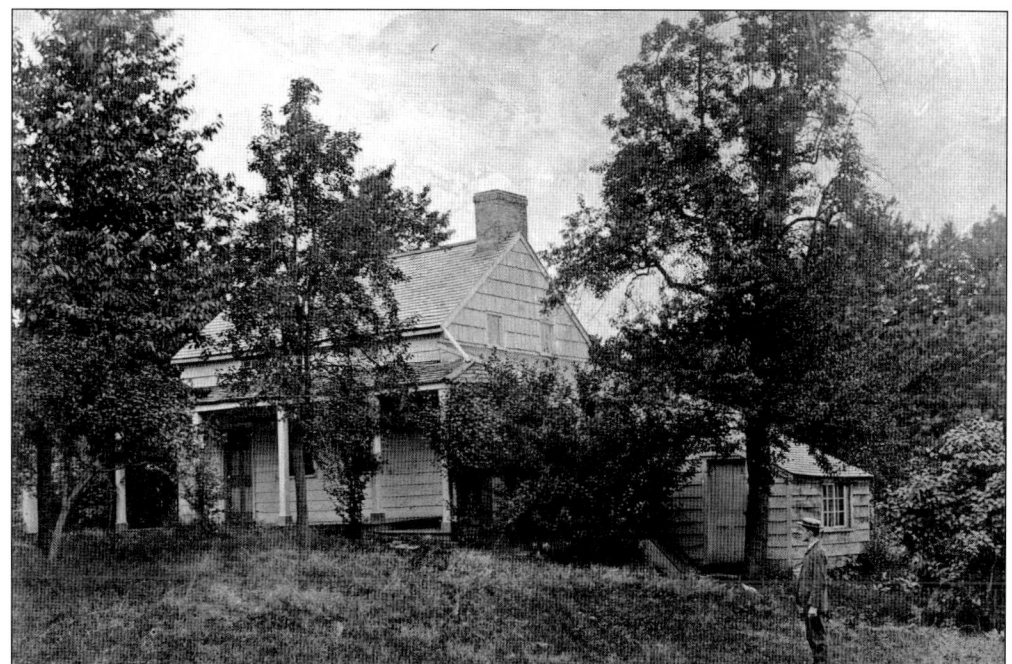

In 1846, Poe moved into this modest cottage in the countryside of Fordham, about 15 miles outside New York City. He believed the fresh country air would improve his wife's health. Virginia was suffering from tuberculosis. Poe lived in the house with his wife, mother-in-law, a cat, and some birds. The photograph dates to the 1880s.

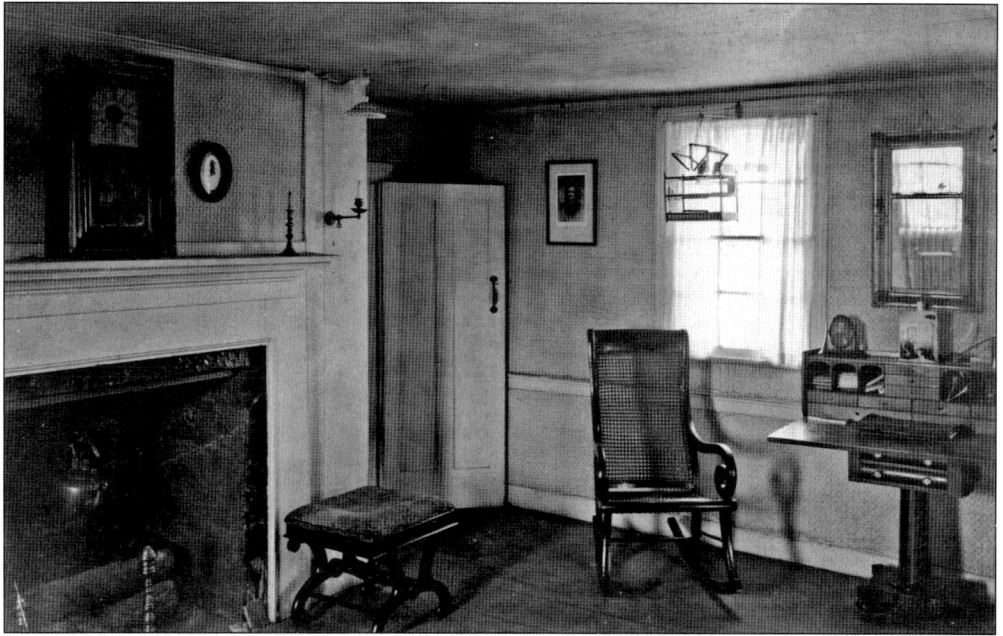

This 1920 photograph by Charles W. Stoughton depicts Poe's study from his Fordham cottage. A visitor to Poe's cottage described Poe sitting in this chair and writing with his cat Catarina perched on his shoulder. In this house, Poe wrote his classic poem "Annabel Lee" as well as his last book, *Eureka*.

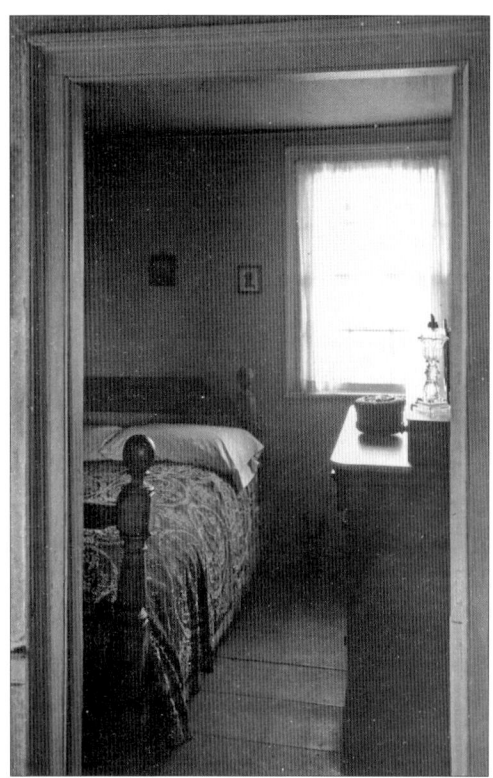

Struggling to sell his stories and articles in order to support his small family, Poe kept his wife warm in this bed by covering her with his coat while his cat slept on her chest. A concerned friend, Marie Louise Shew, volunteered her time to care for Virginia during her final illness. The photograph was taken in 1920 by Charles W. Stoughton.

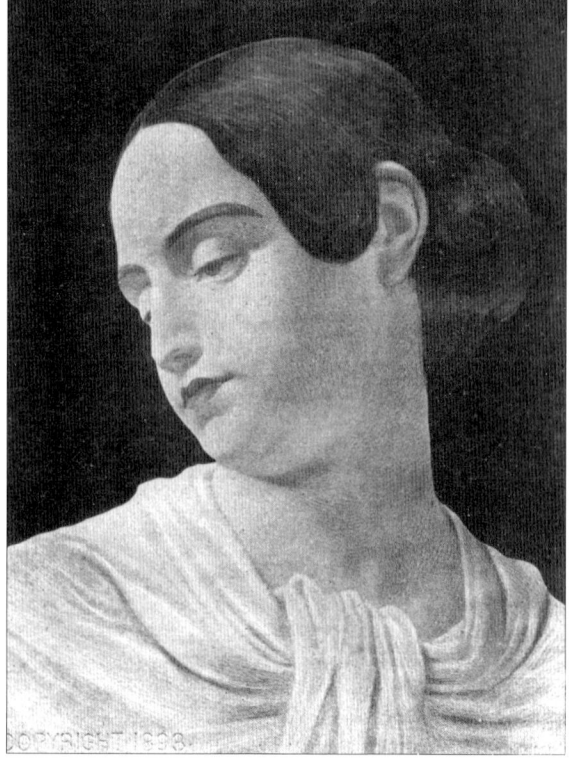

Virginia died of tuberculosis on January 31, 1847, at the age of 24, the same age at which Poe's mother and brother had died. A sketch was made of her shortly after her death. Not wishing the public to see her in such a condition, the Poe family kept the image private for decades before the owner, Amelia Poe, released this photograph of it in 1893.

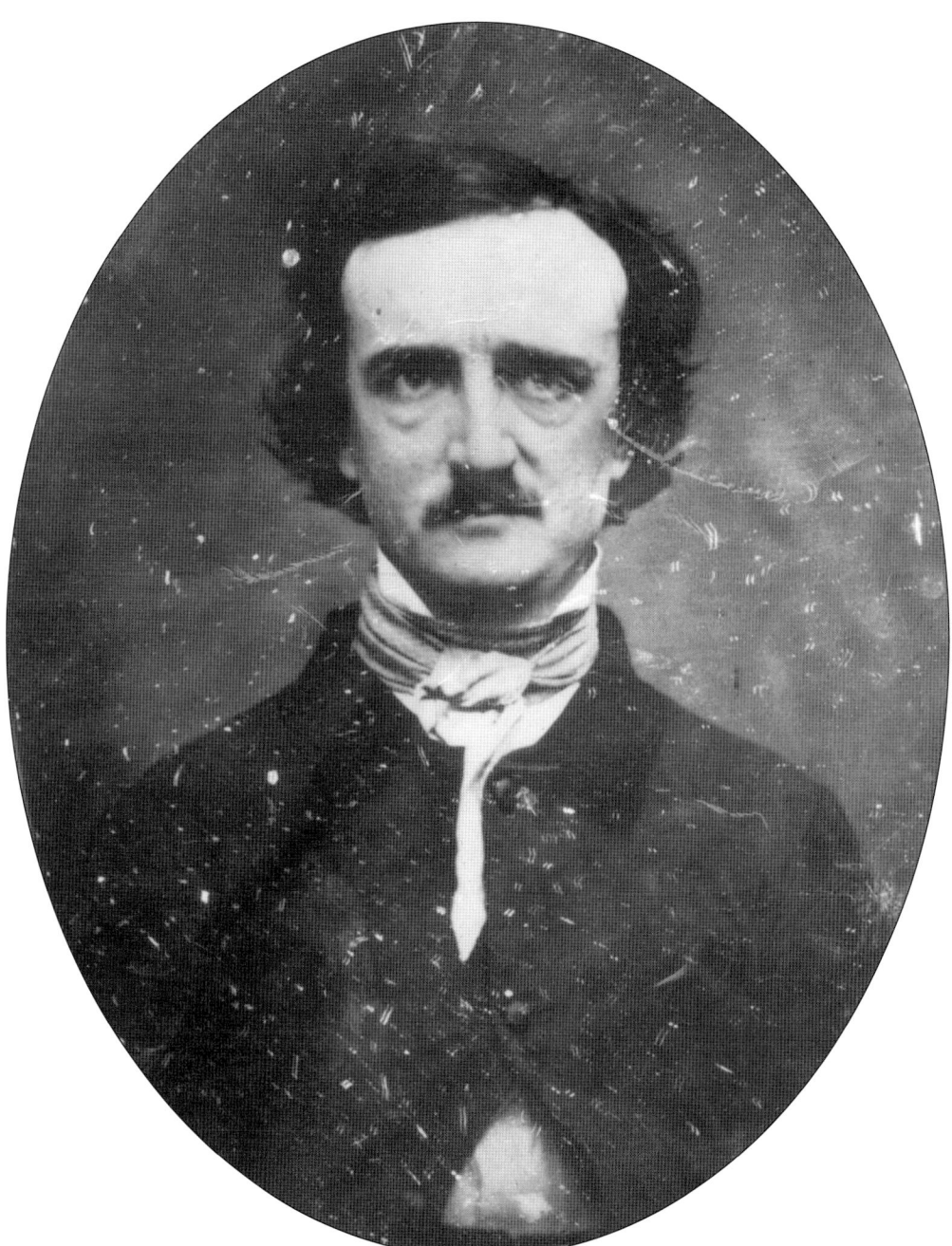

Although one of the best known images of Poe, the "Ultima Thule" daguerreotype shows Poe at perhaps the lowest point in his life. Taken in early November 1848 in Providence by Edwin H. Manchester, this grim image reflects the circumstances under which Poe sat for the photograph. After a proposal to the poet Sarah Helen Whitman had been rejected, Poe attempted suicide by overdosing on the painkiller laudanum four days before this picture was taken. To cheer him up, Poe's friends took him out drinking the night before this daguerreotype was taken. Ten days later, Poe became engaged to Whitman, who owned the original daguerreotype and who named it the "Ultima Thule," a Latin term referring to the ends of the known world.

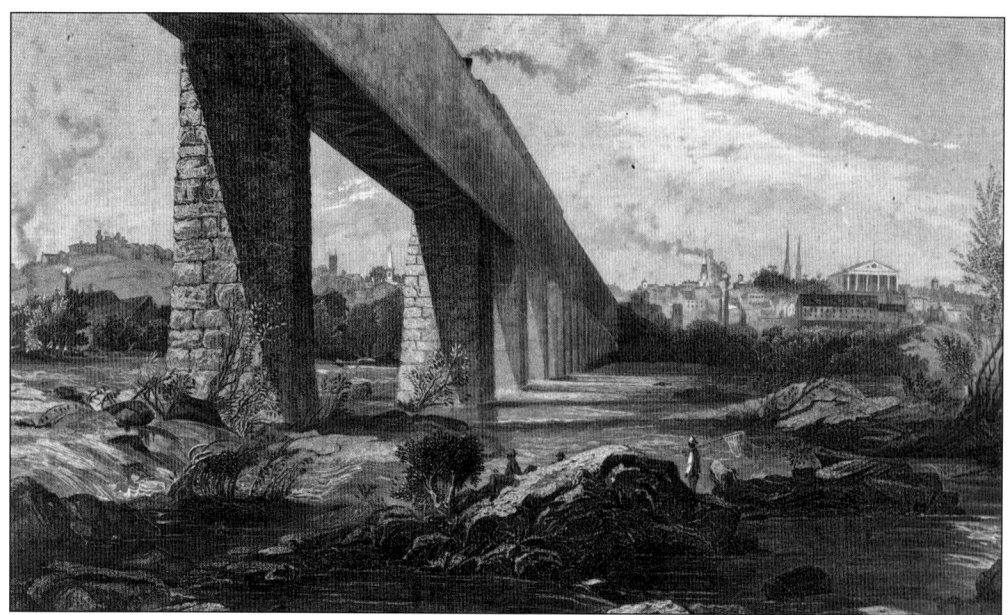

Although this 1871 view of Richmond was engraved after Poe's death, it features two important Richmond landmarks, the Virginia State Capitol and the James River. A notable change since Poe's time is the railroad bridge in the foreground. Trains were beginning to connect the Northeast but were less common in the South until after Poe's death.

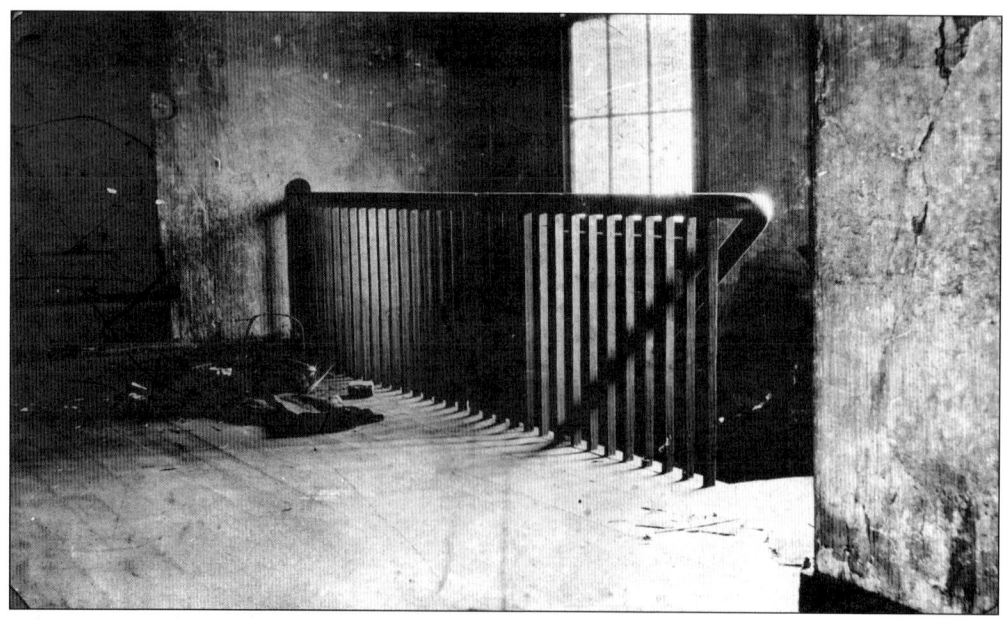

Taken in 1904, this rare photograph depicts the hall of the Swan Tavern, where Poe stayed during his last visit to Richmond in the summer of 1849. Poe, no doubt, would have walked up and down these stairs during his stay. After his death, his trunk of possessions was found in storage at the tavern.

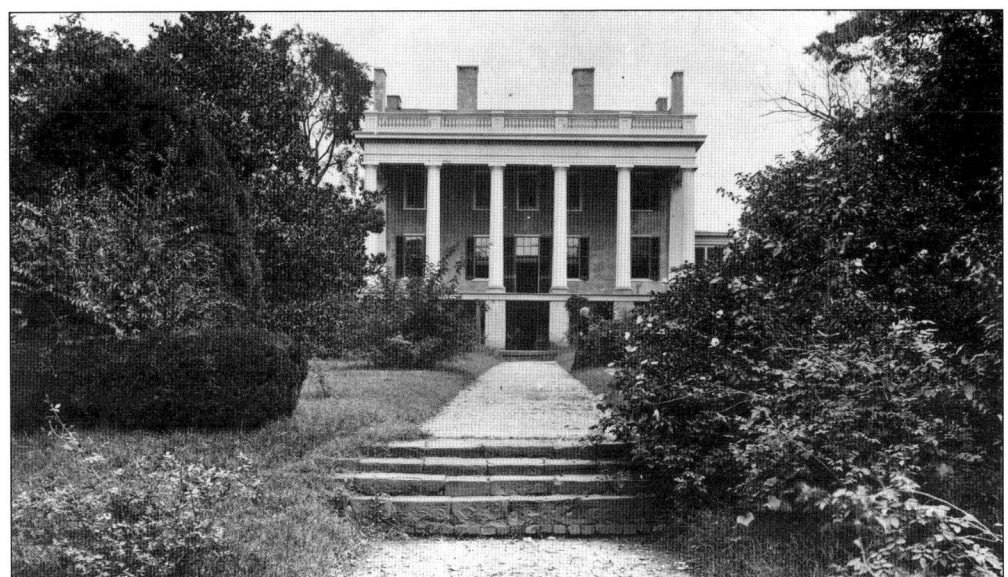

The Van Lew family lived in this grand manor on Church Hill. Located a block from St. John's Church and the Elmira Shelton House, this mansion would have been a regular sight on Poe's walks through the neighborhood. Van Lew family tradition relates that Poe read *The Raven* for the family. The woman in the garden is Elizabeth Van Lew, who was a Union spy during the Civil War. The home was demolished in 1911.

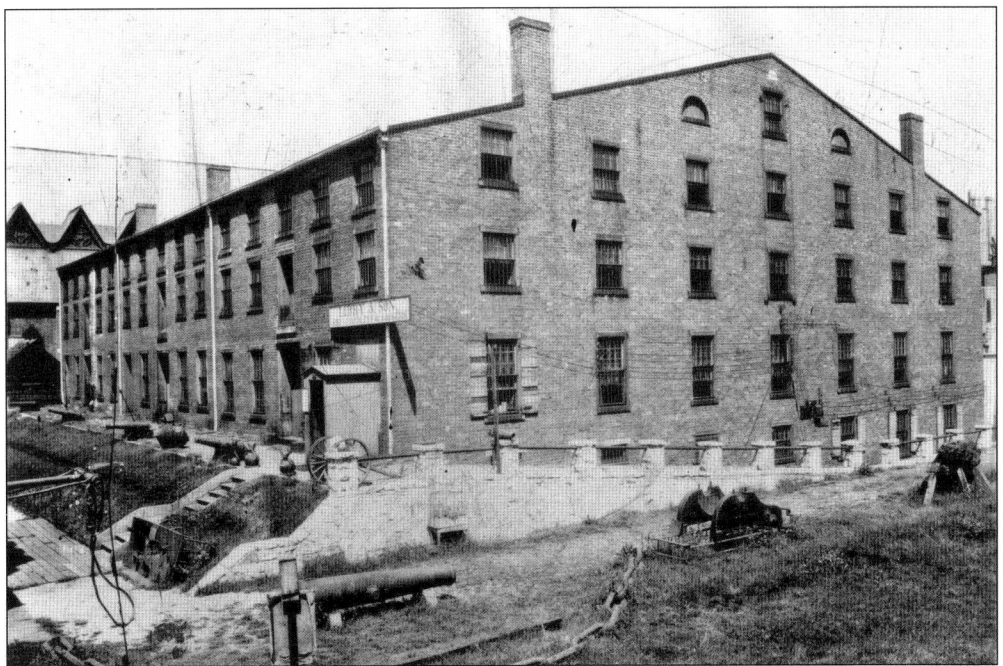

During Poe's lifetime, the Libby Warehouse on Cary Street was little different from other large warehouses along the James River. During the Civil War, the building was taken over by the Confederate government and used as a prison for Union officers. The structure was thenceforth known as Libby Prison. The building became infamous when in 1888 the building was disassembled and reconstructed at the Chicago World's Fair.

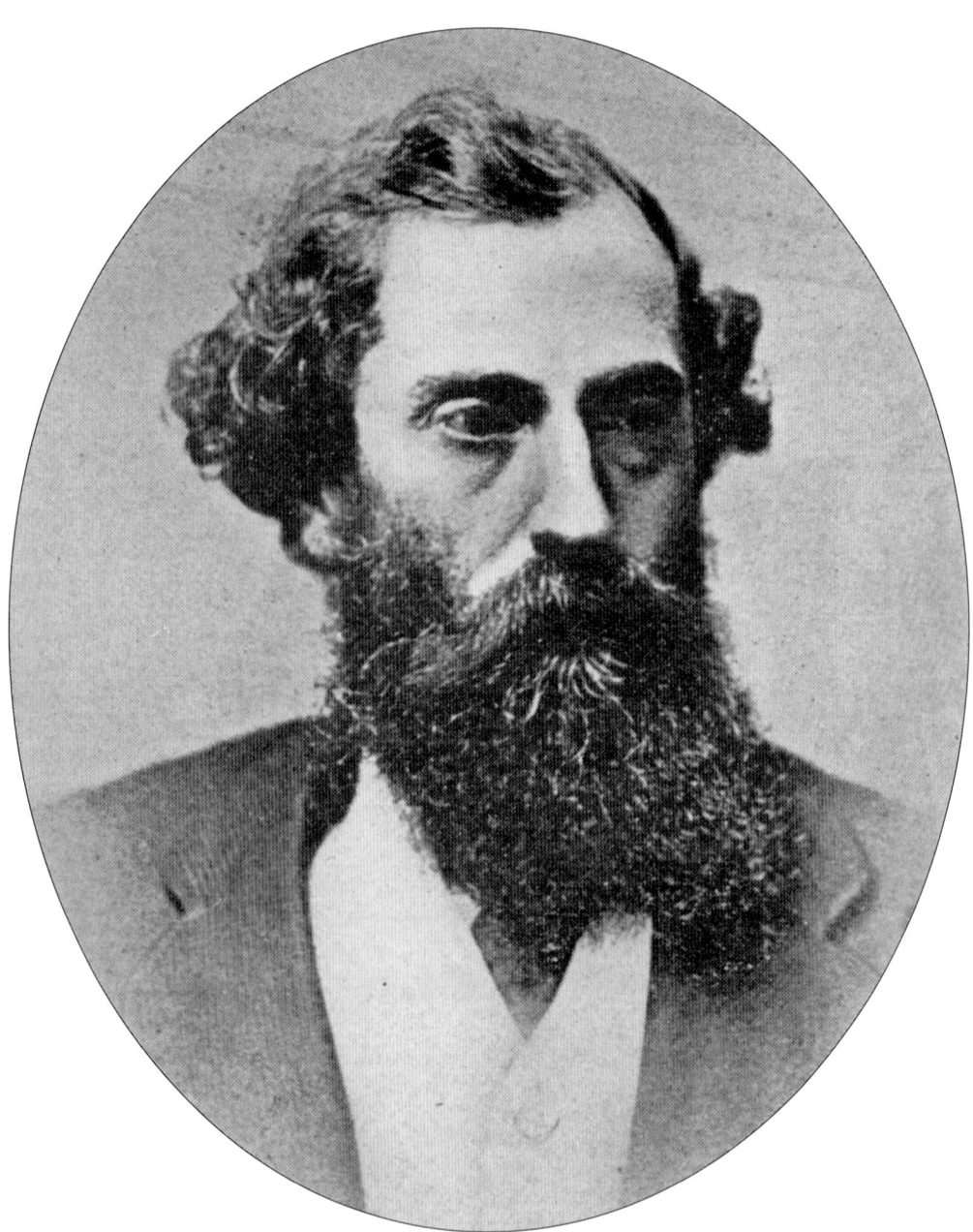

John Rueben Thompson became the editor of the *Southern Literary Messenger* in 1847. By his account, Thompson was informed that the writer Edgar Allan Poe was "wandering around" Rocketts Landing, "a rather disreputable suburb of Richmond," in 1848. Thompson spent the afternoon searching for him without success. After 10 days, Poe appeared in the *Messenger* office and stated, " 'My name is Poe,' without further introduction or explanation." On another occasion, Thompson claimed to have found Poe in a saloon, "mounted on a marble-top table, declaiming passages from his then unpublished *Eureka* to a motley crowd, to whom it was as unintelligible as so much Hebrew." Thompson soon began publishing Poe's articles in the *Southern Literary Messenger*, and Poe's articles continued to appear in the magazine until his death the following year. After Poe's death, Thompson lectured widely on "The Genius and Character of Edgar Allan Poe."

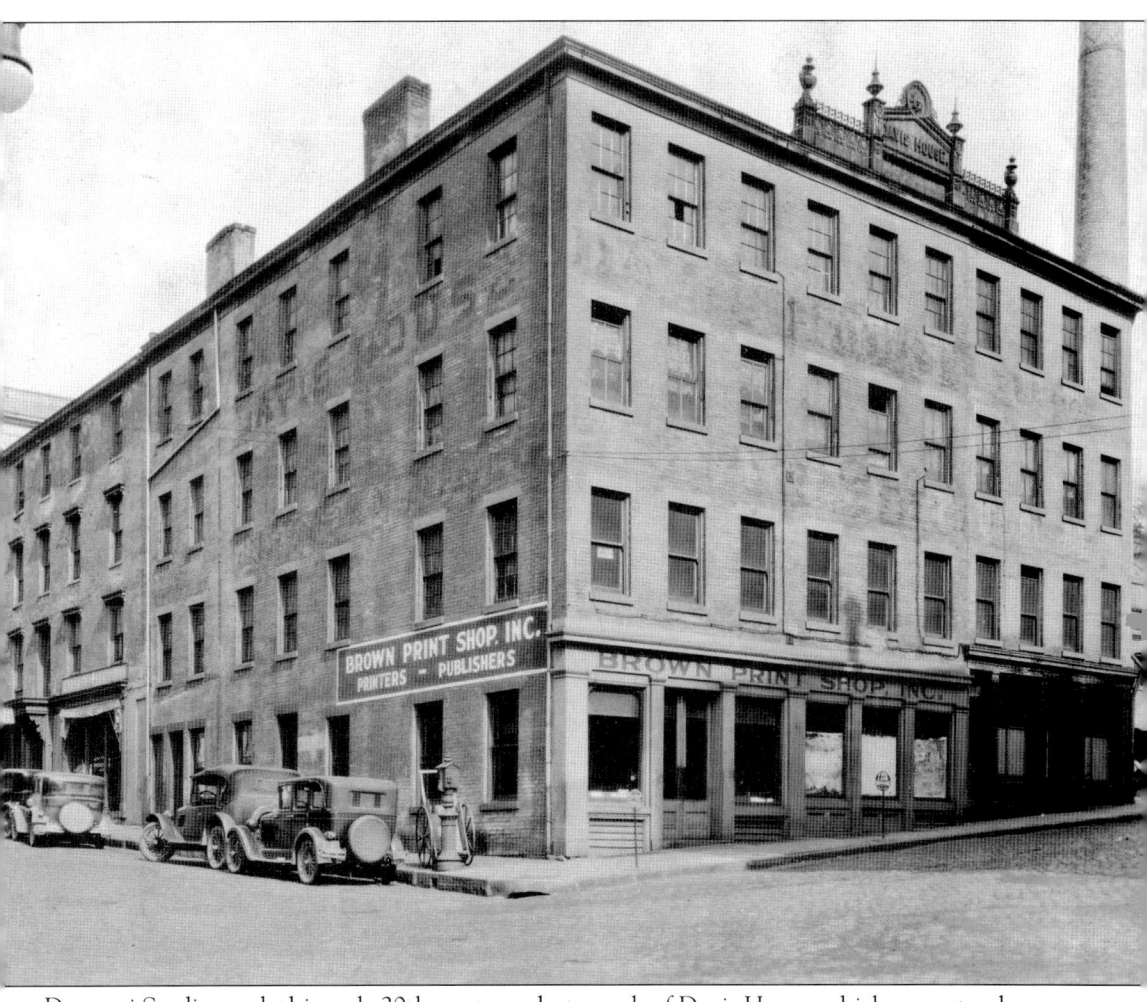

Dementi Studios took this early-20th-century photograph of Davis House, which once stood on the northwest corner of Governor and Franklin Streets. The *Southern Literary Messenger* moved its editorial offices to the second floor of this building, and it was here Poe visited the new editor of the journal, John R. Thompson, in 1848. Before Poe left Richmond for the last time in September 1849, he gave Thompson a copy of his unpublished poem "Annabel Lee."

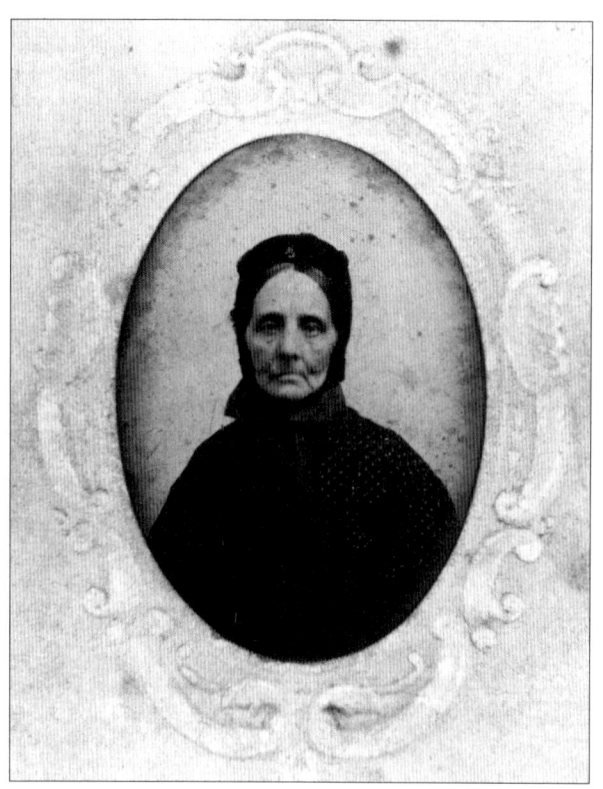

This 1865 tintype and this albumen print photograph taken about 1870 both show Poe's only sister, Rosalie Mackenzie Poe. Rosalie was separated from her siblings at the age of one when their mother died. Edgar Poe was sent to live with the Allan family, and Rosalie grew up in the home of the Allans' friends the Mackenzies. Although Poe traveled from city to city for much of his adult life, Rosalie spent most of her life in Richmond. She regularly wrote to him to request his autograph to give to friends. When asked for an autograph, Rosalie would sign photographs and books "Rose Poe, Sister of the Poet."

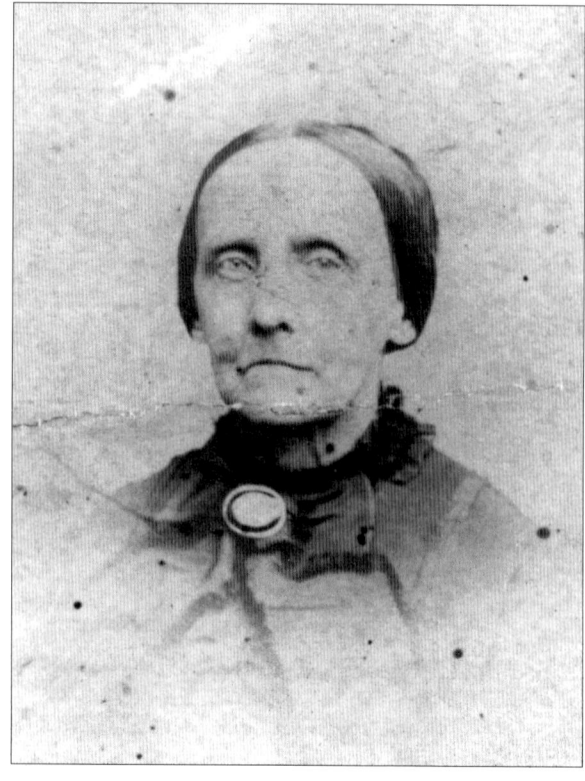

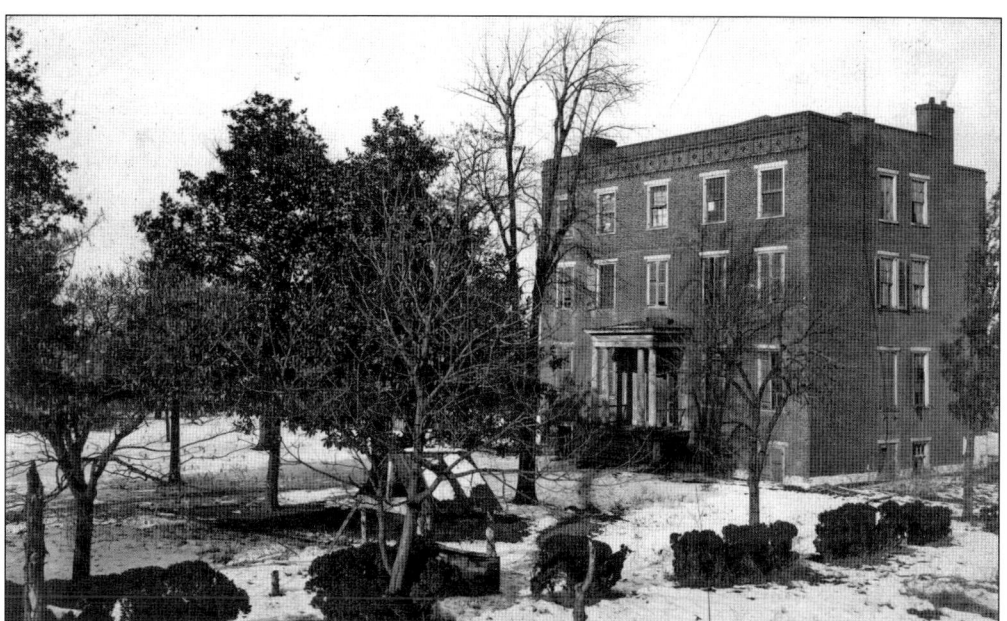

Poe's sister lived in this rural home, Duncan Lodge, with the Mackenzie family. By the time this photograph was taken in the late 19th century, a third story had been added to drastically change the appearance of the house from what Poe would have seen on his visits to the building. Duncan Lodge was demolished in 1906.

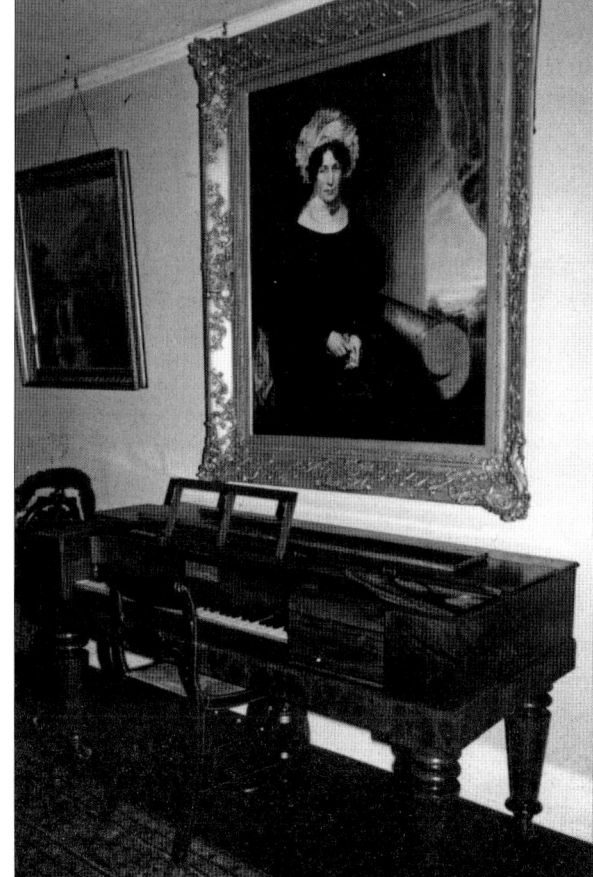

This piano, made between 1838 and 1840, is the one Poe's sister, Rosalie, played at her Richmond home Duncan Lodge, where she lived with her foster mother, Jane Scott Mackenzie. The Mackenzies lost their fortune after the Civil War, and Rosalie Poe gave her piano to her doctor to pay off a debt.

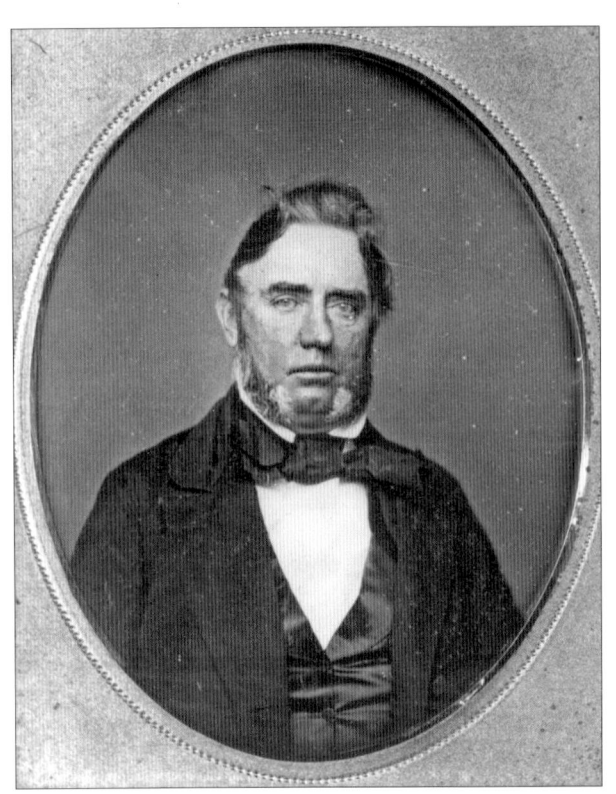

Rosalie Poe's foster brother John Hamilton Mackenzie was a lifelong friend of Edgar Poe's. This daguerreotype shows his in his middle age, while the albumen print reproduced below represents him in later years. When his father, William Mackenzie, died in 1829, John Hamilton Mackenzie became Rosalie Poe's legal guardian. Because he had known Poe, Mackenzie was called upon by biographers to provide insight into the life of his friend.

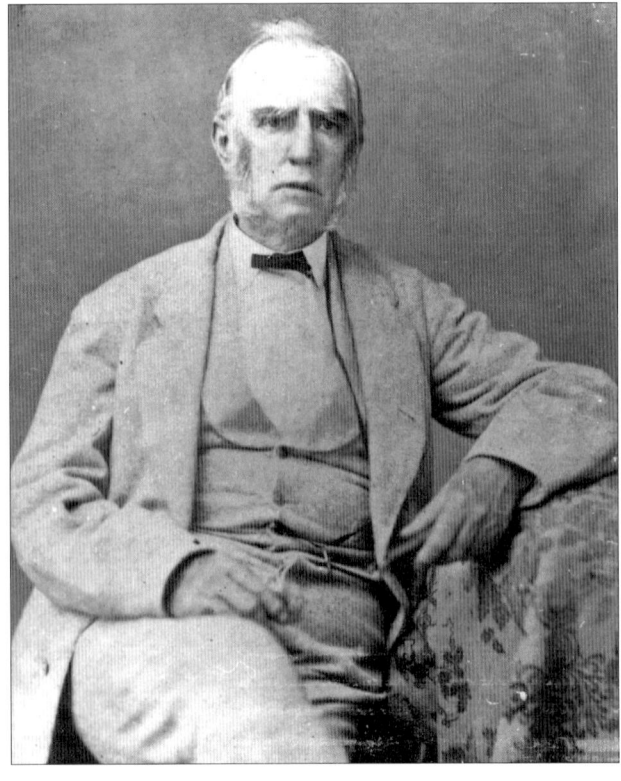

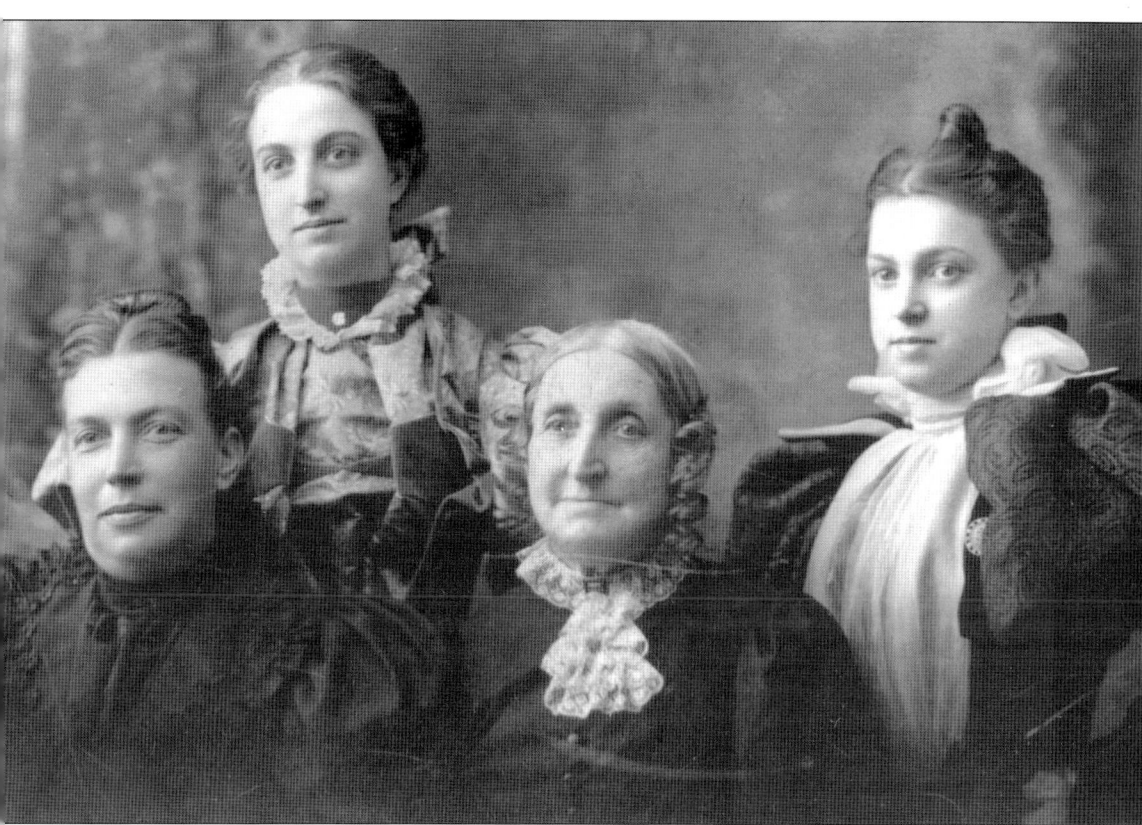

John Hamilton Mackenzie's second wife, Louisa Lanier Mackenzie, is seated at the center of this undated 19th-century portrait. Seated on the left is her daughter Flora Latham Mack, whose daughters Mary (left) and Grace stand behind her. In his final years, John H. Mackenzie gave his daughter Flora Mack two boot hooks that had been left at the Mackenzie home by Edgar Poe. A photograph of the boot hooks, which are now in the Poe Museum, appears on page 78. Mackenzie relatives also sold or donated several other pieces of furniture, silver, and artwork to the Poe Museum.

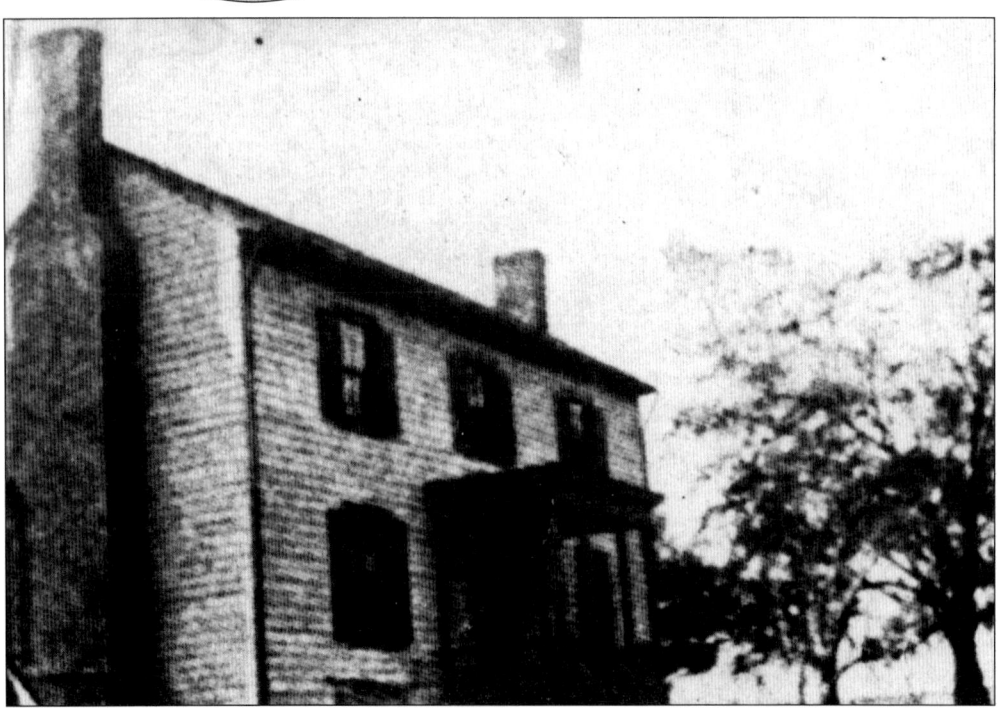

Susan Archer Talley Weiss was a close friend of Poe's sister and often entertained Poe at her home, Talavera, in the summer and fall of 1849 during Poe's last visit to the city. In a later account, Weiss described one of Poe's readings in which he attempted to read "The Raven" with the utmost solemnity while a moth was fluttering about his face.

This early view of the Talley residence, Talavera, reveals the appearance of the farm house before late-19th-century additions altered its appearance. Poe was a regular guest of the Talleys and gave his last private reading of "The Raven" in the parlor. According to Talley family member Susan Archer Talley Weiss, Poe's performance was so terrifying that the servants in attendance fled the room.

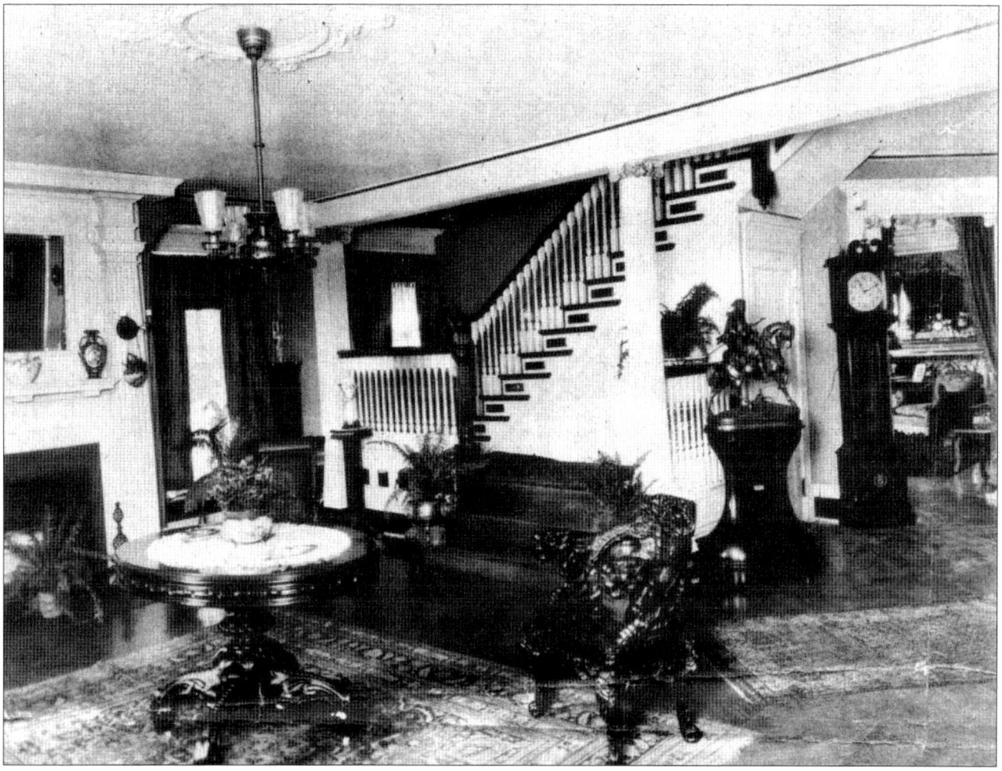

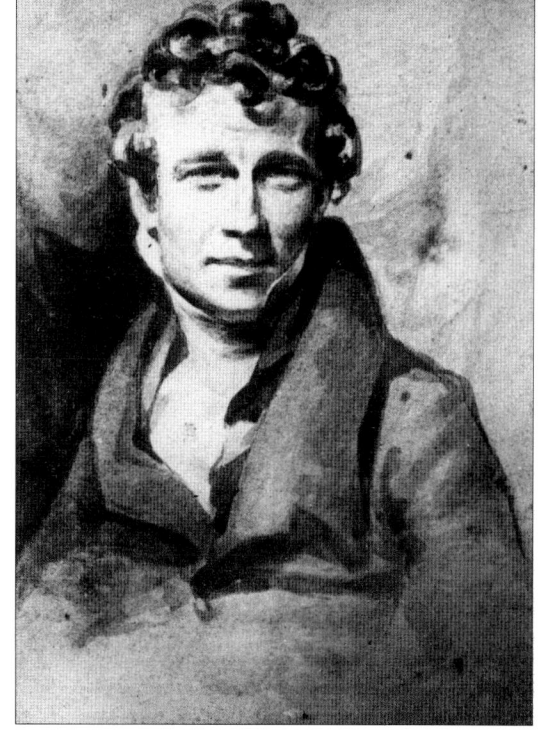

This is a 1921 photograph of the reception hall of Talavera, the home in which Poe gave his last private reading on September 25, 1849. Susan Weiss, who was present at the performance, later recounted that Poe told her that evening that the last few weeks he had spent in Richmond had been "the happiest he had known for many years." He died two weeks later.

Robert Matthew Sully was an artist born in Petersburg, Virginia. Sully was a friend of Edgar Allan Poe and painted a portrait of his wife, Virginia Clemm, in 1836. Sully painted portraits of many of the people Poe knew, including Poe's foster mother, Frances Allan, and Poe's sister's foster mother, Jane Scott Mackenzie.

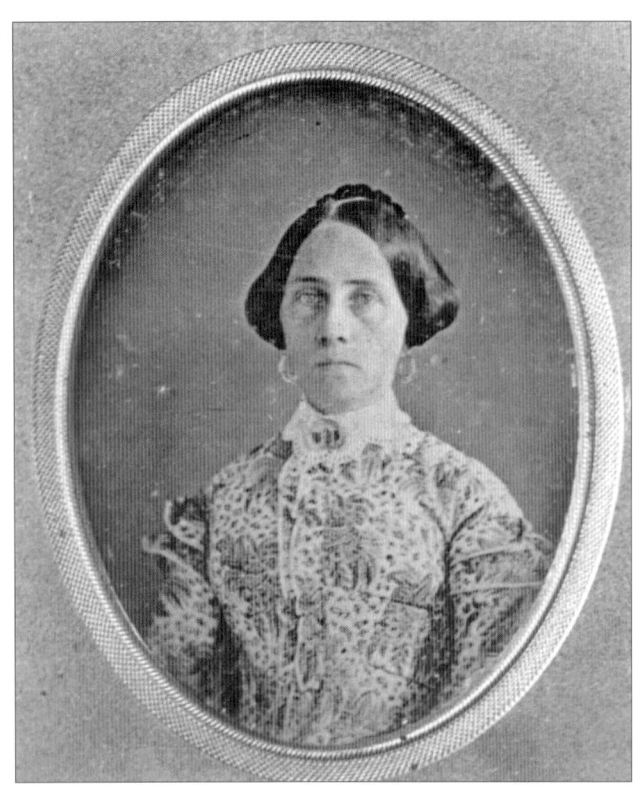

Two daguerreotypes from the early 1850s depict Elmira Royster Shelton, who was Poe's first fiancée in 1826 when he was 17. After her father broke off the engagement, she married Alexander Shelton in 1828. When Poe married his cousin Virginia Clemm in 1836, the Sheltons saw the newlyweds at a party. According to Elmira Shelton, seeing the couple was "almost agonizing;" she reminded herself she was a married woman and "banished" her feelings for Poe as "[she] would a poisonous reptile." Thirteen years later, Elmira Shelton was engaged to Poe again when he was 40, but he died before the wedding could take place. These photographs were taken a few years after Poe's death. According to Poe's friend Susan Talley, Shelton had large blue eyes, straight features, and a stern countenance.

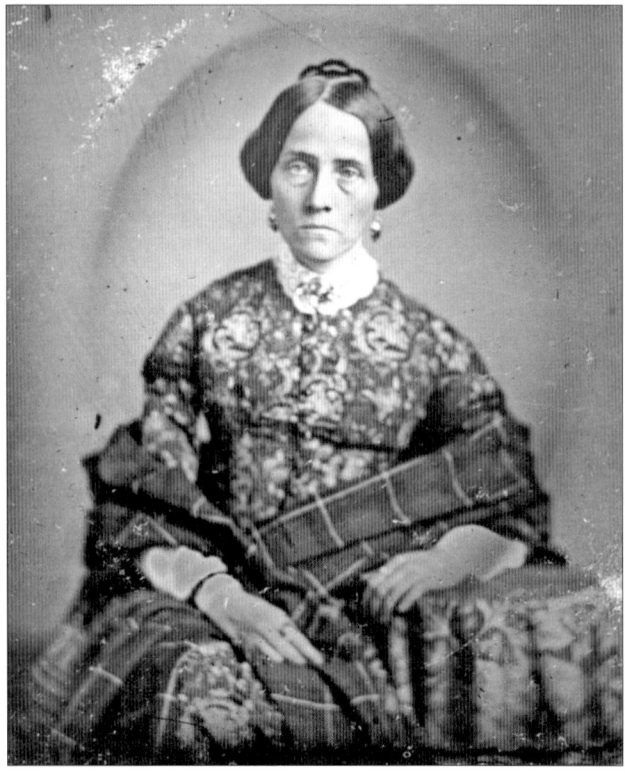

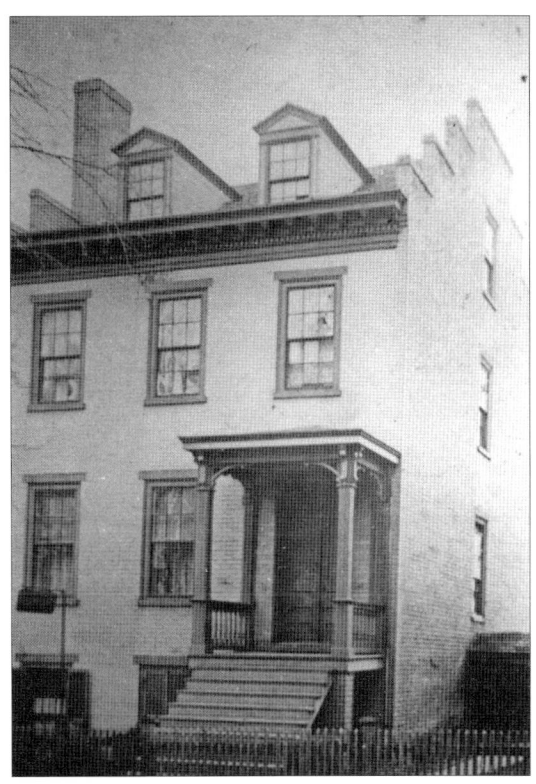

Elmira Royster Shelton was living in this house on Church Hill while Poe was courting her in 1848 and 1849. Although she had inherited a considerable fortune from her late husband, Alexander Shelton, Elmira rented this home. A frequent visitor to the house, Poe spent time there on his last night in the city. The 19th-century photograph with the picket fence in front of the yard gives a better impression of the house's appearance during Poe's time. The iron fence depicted in the 20th-century view was a later addition. In the 20th century, the house was acquired by the Historic Richmond Foundation, which occupied and maintained it for several years.

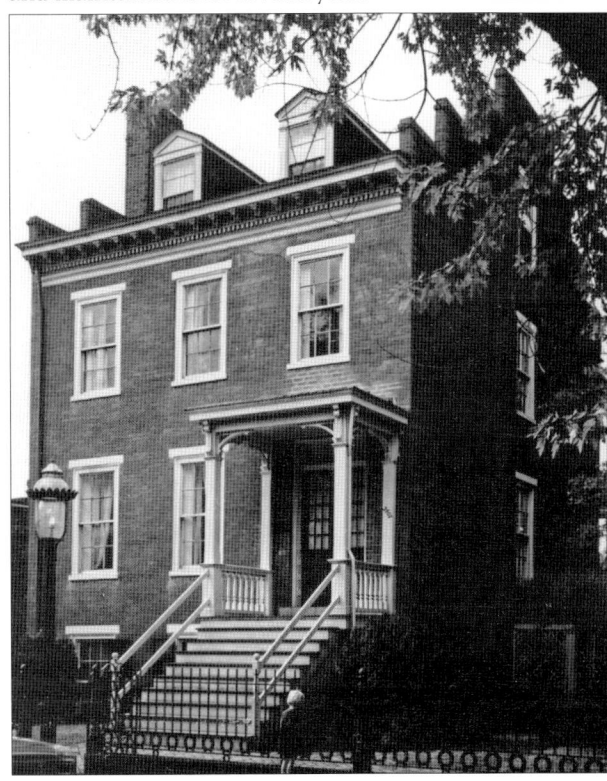

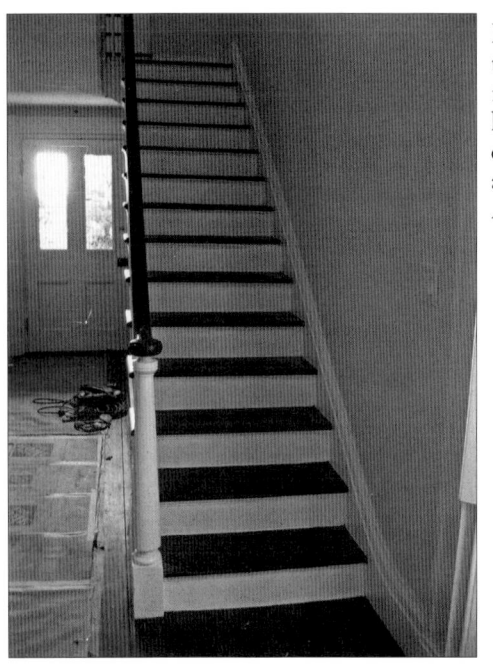

In July 1848, the widow Shelton came down these stairs in her East Grace Street home to investigate an argument she heard someone having at the front door with her maid. Shelton discovered the intruder was Poe, who had arrived unannounced after an 11-year absence. As a proper lady, Shelton told Poe to leave.

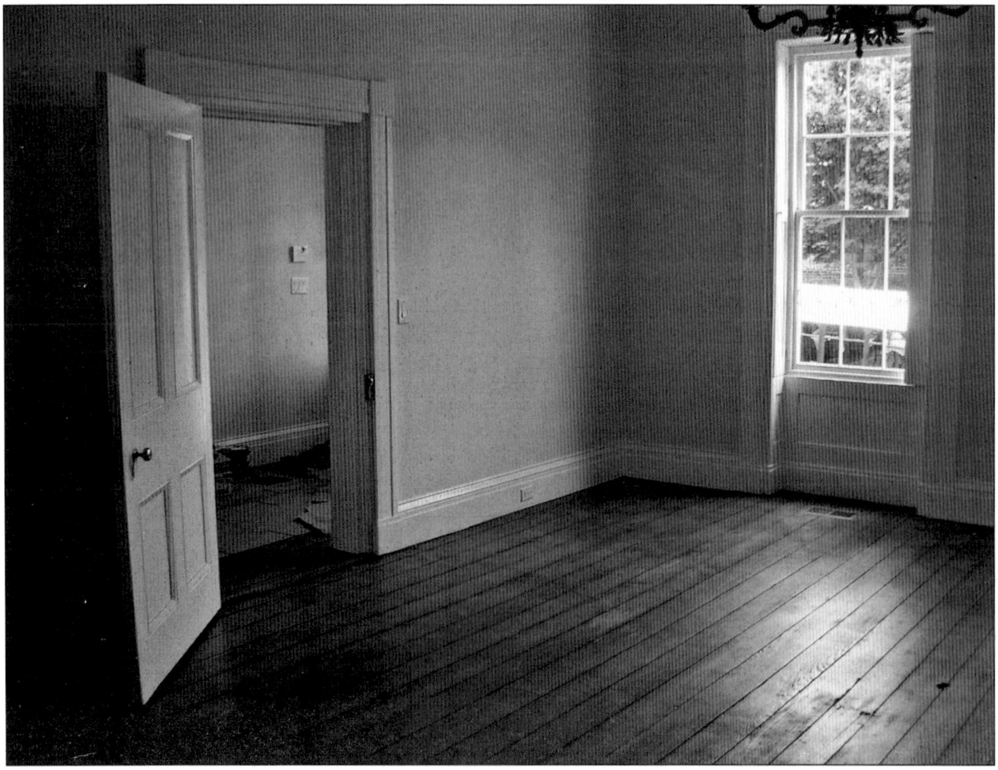

Poe proposed to Elmira Shelton in her parlor (seen here while undergoing restoration) in July 1849. Her first response was to laugh at him. In an 1875 interview with Edward Valentine, Shelton related, "I told him if he would not take a positive denial he must give me time to consider of it—and he said that a love that hesitated was not a love for him."

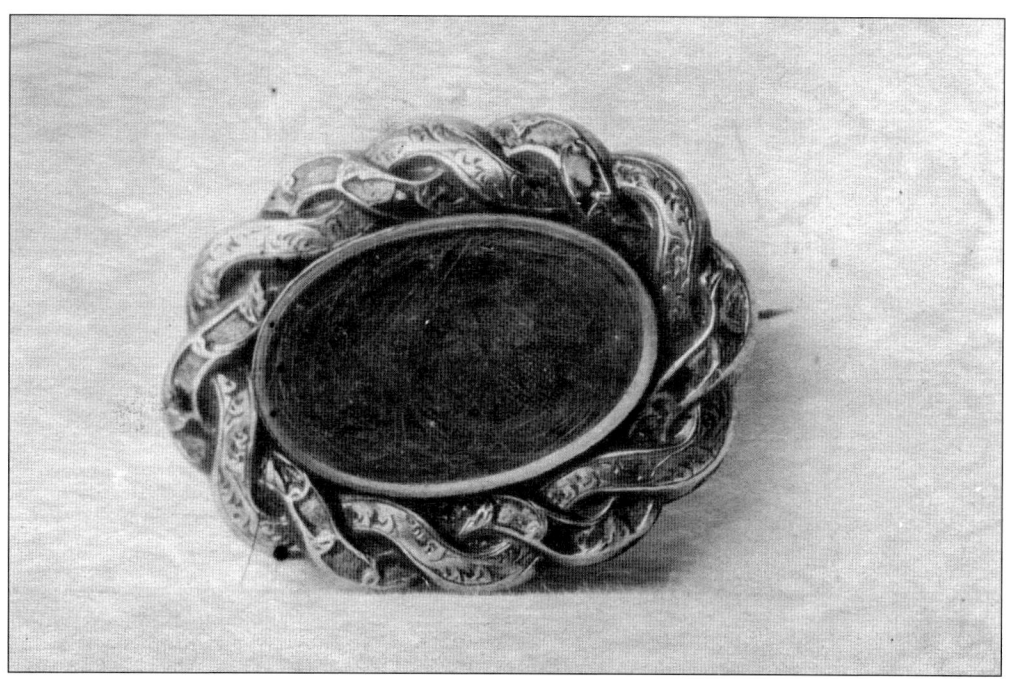

Poe gave this brooch to Elmira Shelton at the time of their second engagement in 1849. The top is engraved with Poe's and Shelton's initials. The brooch opens to reveal a lock of Poe's hair. Poe first proposed to Shelton in July 1849, but she had hesitated to reply. Though her feelings for him appear to have been genuine, her first husband, Alexander Shelton, had left a stipulation in his will stating that if she were to remarry after his death she would lose three-quarters of the fortune he had left her and cease to be the executor of his estate. That Shelton had accepted Poe's marriage proposal is evident in a letter she wrote to Poe's aunt Maria Clemm on September 22, 1849.

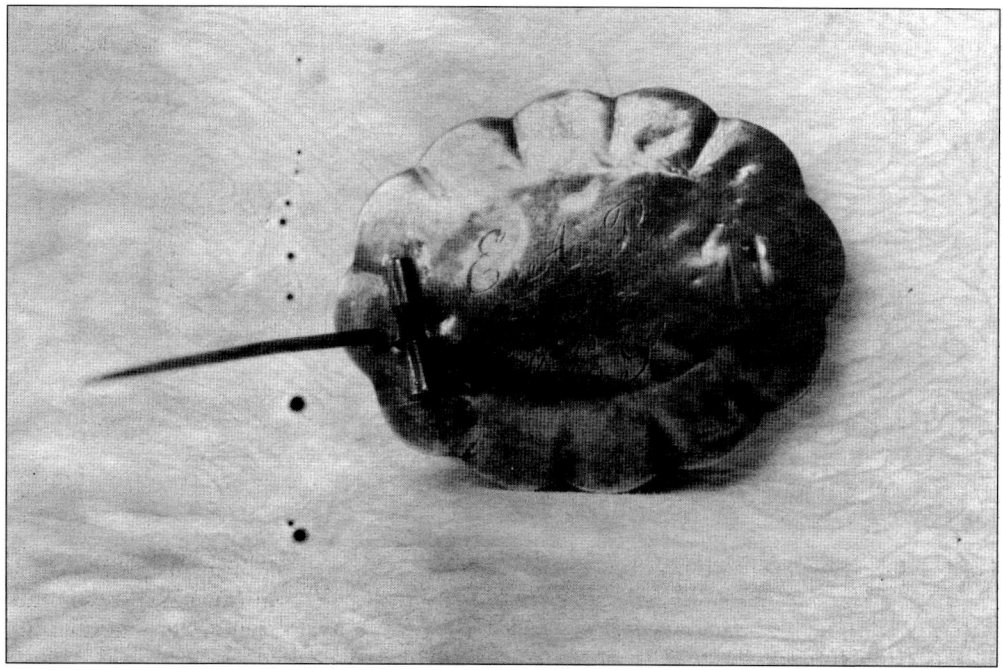

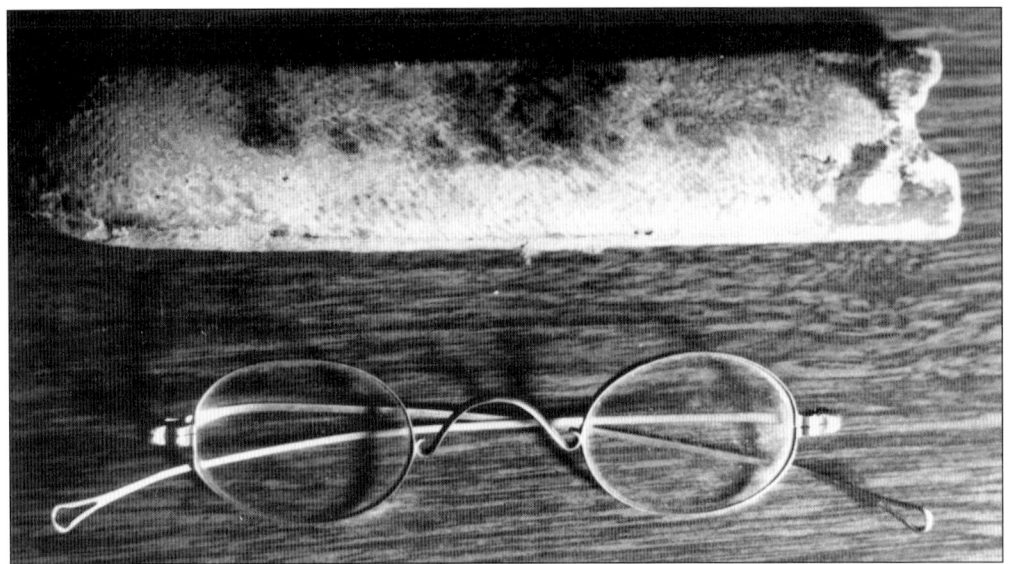

Elmira Shelton wore these glasses, which she kept in the leather case also visible in this photograph. The pieces were given to the Poe Museum by Shelton's descendants along with a daguerreotype of Shelton and a miniature portrait of her father, James Royster.

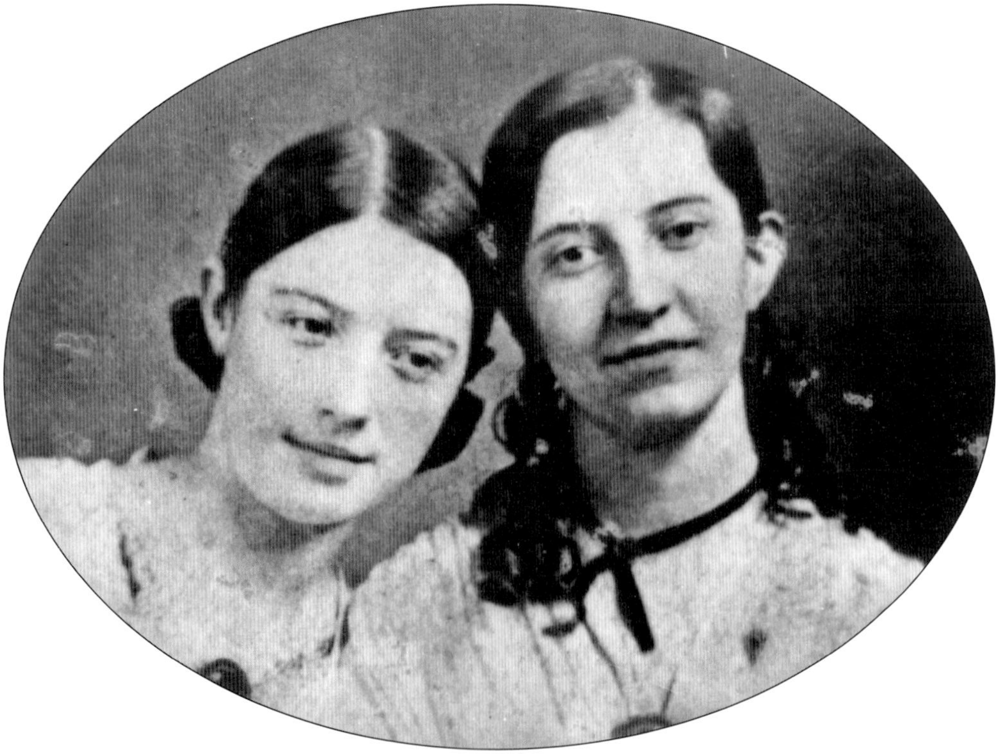

This 19th-century photograph on metal depicts Elmira Shelton's daughter Ann Elizabeth Shelton (left) and the latter's cousin, Lucy Bohannan. Both Ann Shelton and her brother, Southall Bohannan Shelton, opposed her mother's relationship with Poe. They may have shared the opinion of some Richmonders who believed Poe wanted to marry Elmira Shelton for her money.

Elmira Shelton's daughter, Ann Elizabeth Leftwich (née Shelton), appears in later life in this 19th-century albumen print by Virginia Art Studio of Richmond. Her mother had not remarried after Poe's death, and Poe's name was rarely spoken in the house. Leftwich's children knew nothing of their grandmother's relationship with Poe until after her death, when it appeared in her obituary.

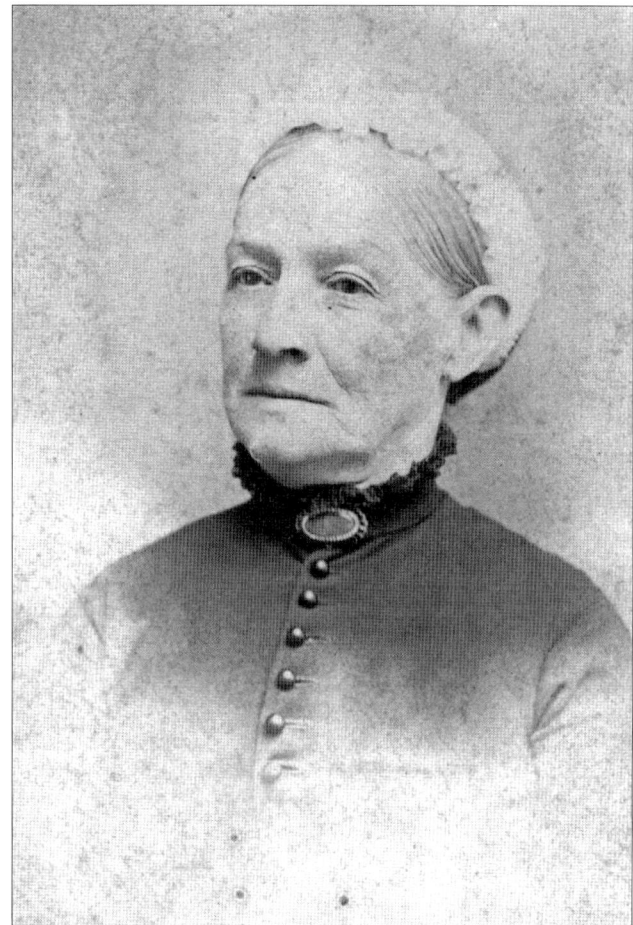

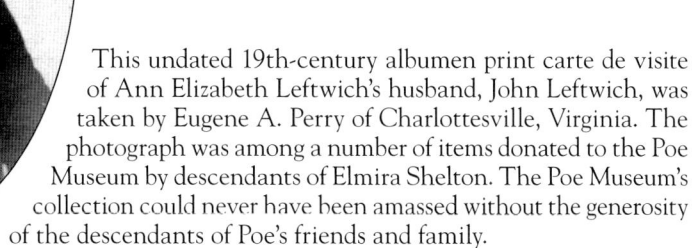

This undated 19th-century albumen print carte de visite of Ann Elizabeth Leftwich's husband, John Leftwich, was taken by Eugene A. Perry of Charlottesville, Virginia. The photograph was among a number of items donated to the Poe Museum by descendants of Elmira Shelton. The Poe Museum's collection could never have been amassed without the generosity of the descendants of Poe's friends and family.

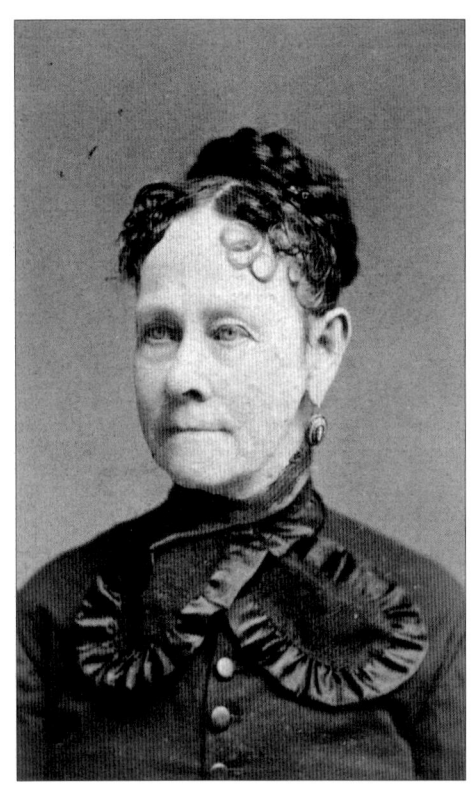

Elmira Shelton's sister Lucy Pierce is depicted in these 19th-century photographs. The seated portrait is dated 1880, and the close-up, taken at the New York Art Gallery of Richmond, was likely taken around that time. Pierce's opinion of her sister's relationship with Edgar Allan Poe is unknown. Like her sister, Pierce declined to discuss the matter publicly. After refusing several requests for interviews, Shelton finally agreed to speak about Poe with Richmond historian Edward Valentine in 1875. During the interview, she denied having been engaged to Poe at the time of his death, but her letters written at the same time tell a different story.

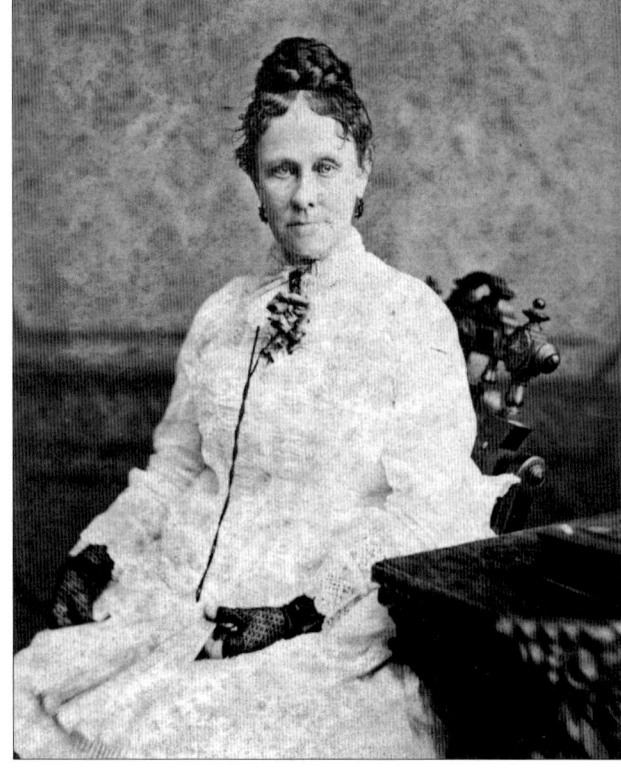

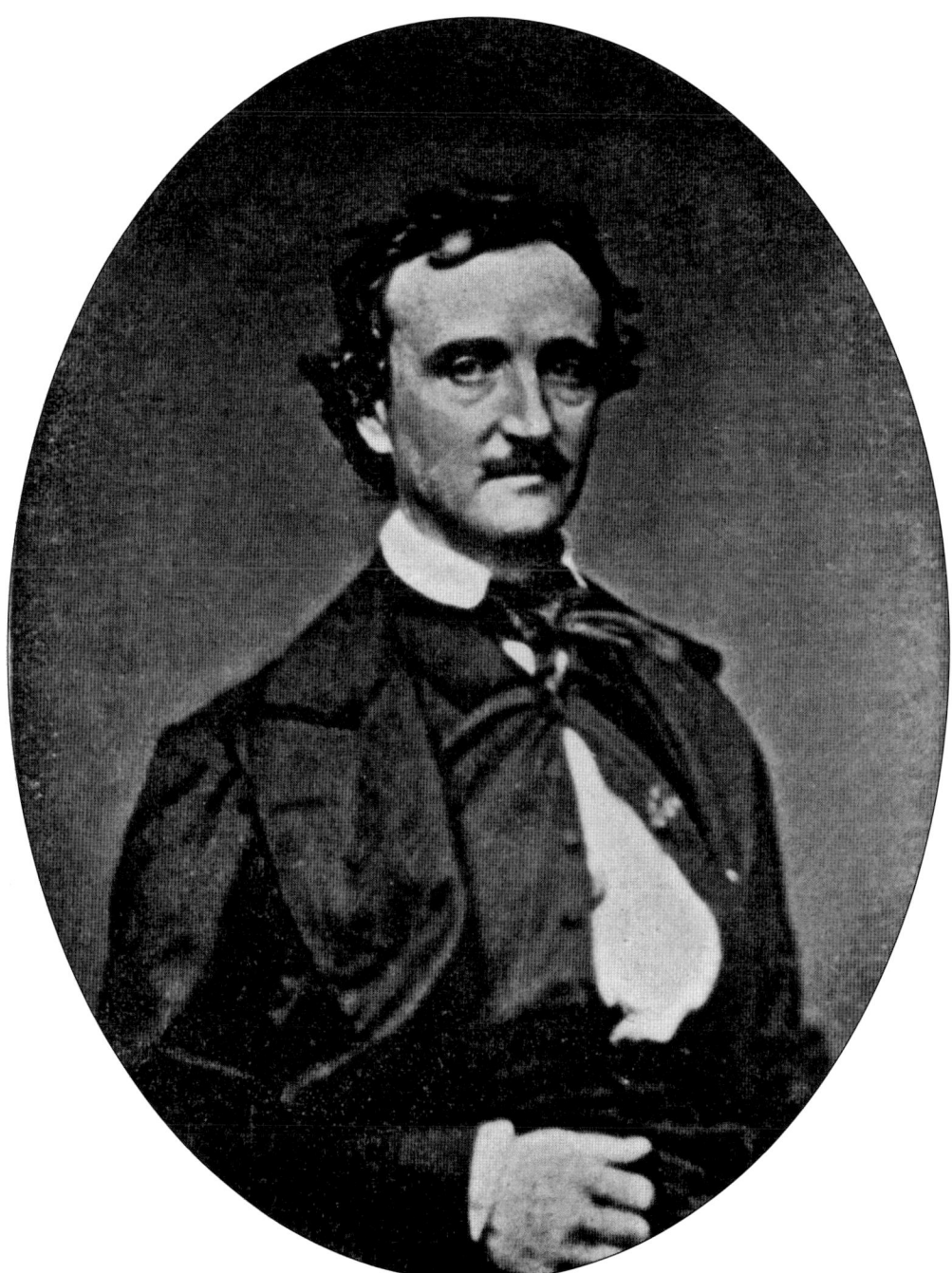

This daguerreotype of Poe was taken in 1849 in Richmond about three weeks before his death. The present plate and a similar photograph taken at the same sitting were the last pictures taken of the literary figure. The photographer, William Pratt, operated a daguerreotype studio on Main Street and recounted that he saw Poe walking down the street and asked him to pose for a picture. Poe, who probably could not afford a daguerreotype, left the pictures at the studio. Elmira Royster Shelton, the woman to whom Poe was engaged at the time of his death, owned one of the daguerreotypes, and Pratt proudly displayed the other in the front window of his studio.

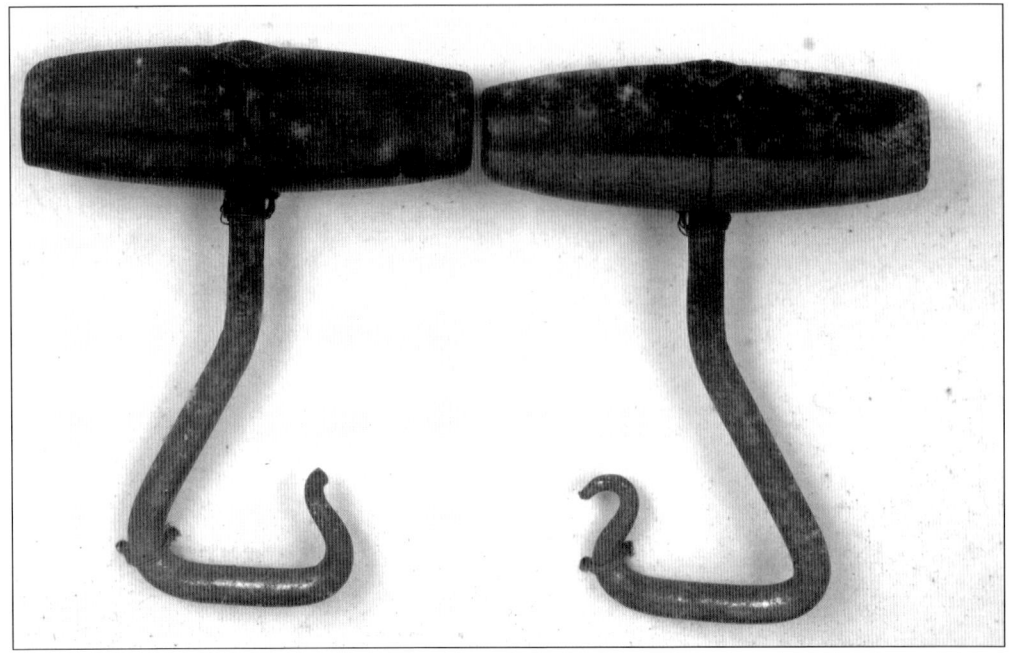

According to the certificate of authenticity, Poe habitually carried these boot hooks with him. On his last visit to Richmond, he left them at Duncan Lodge, the home of his sister, Rosalie Poe, and her foster brother John Hamilton Mackenzie kept them as a souvenir of his friend, the famous poet.

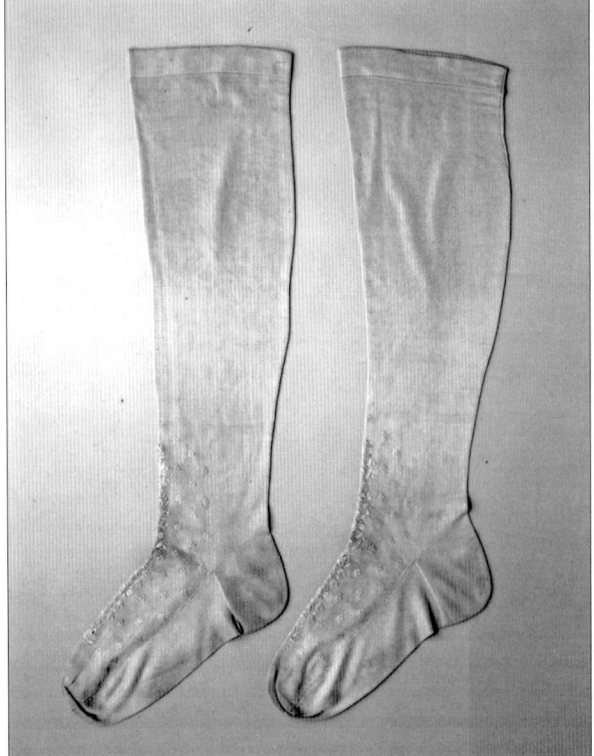

Poe's silk socks were photographed by Dementi Studios around 1997, when they entered the Poe Museum. These pieces came from a trunk of Poe's possessions his mother-in-law, Maria Clemm, kept after his death. Before she died, Clemm left it with a relative, Elizabeth Poe Herring, through whose family the trunk passed before the contents were given to the Poe Museum. The trunk was given to charity and presumed lost.

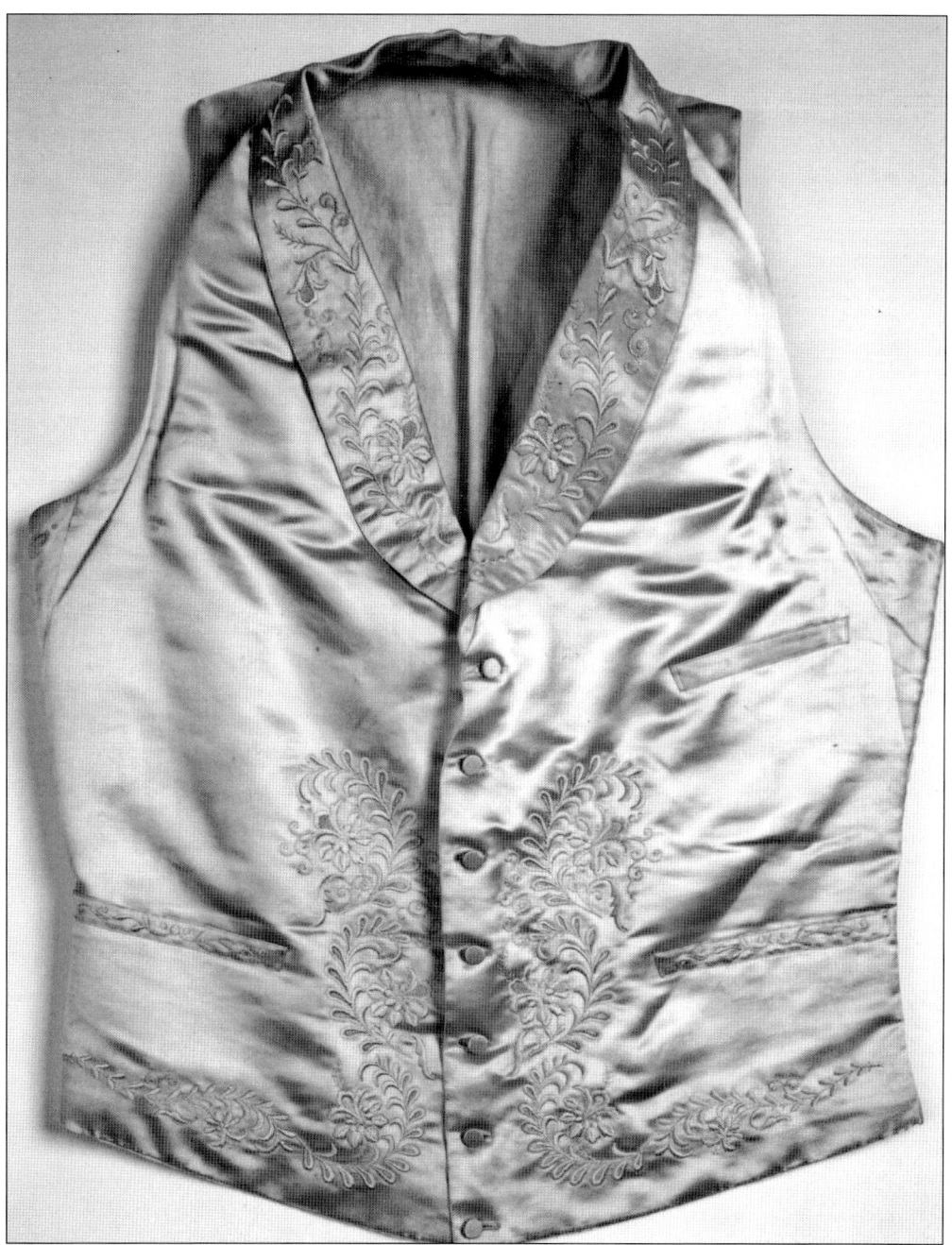

This photograph shows Poe's embroidered silk vest shown on display at the Poe Museum. Because of the quality and expense of such a vest, Poe probably only wore it for special occasions, such as his lectures and poetry readings. The vest was kept in a trunk of the author's possessions after his death and passed down through his aunt's family until it was donated to the museum. The donor recalled that her grandmother would take the clothing out of Poe's trunk once a year to show the family. In addition to Poe's vest, this donor also gave the museum Poe's socks and Maria Clemm's stockings and cap. Richmond's Poe Museum is the only public collection to own any of Poe's clothing.

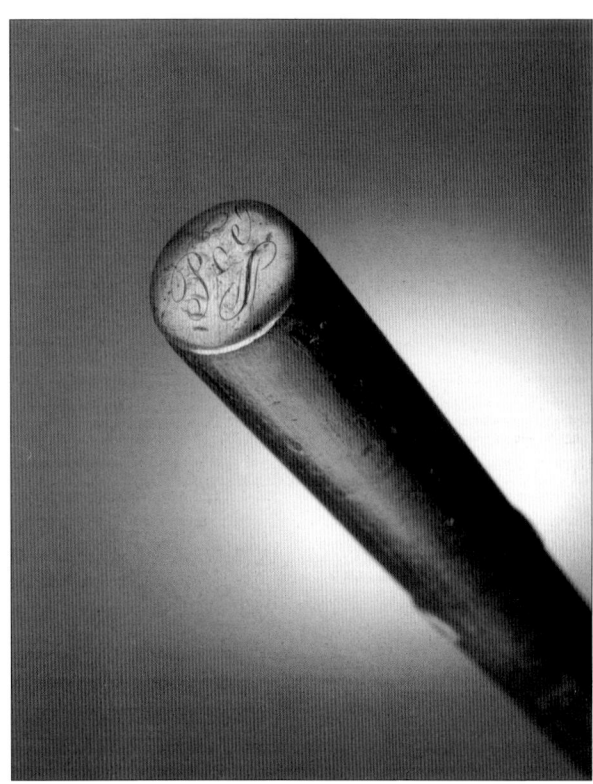

These two 20th-century photographs by Dementi Studios depict Poe's walking stick. The close-up shot focuses on the silver tip inscribed with Poe's name. Poe carried the walking stick on his 1849 visit to Richmond. On his last night in town, he left the home of his fiancée Elmira Shelton and visited his friend Dr. John Carter on Broad Street. After a few hours of conversation, Poe left Carter's house carrying Carter's sword cane and leaving his own. It is unknown why Poe took the wrong cane. After Poe's death, Carter recovered his walking stick but kept Poe's as a souvenir. The walking stick is now in the collection of the Poe Museum.

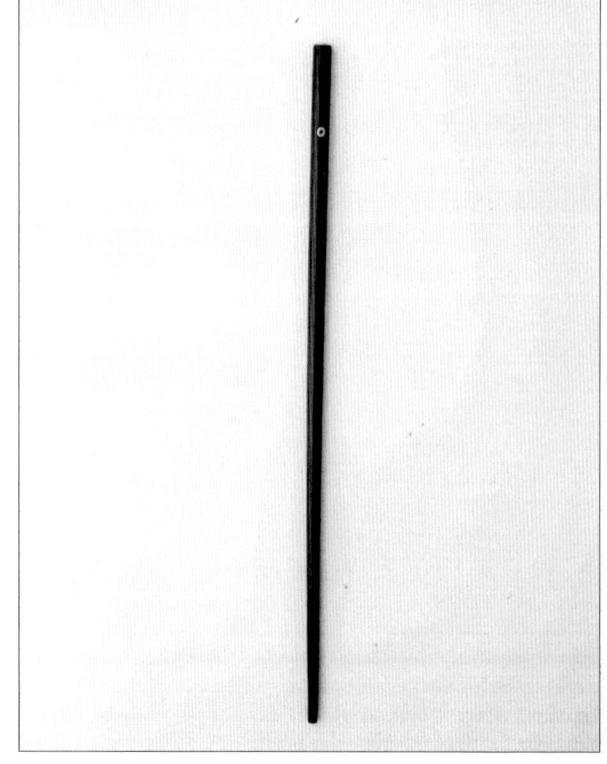

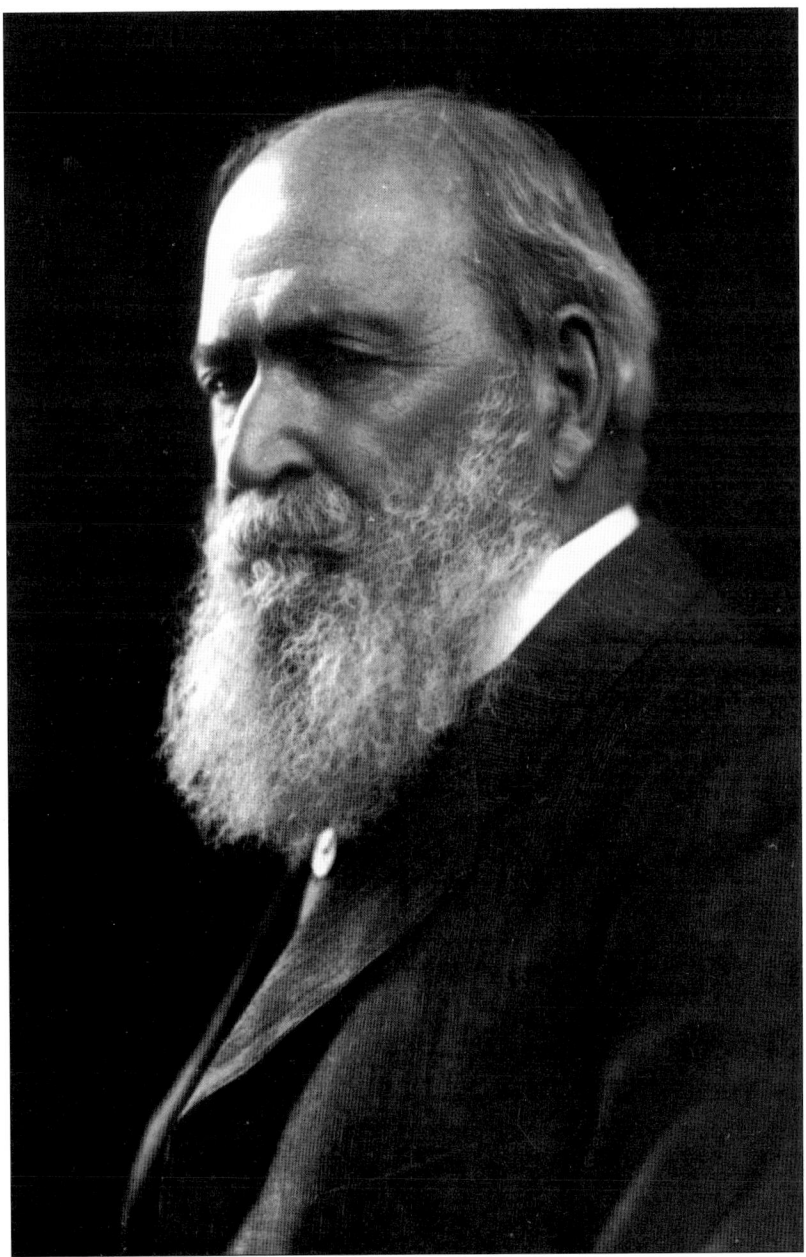

By the time this photograph was taken in the first decades of the 20th century, the subject, Basil Gildersleeve, was one of the dwindling numbers of people who had met the poet. Writing about the experience in 1915, Gildersleeve recalled Poe as "a noticeable man clad in black, the fashion of the times, close-buttoned, erect, forward looking, something separate in his whole bearing." Gildersleeve considered Poe's face "beautifully poetic." He added that Poe's "eyes were fine, the forehead challenged especial attention for its breadth and prominence. The mouth was feminine, and took away from the strength of the countenance; but the whole effect was spiritual. . . . His voice was pleasant. There was nothing dramatic about his recitation." Gildersleeve sent this photograph, along with his description of Poe's appearance, to the Poe Shrine in 1921 but declined an invitation to visit the shrine.

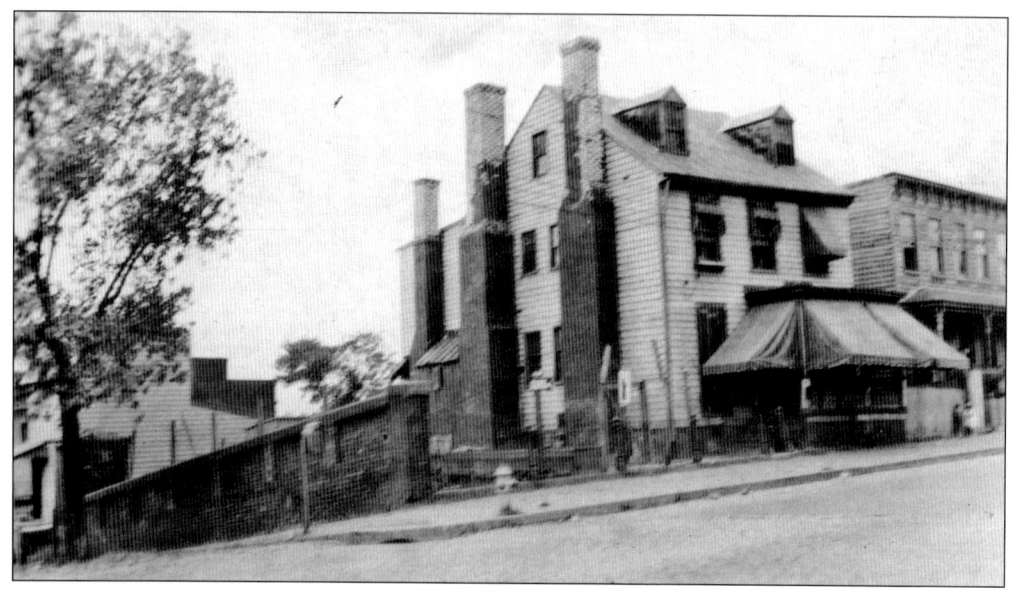

Construction on the John Woodward House began by 1799, and it remains one of the oldest frame houses in the city and the sole survivor of the bustling port of Rocketts Landing. Poe left Richmond for the last time aboard the steamship *Pocahontas*, which departed from Rocketts Landing at four in the morning on September 27, 1849.

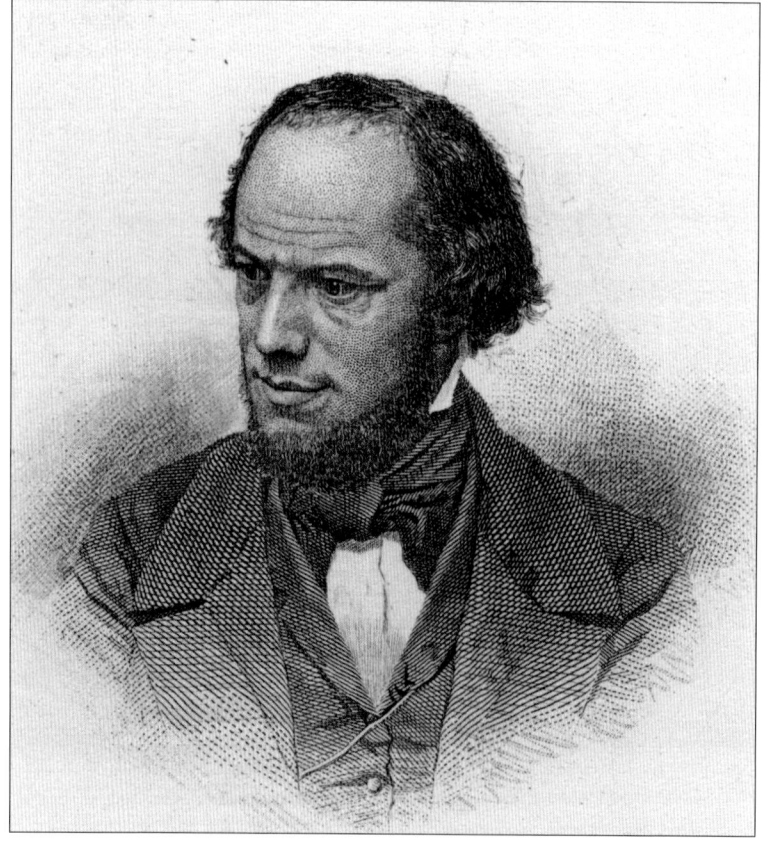

Rufus Wilmont Griswold was a popular anthologist and editor in Poe's time. Griswold's 1842 anthology *The Poets and Poetry of America* included three of Poe's poems: "Coliseum," "The Haunted Palace," and "The Sleeper." Poe repeatedly criticized the volume in lectures and ridiculed Griswold in his tale "The Angel of the Odd." Griswold retaliated after Poe's death by writing a biography portraying Poe as an insane drunk with no morals.

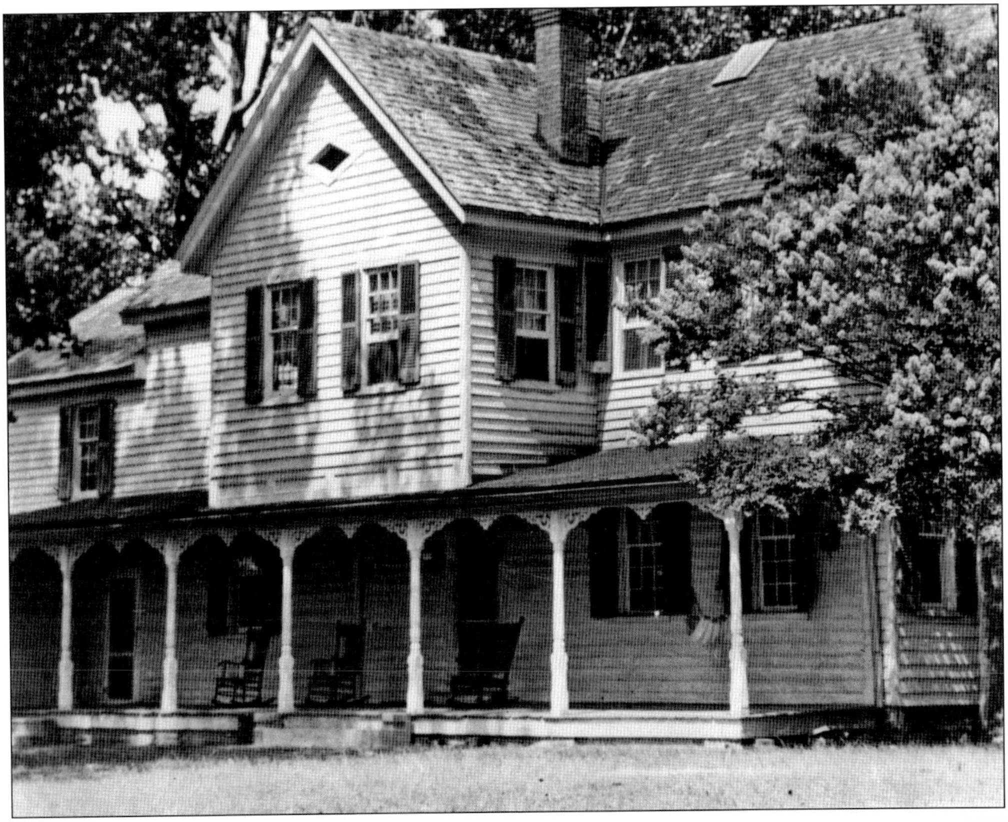

This 1926 photograph by Archer Jones depicts Oakwood, the Matthews County residence of Jane Mackenzie Byrd Miller, granddaughter of William and Jane Scott Mackenzie, Rosalie Poe's foster parents. After the death of her foster mother in 1865, Rosalie lived with various Mackenzie relatives and spent time at Oakwood. After her death, Rosalie left at Oakwood a trunk her famous brother had owned.

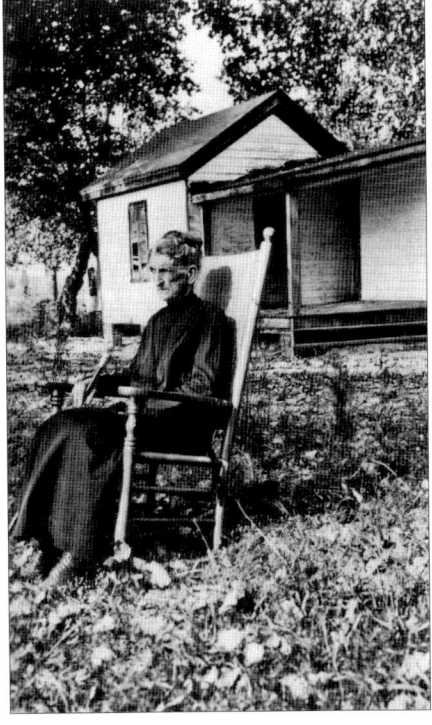

Archer Jones took this photograph of Jane Mackenzie Byrd Miller in 1926. Through Poe's sister, Miller had acquired Edgar Poe's trunk, which she sold to the Poe Museum for $35 in 1922. She also helped expand the newly established Poe Museum's collections by offering furniture and portraits that had once resided in the Mackenzies' Richmond home, Duncan Lodge.

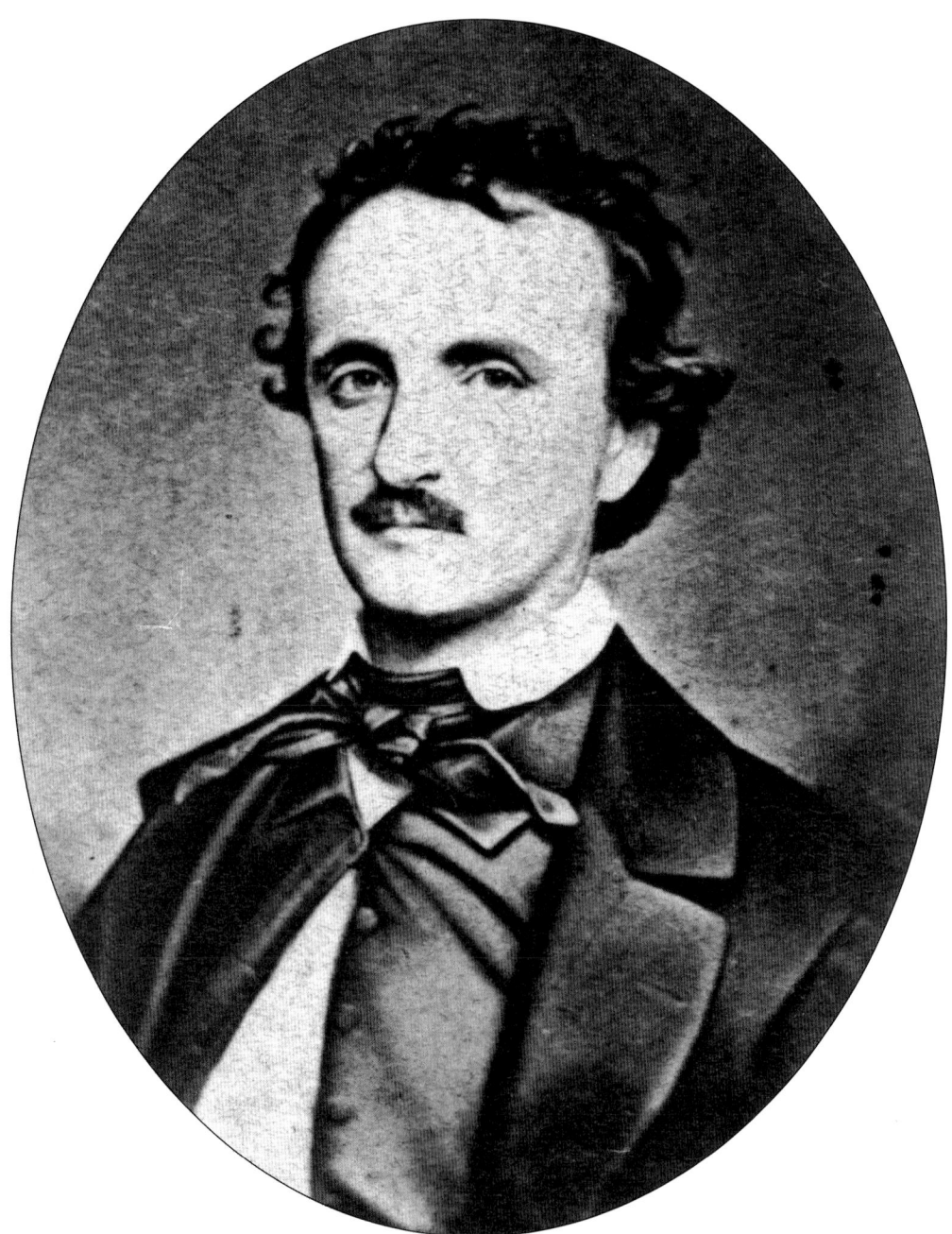

This 1870s albumen print carte de visite of Poe was found among Elmira Shelton's possessions by her descendants, who donated it to the Poe Museum. The photograph was taken by Lee Studios of Richmond of an 1868 pastel portrait by Oscar Halling, so Shelton would have acquired it at least 20 years after Poe's death, by which time she had denied she was ever engaged to him.

Four

THE POE SHRINE

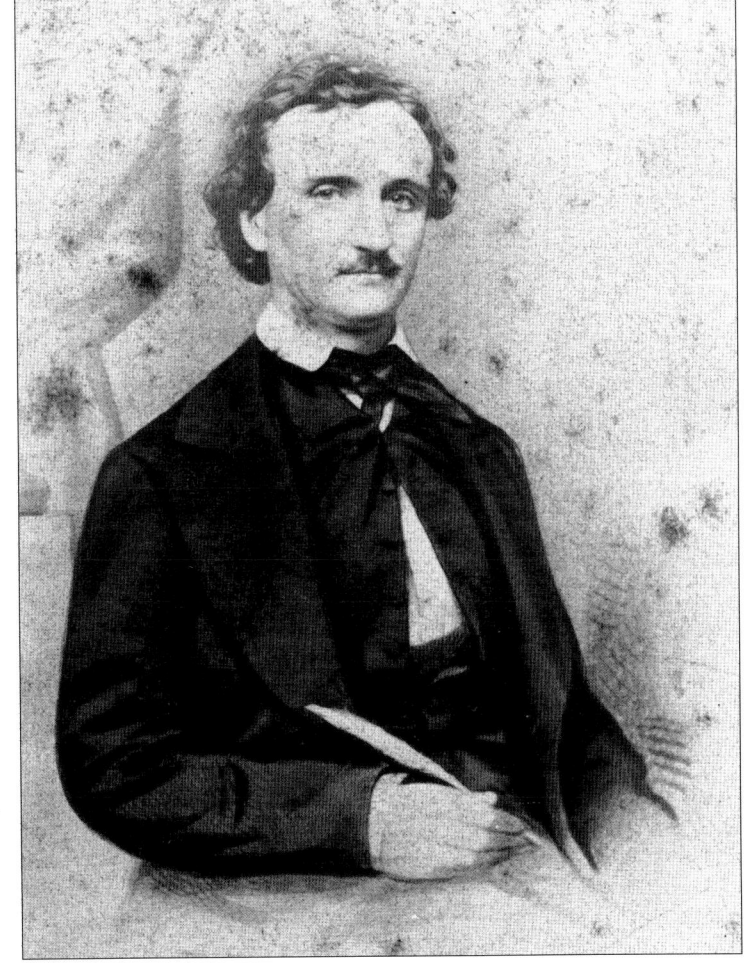

This altered photograph of Poe was published in 1877 as the "Memorial Portrait." The photographer, Daniel Bendann, copied an earlier daguerreotype of Poe, and an unknown artist added a quill pen to Poe's hand and a curtain to the background. Two years before this image was published, Poe's previously unmarked grave was relocated and finally designated with a large monument. The photograph first appeared in a book commemorating the dedication of that monument.

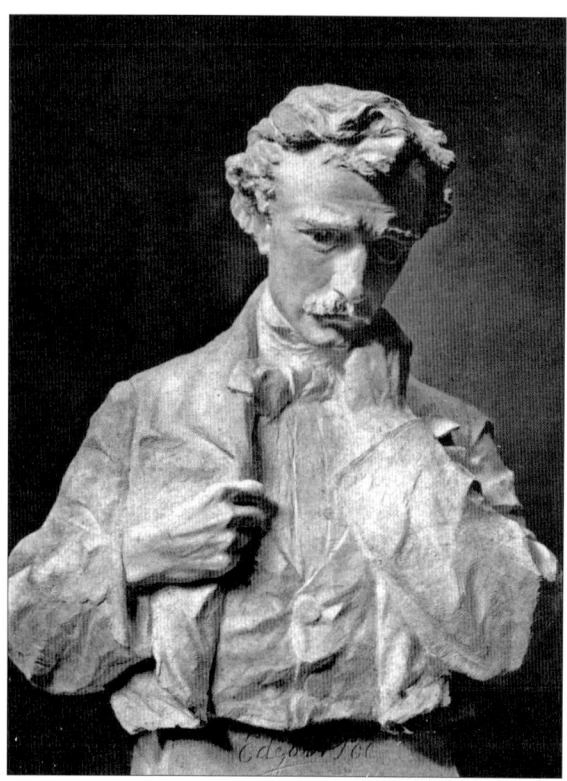

The Hungarian sculptor George Julian Zolnay sculpted this bust in 1898 for Poe's alma mater, the University of Virginia. The bust was unveiled in 1899 on the 50th anniversary of Poe's death. Five years later, in 1904, the university further honored Poe by establishing the Raven Society, an honor society named after his most famous poem.

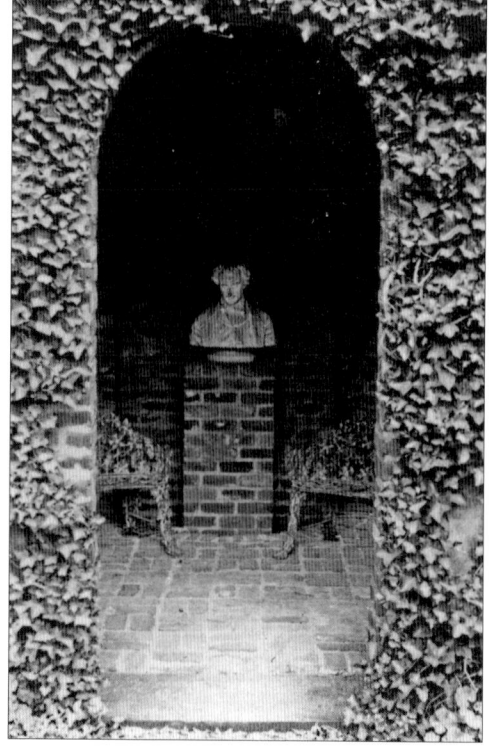

Created by Edmund Quinn in 1908, this bust was officially unveiled on the centennial of Poe's birth—January 19, 1909—as part of a celebration honoring the poet. Observances took place throughout the nation as Poe entered his second century. Poe's popularity continued to rise over the course of the 20th century.

Former lieutenant governor of Virginia and member of the State Corporation Commission Joseph E. Willard was among Poe's admirers who sought to erect a statue of Poe in Richmond. In 1906, he and other prominent citizens established the Poe Memorial Association for that purpose, but, unable to raise the necessary funds, the association never built the statue.

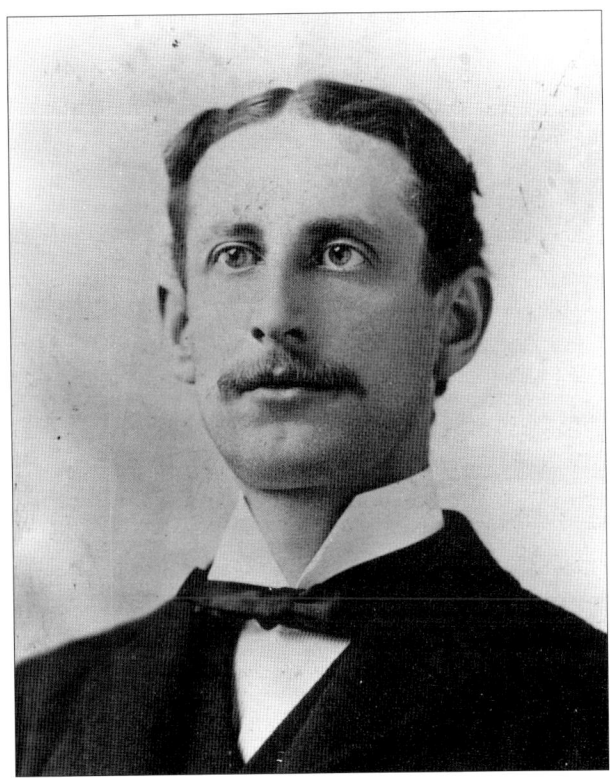

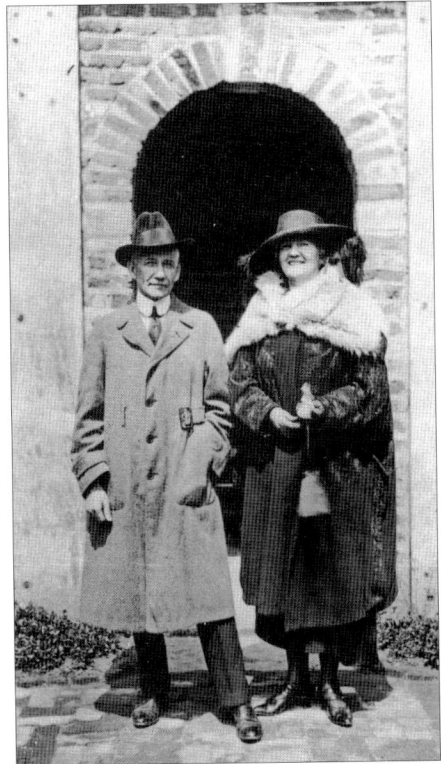

Archer and Annie Jones pose in front of the recently completed Poe Shrine in this 1922 photograph. A devoted preservationist, Archer Jones wanted to save the Old Stone House from destruction by converting it into a museum of Colonial history. After meeting Poe collector James Whitty, the Joneses decided to use the property to create a Poe Shrine instead.

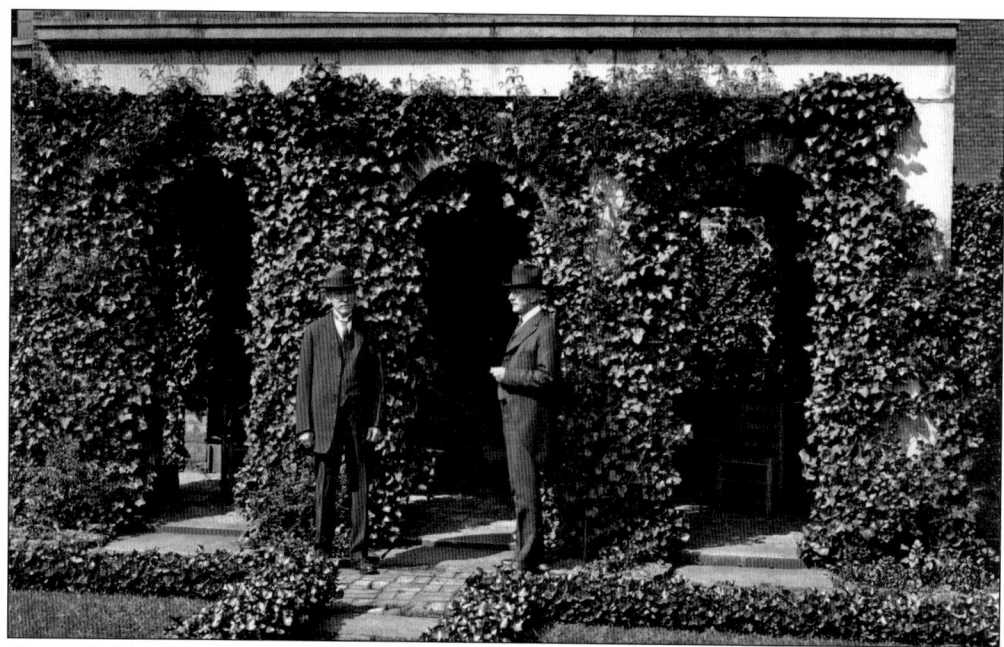

Granville Valentine (left) and Robert A. Lancaster stand before the Poe Shrine in this 1930 photograph. Even before Valentine became a supporter of the Poe Shrine, he personally purchased the Old Stone House and donated it to the Association for the Preservation of Virginia Antiquities to save the Colonial-era structure from demolition. Lancaster is the author of *Historic Virginia Houses and Churches*.

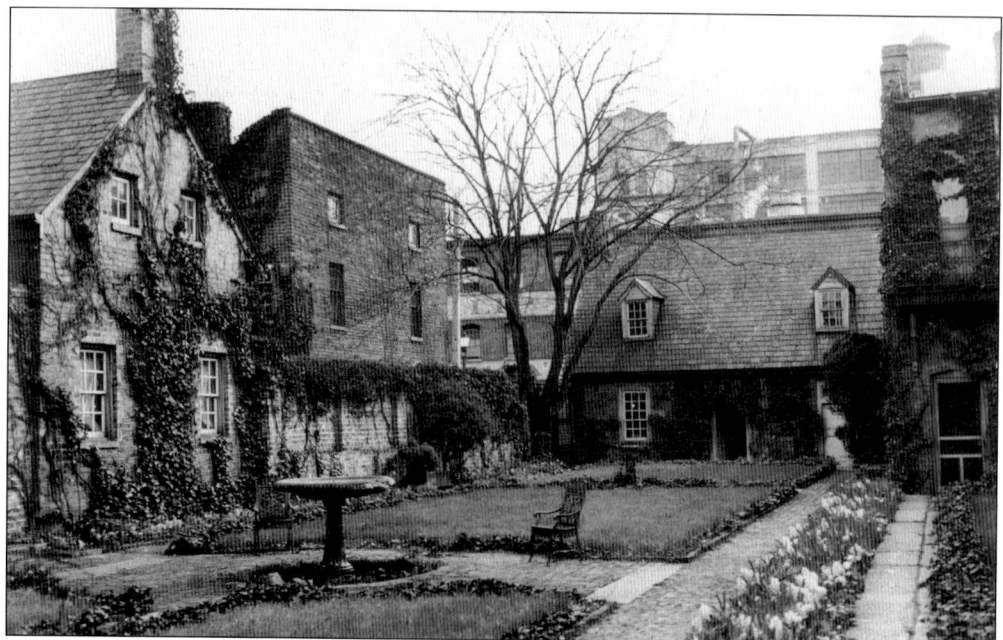

The Old Stone House overlooks the Enchanted Garden in this 20th-century photograph. As the only pre–Revolutionary War home in downtown Richmond, as well as the oldest house still standing in the original city limits, the structure is of interest both to students of Poe and to those interested in the city's Colonial past.

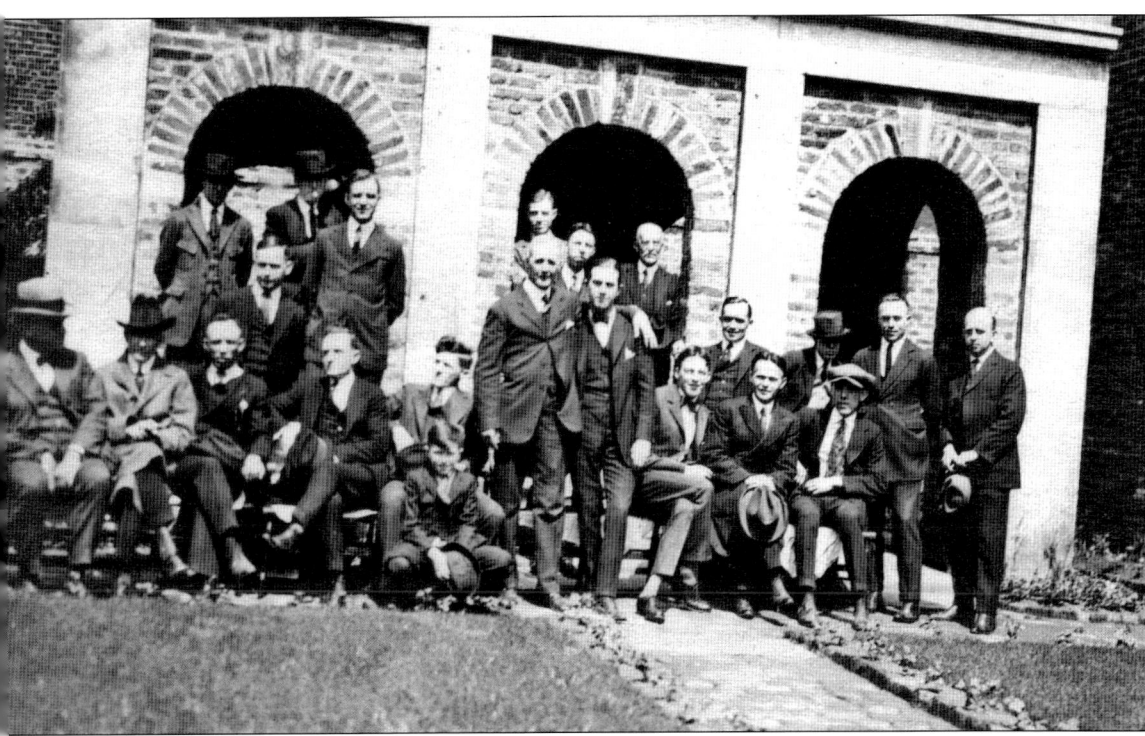

The male founders of the Poe Shrine strike a casual pose in this slightly askew image taken at the Shrine's April 1922 opening. Though most of the figures in this photograph are unidentified, Steven Hughes is recorded as the third man from the right, and Archer Jones is recognizable as the second man from the left in the first row. Granville Valentine is probably the man with the mustache under the central arch. Among those present at the opening of the Poe Shrine were Virginia governor E. Lee Trinkle, Poe biographer George Woodberry, and historian Douglas Southall Freeman. Although it is uncertain how many attended the opening ceremonies, the charter members of the organization included descendants of Elmira Royster Shelton, Jane Stith Craig Stanard, Susan Archer Talley Weiss, and Rufus W. Griswold. The sculptor Edward Valentine, who provided the closing remarks, was the only one present who had ever actually seen Poe.

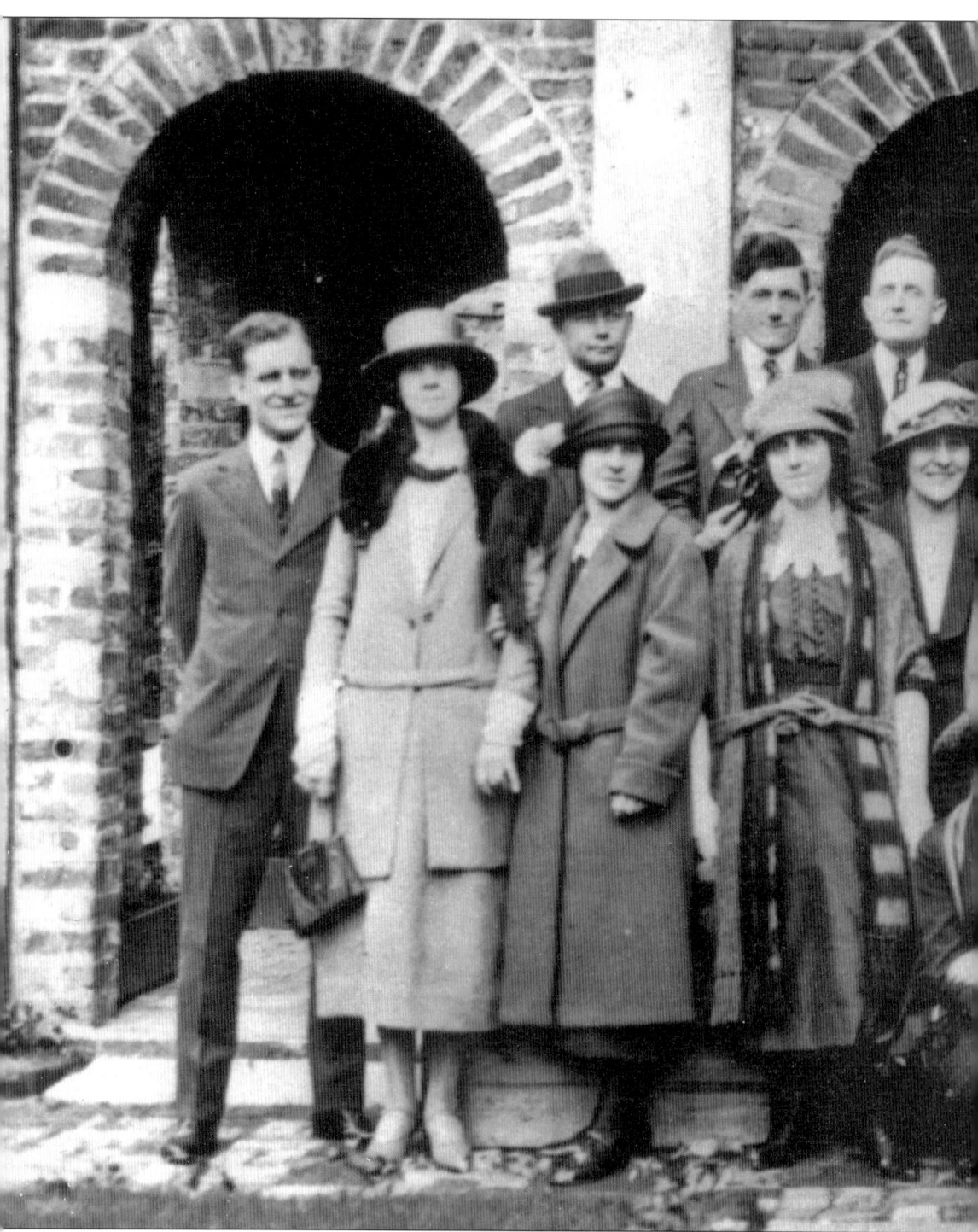

In April 1922, the founders of the Poe Shrine pose in front of the recently constructed shrine made from bricks and granite salvaged from the *Southern Literary Messenger* building. Among those present at the opening ceremonies were preservationists Archer and Annie Jones and the eccentric Poe collector James H. Whitty, the first president of the Poe Foundation, the organization

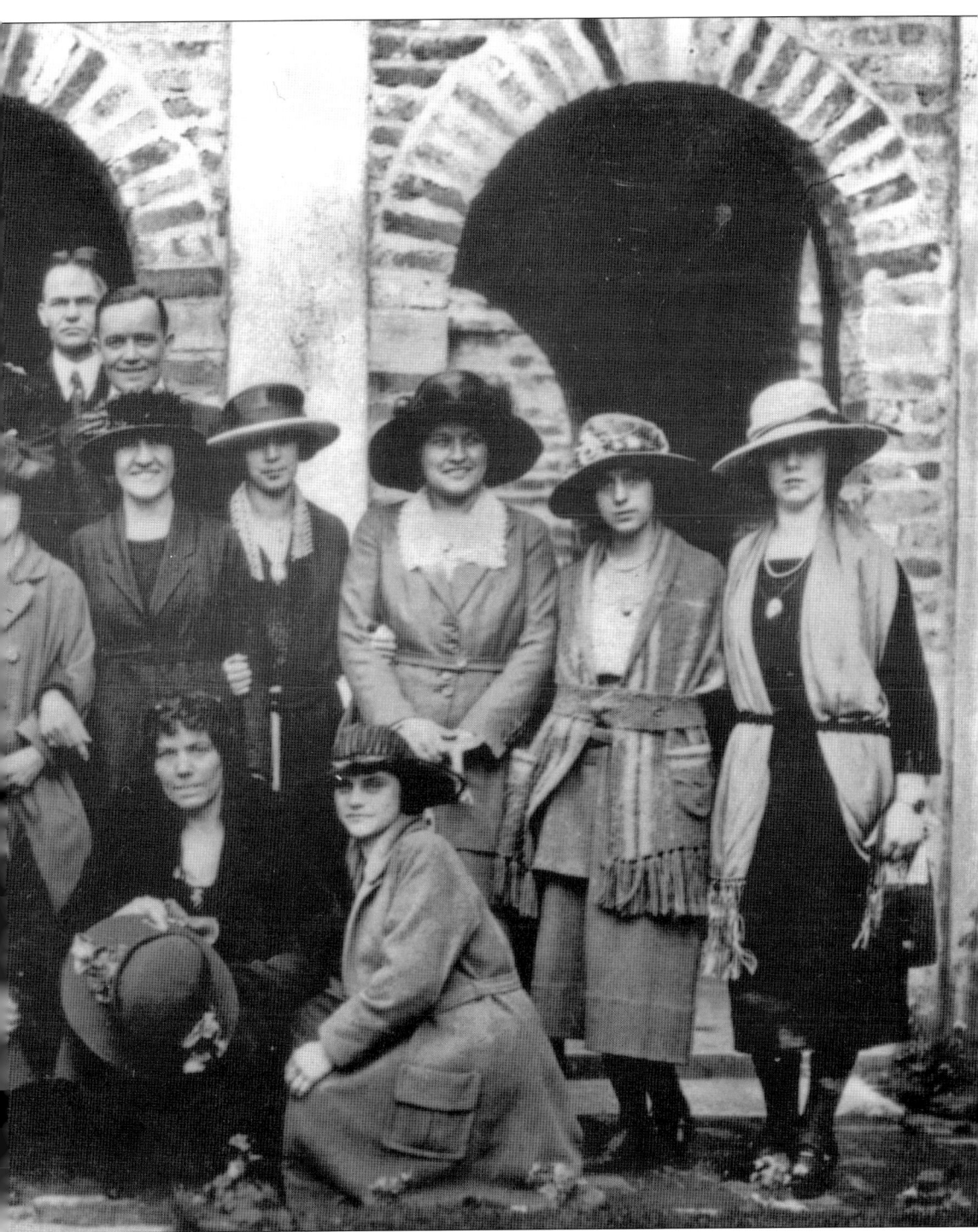

that operates the Poe Shrine. Within two years, Whitty would be banned from the museum, and Jones would commit suicide three years later. In spite of its rocky start, the Poe Foundation still maintains the Poe Shrine, which has since changed its name to the Edgar Allan Poe Museum.

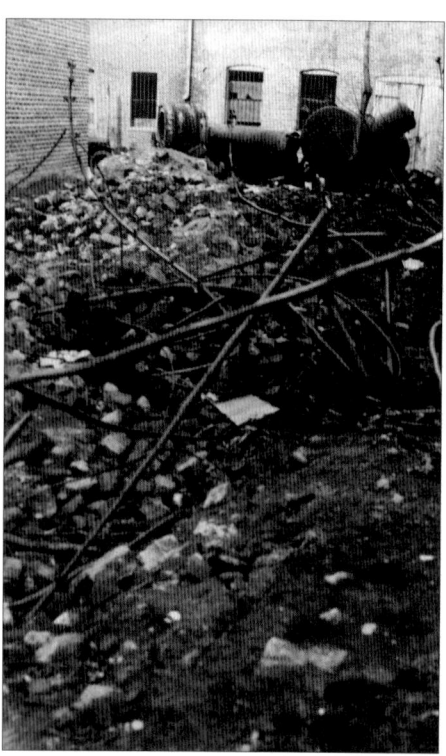

This 1921 photograph shows the junkyard that once stood behind the Old Stone House, which had been abandoned a few years earlier. A year after this picture was taken, the yard would reopen as a garden planted in honor of Poe and named the Enchanted Garden after a line from Poe's 1848 poem "To Helen."

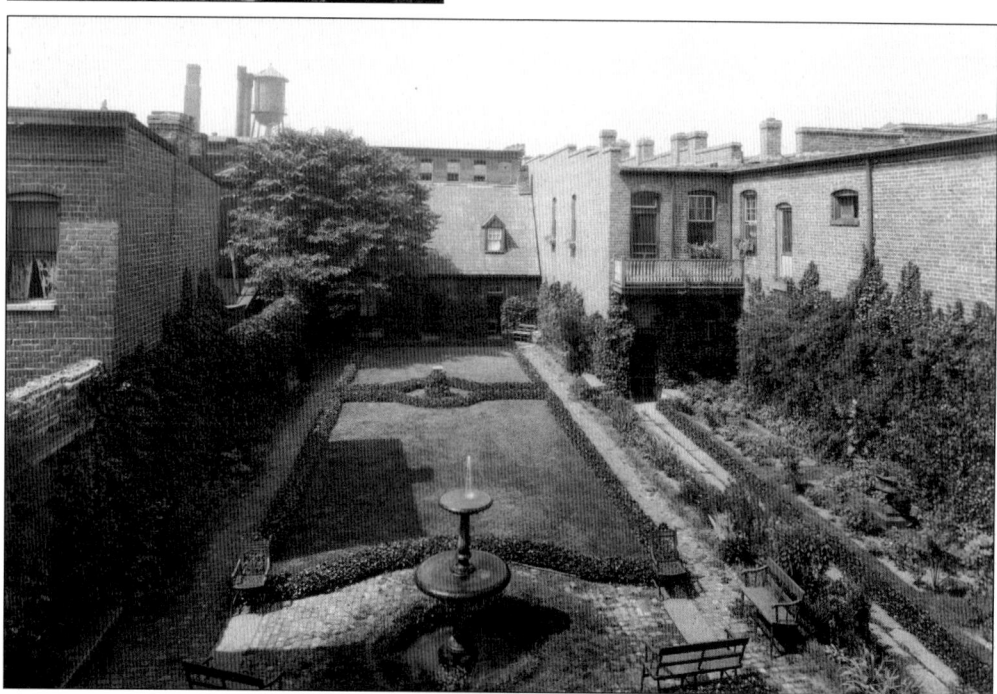

This photograph of the Poe Museum's Enchanted Garden was taken from atop the Poe Shrine in 1927. The layout of the garden was based on the description in Poe's poem "To One in Paradise." The poem was believed to be a description of the garden in which a 16-year-old Poe and his fiancée Elmira Royster once met to keep their relationship a secret from her father.

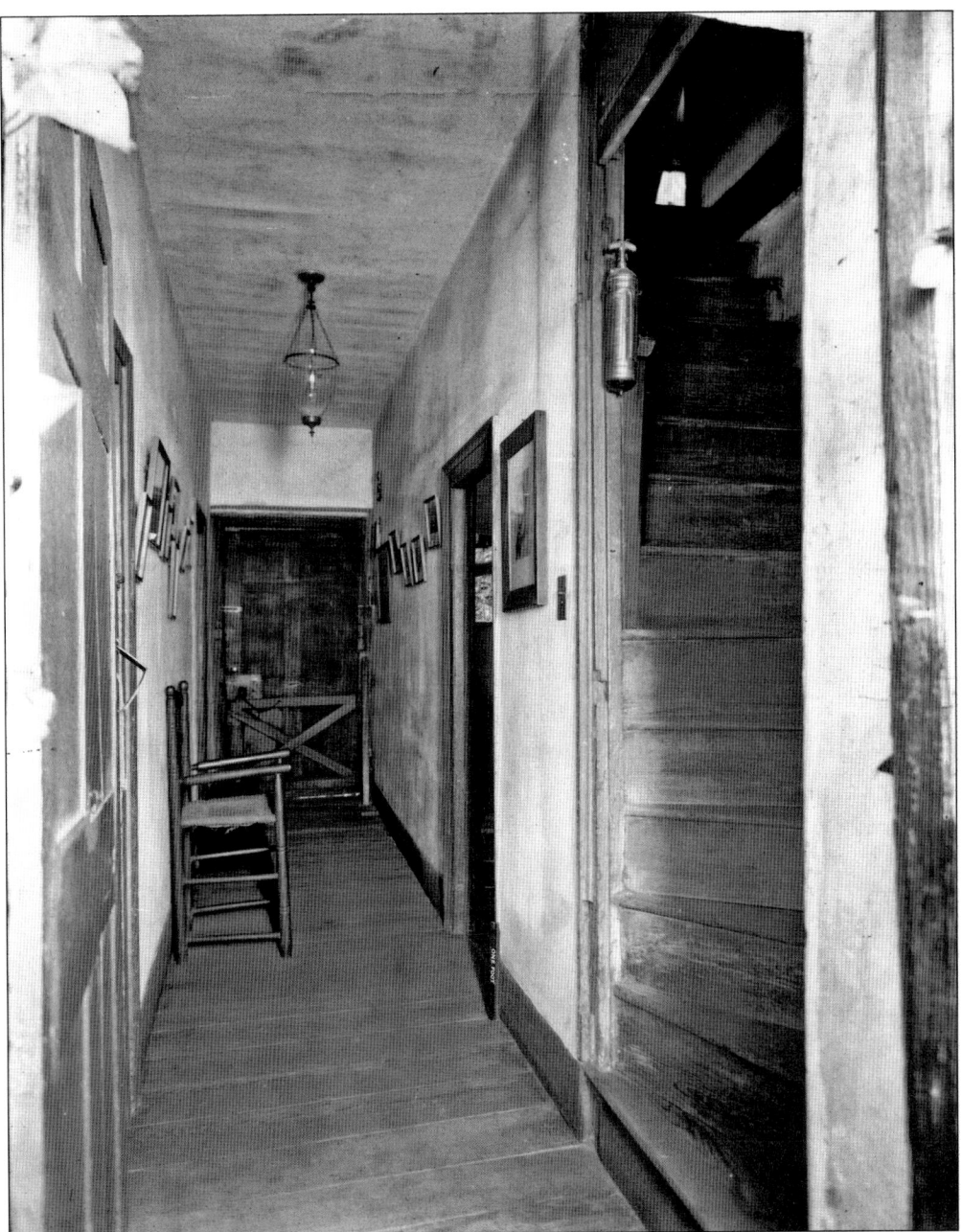

As the entrance to the Poe Shrine, the Old Stone House was filled with Edgar Allan Poe artifacts and memorabilia. This 1927 photograph depicts the early days of the Poe Shrine, which did not acquire the present name of the Poe Museum until later. Visitors entered the complex through this narrow hallway, which ran from the front door to the back and then opened onto the garden. Such literary figures as Gertrude Stein, H. P. Lovecraft, Carl Van Vechten, and Henry Miller walked this passage lined with portraits of Poe and the places he knew. The room to the right contained a 16-foot-long model of the city as it would have appeared during Poe's lifetime. The chair in the hallway was one of many period pieces the museum acquired before it was able to collect more furniture from Poe's home.

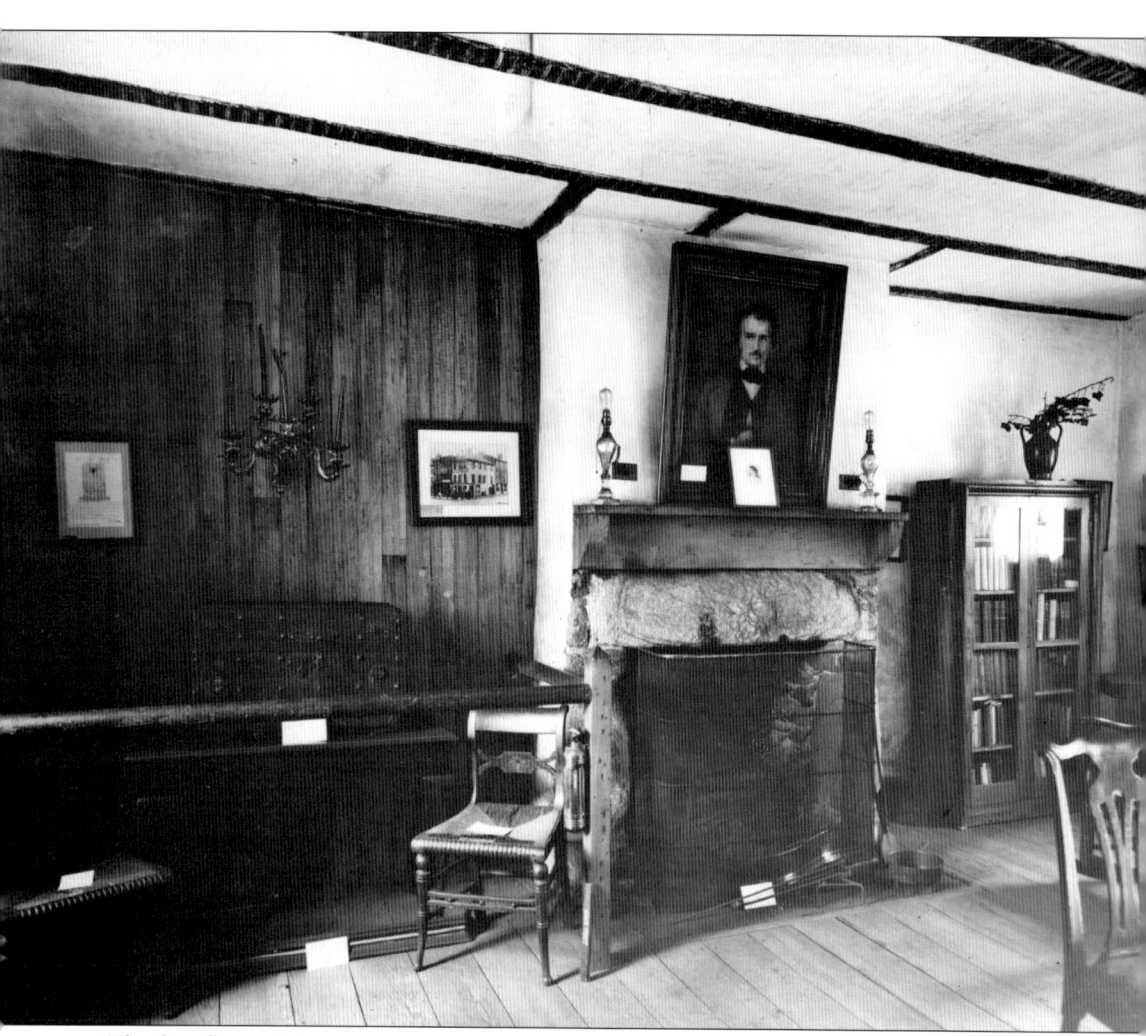

The first floor of the Stone House consisted of two rooms. The one represented here held Poe's trunk (left) on a table in front of wood paneling salvaged from the *Southern Literary Messenger* building. Both the sconce on the paneling and the chairs flanking the trunk came from the Allan mansion, Moldavia. The frame on the wall on the left side of the picture contains a lock of Poe's hair taken at the time of his death by his friend Joseph Snodgrass. The bookcase on the right side of the room was constructed using lumber salvaged from the offices of the *Southern Literary Messenger*. During the renovation of the Old Stone House, missing or broken locks, doorknobs, and hinges were replaced with ones taken from the *Messenger* building and the Craig House. Among the treasures to be found at the Poe Shrine in those years were a buffalo robe used by Poe and several manuscripts loaned to the shrine by the grandchildren of Poe's literary executor, Rufus Griswold.

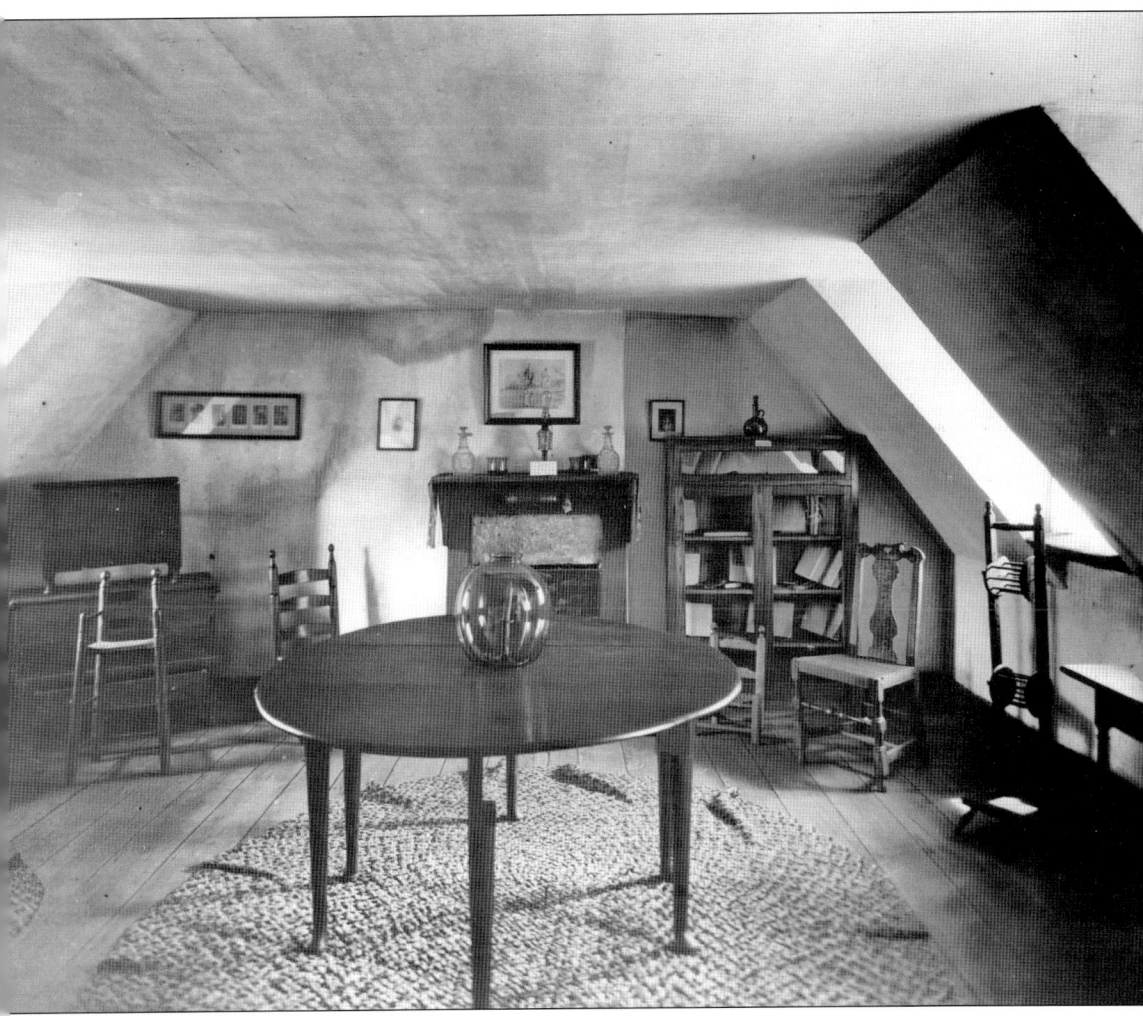

Accessible only by a steep, narrow staircase, the second floor of the Old Stone House is no longer open to visitors. When this 1927 photograph was taken, it contained a display of Poe artifacts, including a table (center) from the Allan house Moldavia. The bookcase to the right of the fireplace was one of 11 the Poe Shrine made from the lumber salvaged from the *Southern Literary Messenger* building. The china and glassware on the bookcase and mantle were formerly owned by Poe's foster parents, the Allans. The small painting on the wall behind the bookcase was once owned by Poe and was painted by his friend Robert Sully. Above the fireplace hangs a photograph of Poe's friend Susan Archer Talley Weiss and a watercolor of her house, Talavera, in which Poe gave his last reading of "The Raven" in 1849.

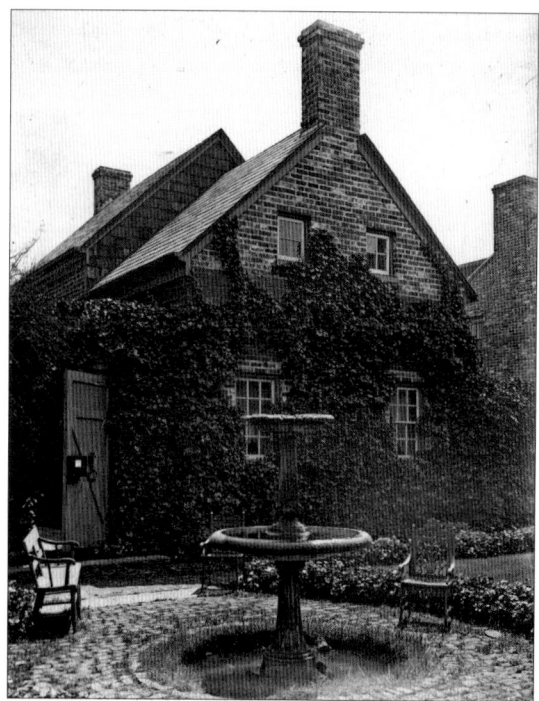

The Poe Museum acquired this late-19th-century structure in 1927 to serve as a tea room for the expanding complex. Visitors to the Poe Museum often tell docents they feel a malevolent presence watching them while they are alone in this building. The space now houses temporary exhibits focusing on Poe's influence on popular culture.

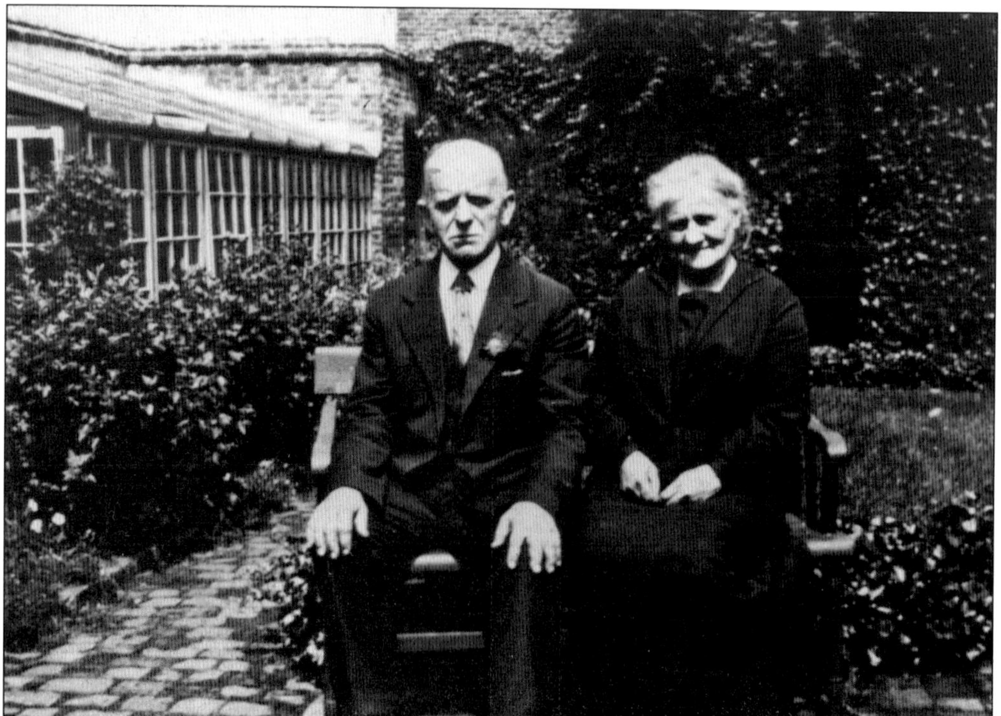

Sitting with his wife in the Enchanted Garden in this photograph taken about 1922, James Priddy was an early caretaker of the Poe Museum. The couple lived on the second floor of one of the museum's buildings, an 1869 structure, which since 1964 has housed Edith Ragland's model of Poe's Richmond in the first floor.

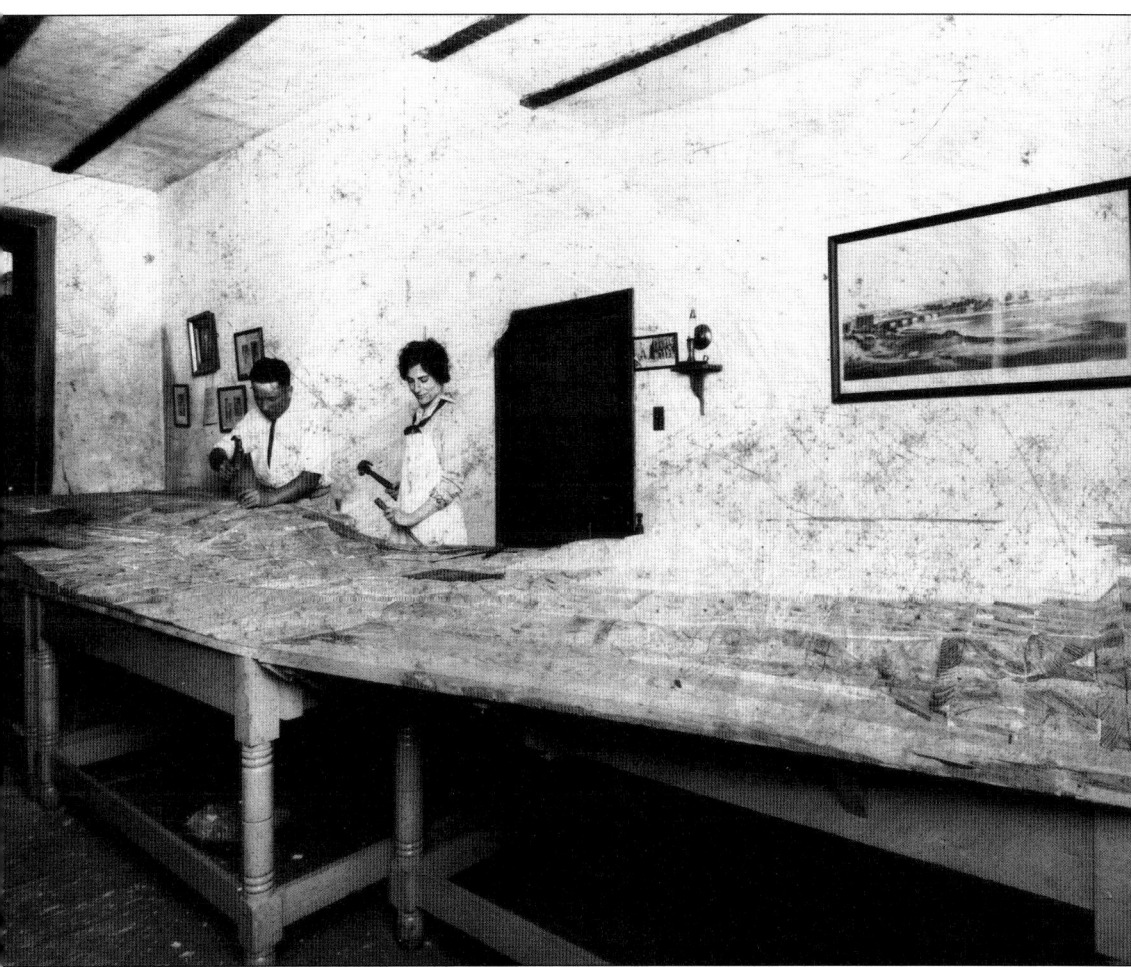

Edith Ragland chisels the wood blocks that will form the base of a 16-foot-long model of Poe's Richmond in this 1924 photograph taken in the Poe Museum's Old Stone House. Since much of Poe's Richmond had already been lost by the 20th century, the Poe Museum attempted to use this model to offer visitors a glimpse into the city as he would have known it. Using old photographs, insurance records, and elevation charts accumulated over the course of several years by the sculptor Edward Valentine, Ragland spent three years building the model, which represents 1840s Richmond from Fifth Street to Twenty-Eighth Street and from Marshall Street to the James River.

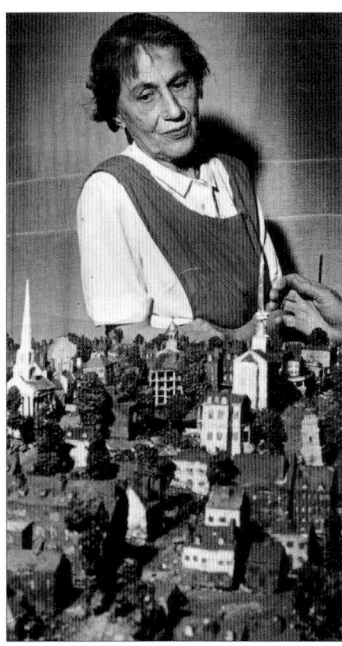

Edith Ragland returned to the Poe Museum, and her model of Richmond, in 1964 when the model was moved from the Old Stone House into another building. In order to move the model, a group of volunteers cut it into three pieces and carried them on their sides through the doors. Many of the buildings fell off in the process, so Ragland was called to put the model back together.

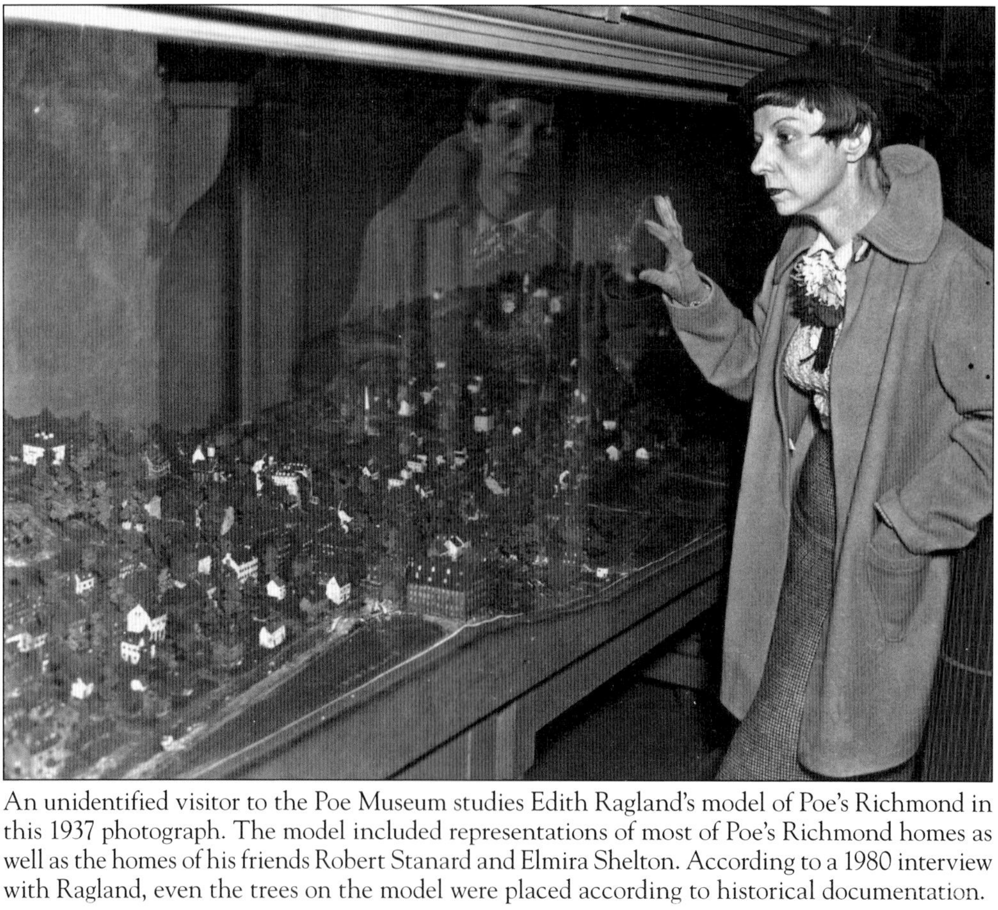

An unidentified visitor to the Poe Museum studies Edith Ragland's model of Poe's Richmond in this 1937 photograph. The model included representations of most of Poe's Richmond homes as well as the homes of his friends Robert Stanard and Elmira Shelton. According to a 1980 interview with Ragland, even the trees on the model were placed according to historical documentation.

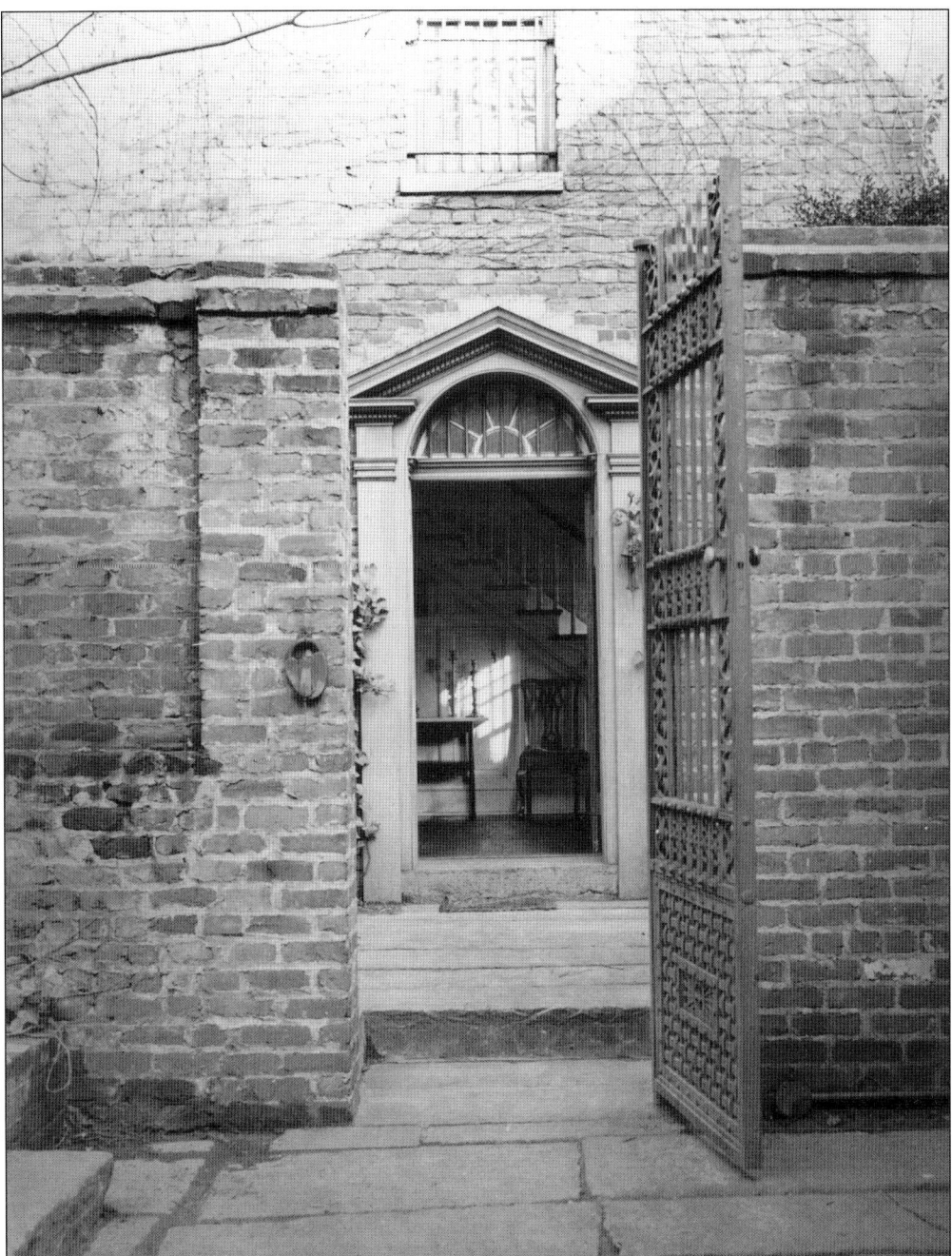

Named in honor of Poe's mother, the Elizabeth Arnold Poe Memorial Building was constructed in 1928 using pieces salvaged from other Richmond buildings associated with Poe. The structure was designed to replicate the small house incorrectly identified as the location of Poe's mother's death. Shortly after this building's completion, Poe's mother's grave at St. John's Churchyard was finally marked.

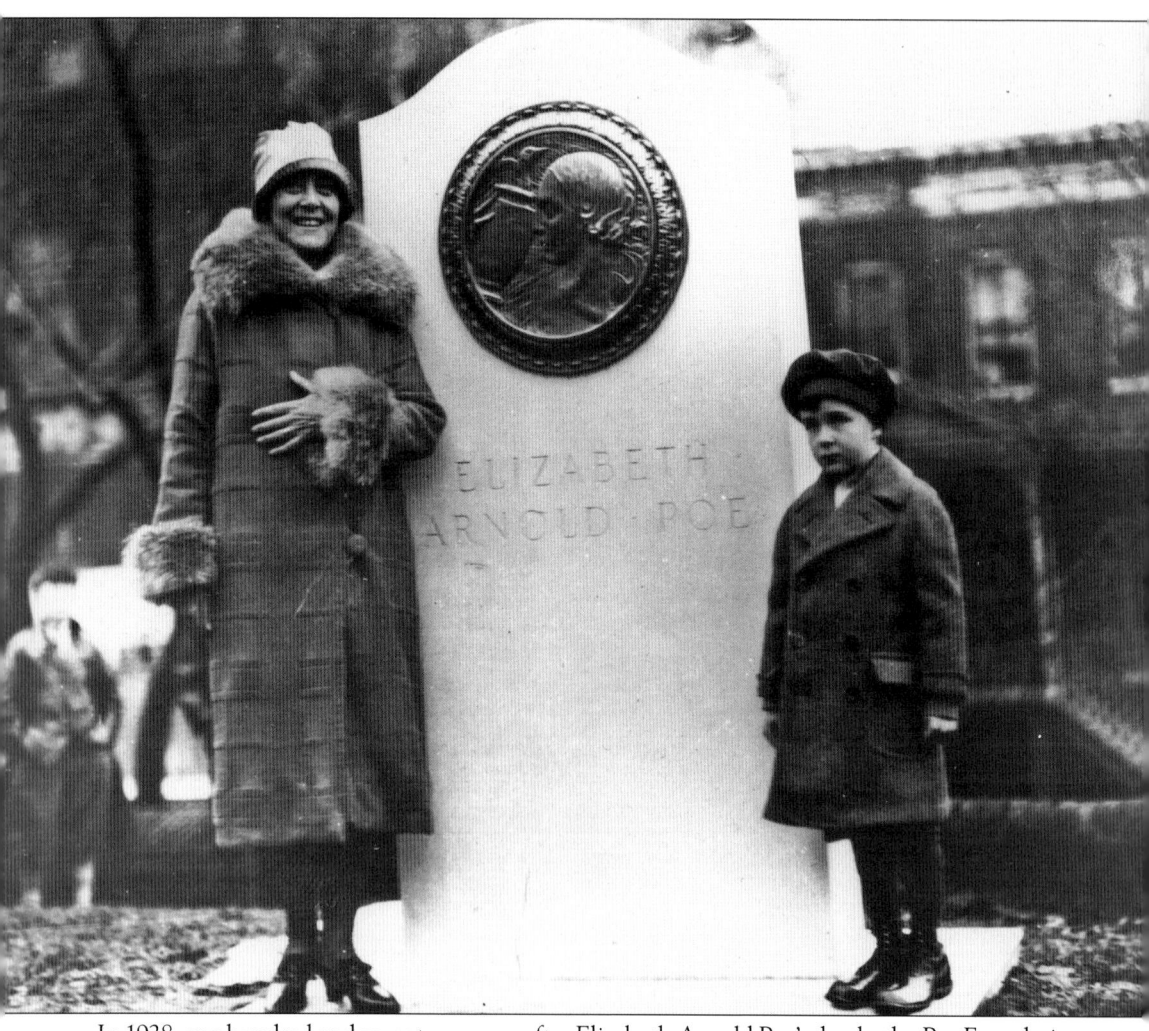

In 1928, one hundred and seventeen years after Elizabeth Arnold Poe's death, the Poe Foundation, the Raven Society, and the Actors' Equity erected this monument on the approximate location of her previously unmarked grave at St. John's Church. Since Elizabeth Poe was an actress, her grave was placed on the edge of the churchyard—far away from the more "respectable" people. The young boy in the photograph, Samuel P. Cowardin III, unveiled the monument in the dedication ceremony, when this photograph was taken. The bronze medallion, entitled "The Birth of Genius," on the front of the monument depicts a woman holding an urn out of which a raven flies. On the reverse side of the monument, another bronze medallion bears a quote from Poe taken from his *Broadway Journal* review of the actress Anna Mowatt, in which Poe states that no earl was ever prouder of his earldom than he was to be the son of an actress. The woman in this photograph is Shakespearean actress Edith Wynne Matthison, who recited this inscription at the ceremony.

An early supporter of the Poe Shrine, Mary Newton Stanard was the author of a biography of Poe entitled *The Dreamer*. She was also married to a direct descendant of Poe's close friend Robert Stanard. Taking an interest in the planting of the Shrine's Enchanted Garden, Mary Stanard listed all the flowers, trees, and shrubs mentioned in Poe's works in hopes of seeing them planted there.

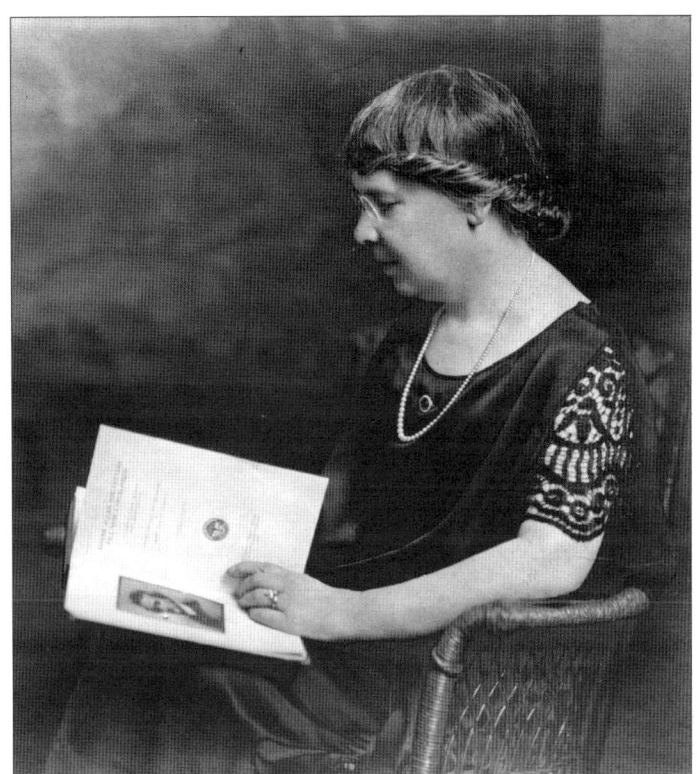

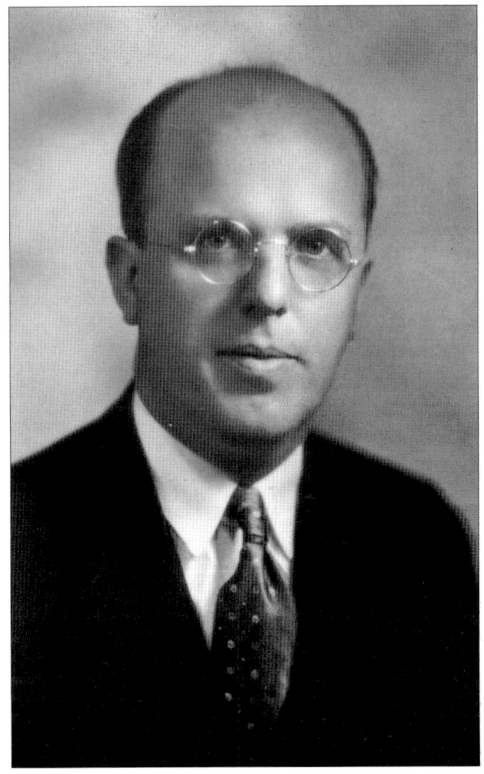

James Rindfleish, a collector of Poe artifacts and memorabilia, supported the Poe Museum and paid to have iron bars installed on the Elizabeth Arnold Poe Memorial Building to protect its contents from burglars. Among his contributions to the museum's collections were the letters and autographs of Poe's contemporaries, including Thomas Dunn English and Anna Stella Lewis.

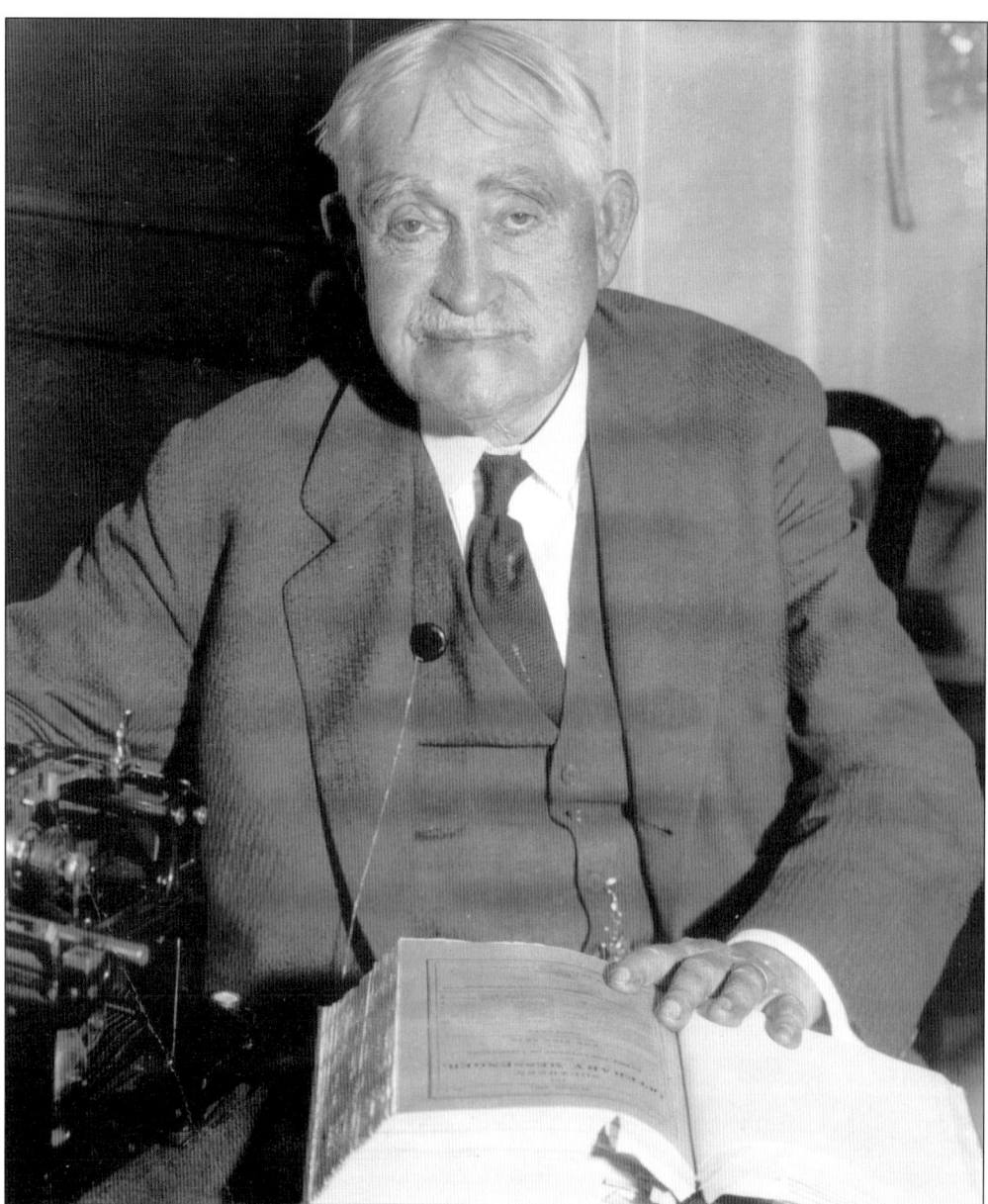

The California psychiatrist John Wooster Robertson was an avid student of Poe and his works. In an attempt to understand Poe's imagination, Robertson wrote the book *Edgar Allan Poe: A Psychopathic Study*, in which he concluded Poe wrote while in an altered state. Robertson continued his Poe research by compiling a bibliography of the first appearances in print of all of Poe's poems and short stories. Additionally, Robertson amassed a large collection of first editions of Poe's works. Among the rarest of the first editions is Poe's book *Al Aaraaf, Tamerlane, and Minor Poems*, of which only 18 copies are known to exist. Another rarity is a copy of Poe's book *Poems*, published in 1831 with the help of Poe's West Point classmates, to whom Poe sold subscriptions to pay for the printing. When Robertson donated these pieces to the Poe Museum over the course of the 1920s and 1930s, they formed the core of the museum's collection.

Julia Sully was the granddaughter of Poe's friend the artist Robert Sully. She became an early supporter of the Poe Museum and donated a small watercolor her grandfather had painted as a gift for Poe. Because Robert Sully knew many of the people in Poe's life, several of the portraits in the Poe Museum were painted by him.

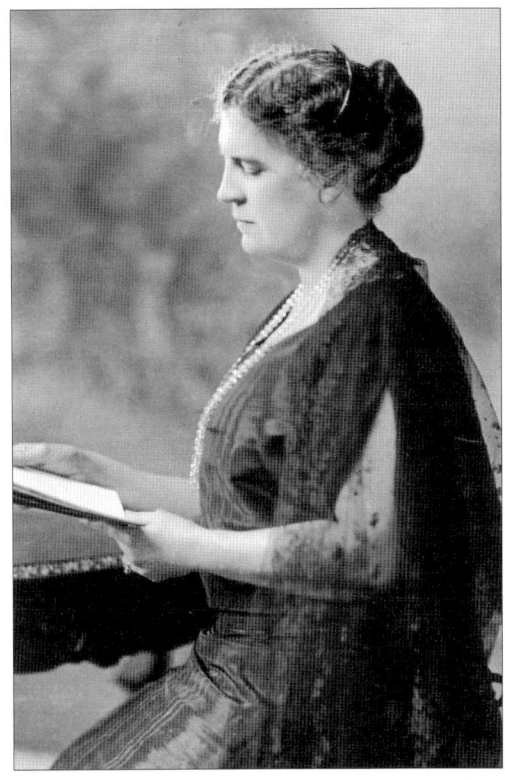

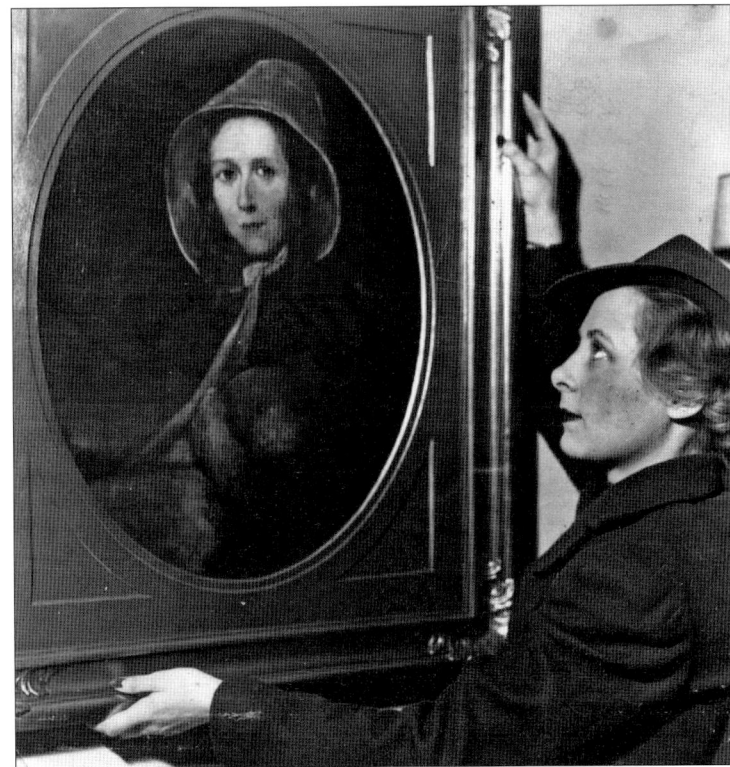

In this 1938 photograph by Dementi Studios, Dorothy Blevin Mathews hangs a painting of Charlotte Sully, sister of Poe's friend Robert Sully. The portrait, painted by Robert Sully, was on loan to the Poe Museum for Poe Memorial Week, an annual observance of Poe's birthday. During the early years of the museum, the organization often borrowed such artifacts and artwork to supplement its growing collection.

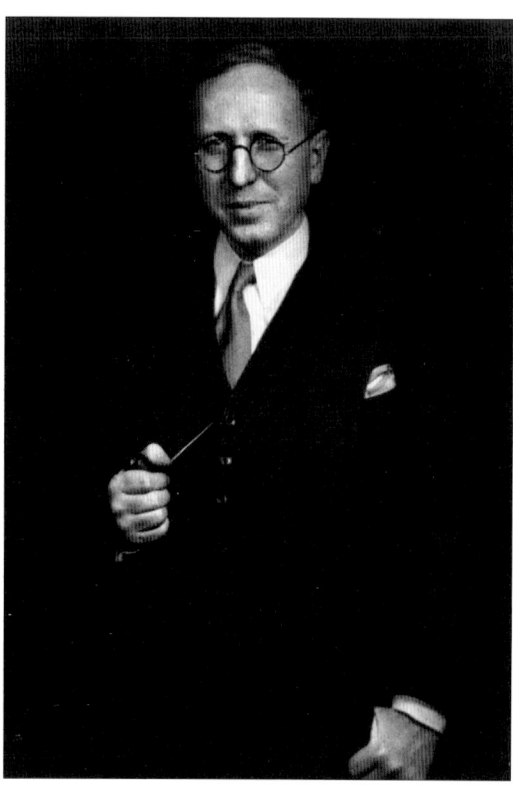

The historian and biographer Douglas Southall Freeman served as president of the Poe Foundation from 1924 until 1947. Freeman wrote Pulitzer Prize–winning biographies of George Washington and Robert E. Lee. One of the most important changes the organization saw during Freeman's presidency was the adoption of the name Edgar Allan Poe Museum in place of the original Poe Shrine.

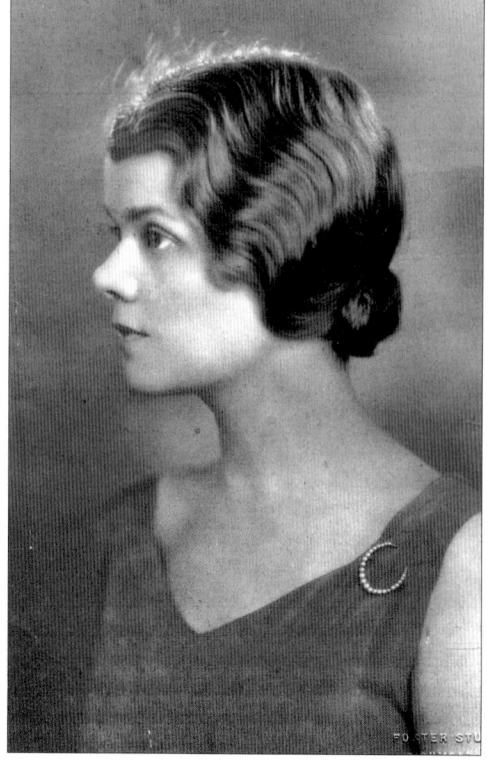

This 1931 image by Foster Studio of Richmond depicts Ann Page Johns, who would serve as president of the Poe Foundation from 1960 until 1964. One of her most important contributions to the museum was moving the large model of Poe's Richmond from the Old Stone House to a building specifically devoted to its display.

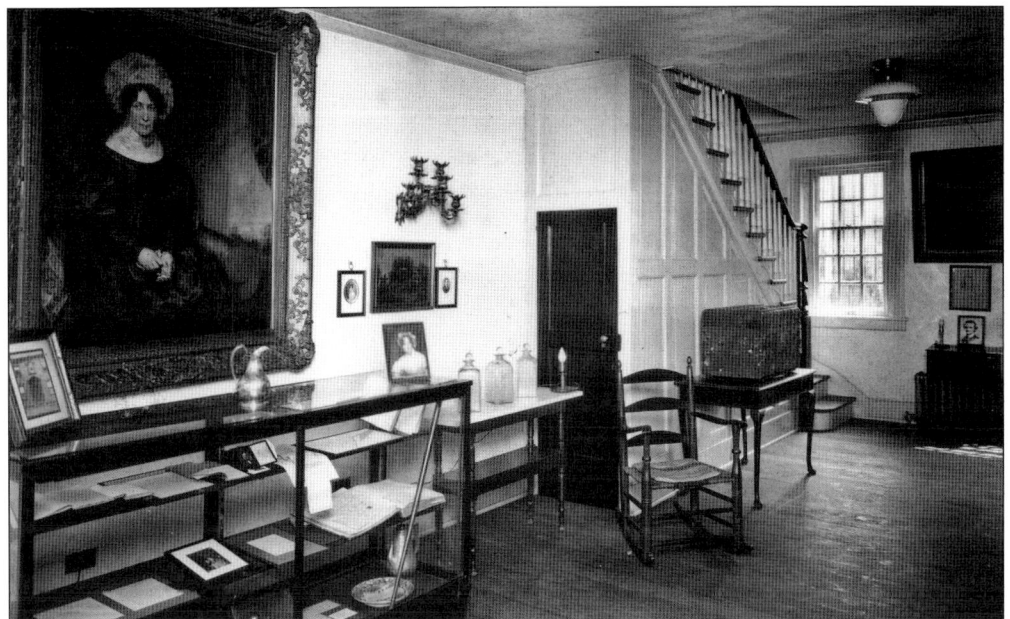

This 1928 image represents an early exhibit in the Poe Shrine's Elizabeth Arnold Poe Memorial Building. The case in the foreground contains an assortment of Poe artifacts, including some of Poe's manuscripts, his walking stick, a soup ladle from his home, and a lock taken from the door of the Craig House.

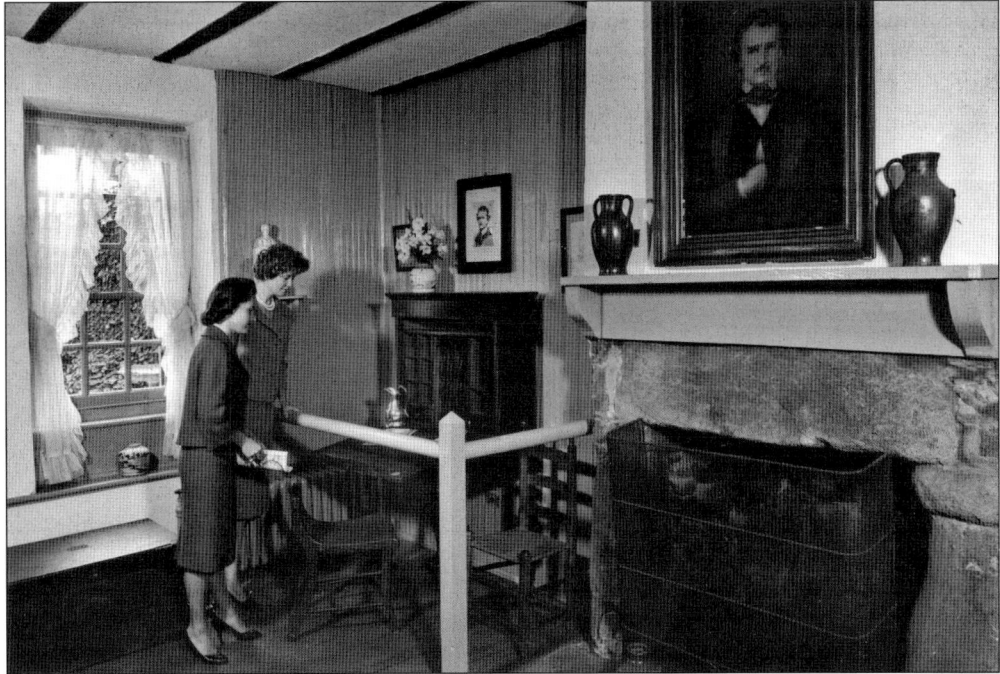

Two unidentified visitors study Poe's chair in this undated photograph taken in the Old Stone House. The portrait over the fireplace was painted in 1921 especially for the Poe Shrine by Mrs. Norman Burwell. It was said to be based on a daguerreotype owned by James Whitty, the first president of the Poe Foundation.

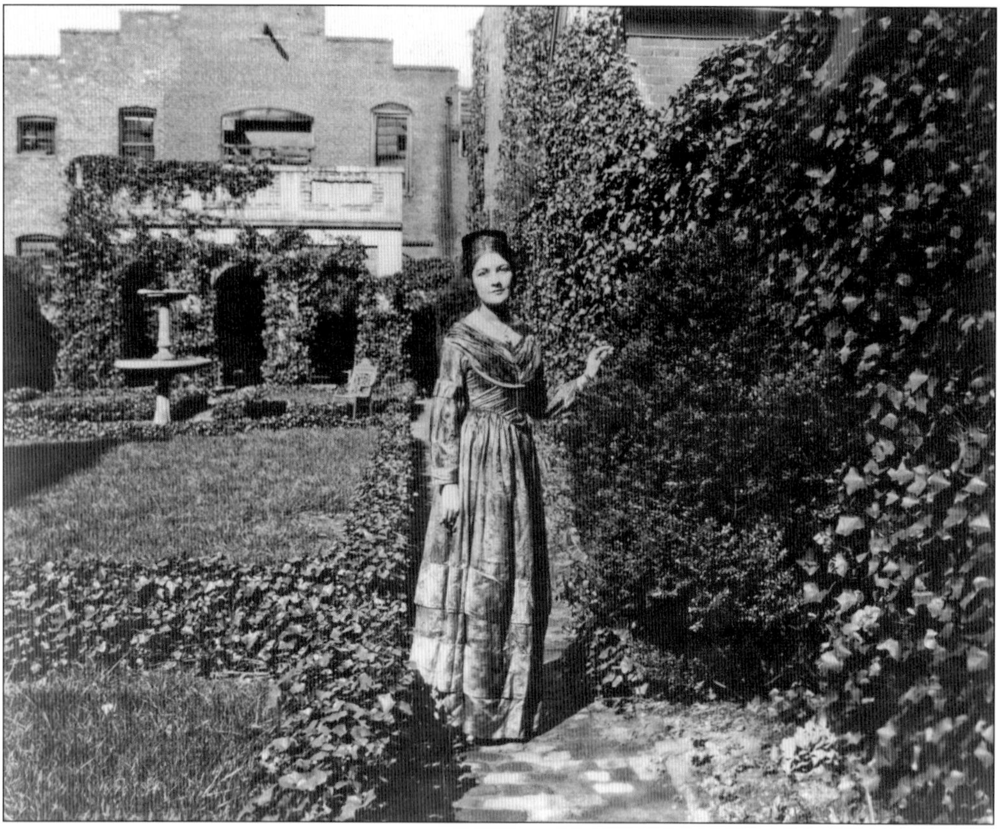

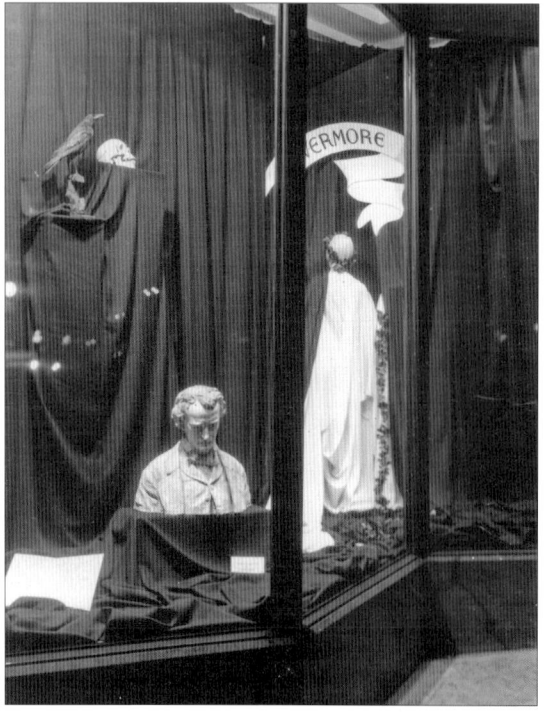

In this 1930 image, Marjorie Blevins poses in the Enchanted Garden in a 135-year-old dress once owned by her great-grandmother. The picture was taken to advertise the upcoming "Adventure Days" historical festival in which the Poe Shrine would be one of the Richmond "beauty spots" open to the public.

During the 1930s, Poe Memorial Week was celebrated annually throughout Richmond. This photograph from 1932 depicts the window of Thalhimers department store, once one of the two most prominent stores in downtown Richmond, decorated with furniture and artifacts from the Poe Museum. In those days, shoppers would travel from as far away North Carolina to spend the day in this store.

Poe family descendant Amelia Poe Woodward looks less than thrilled about posing in the Poe Shrine in the court dress that once belonged to her ancestor Lady Fitzgerald. Since its founding, the Poe Shrine has been supported by Poe family relatives, but it was not until 2004 that a Poe relative, Dr. Harry Lee Poe, became the president of the Poe Foundation.

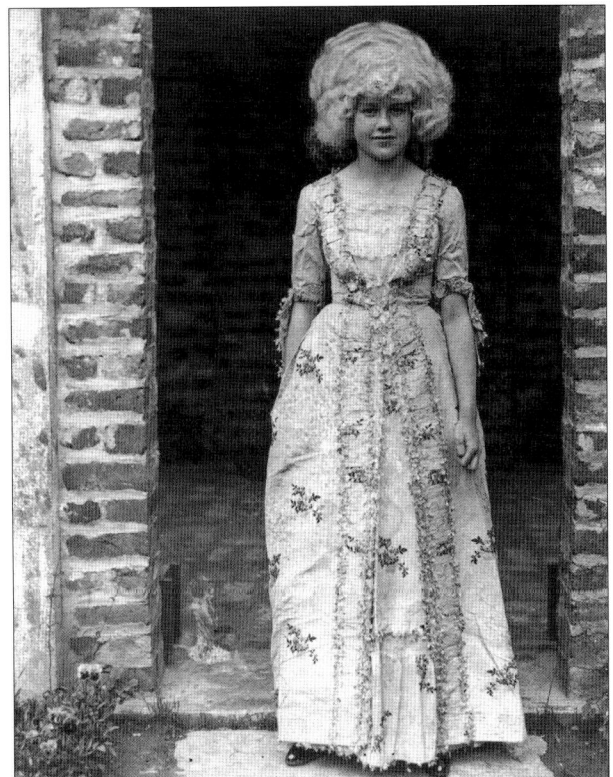

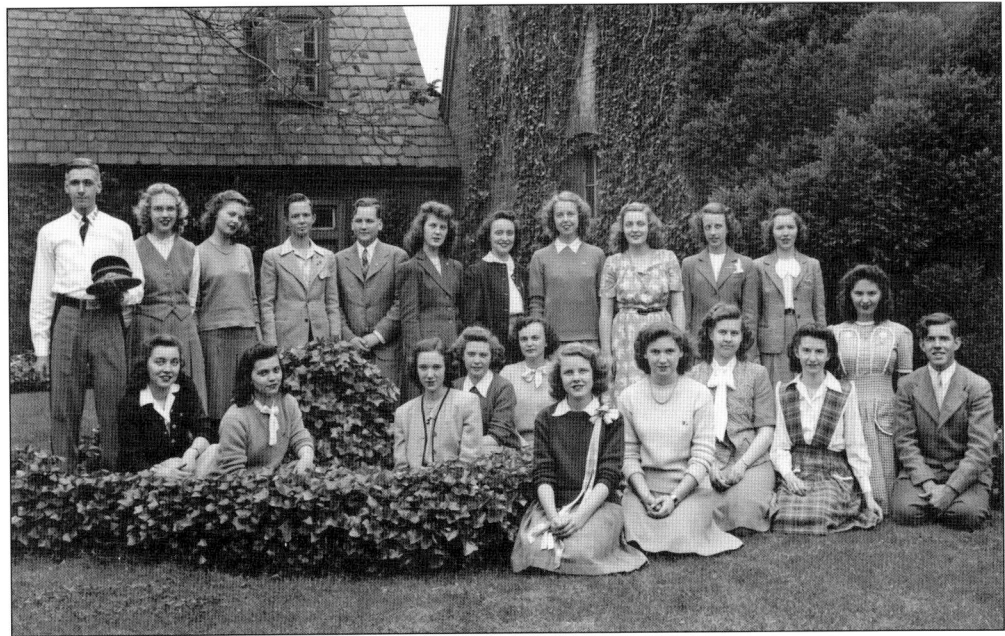

A group from John Marshall High School visits the Poe Museum's Enchanted Garden in this 1945 photograph. Each year, the Poe Museum hosts school group tours for groups from around the world. Because Poe is an internationally known figure, it is not uncommon for students from as far away as France, Germany, and Korea to visit.

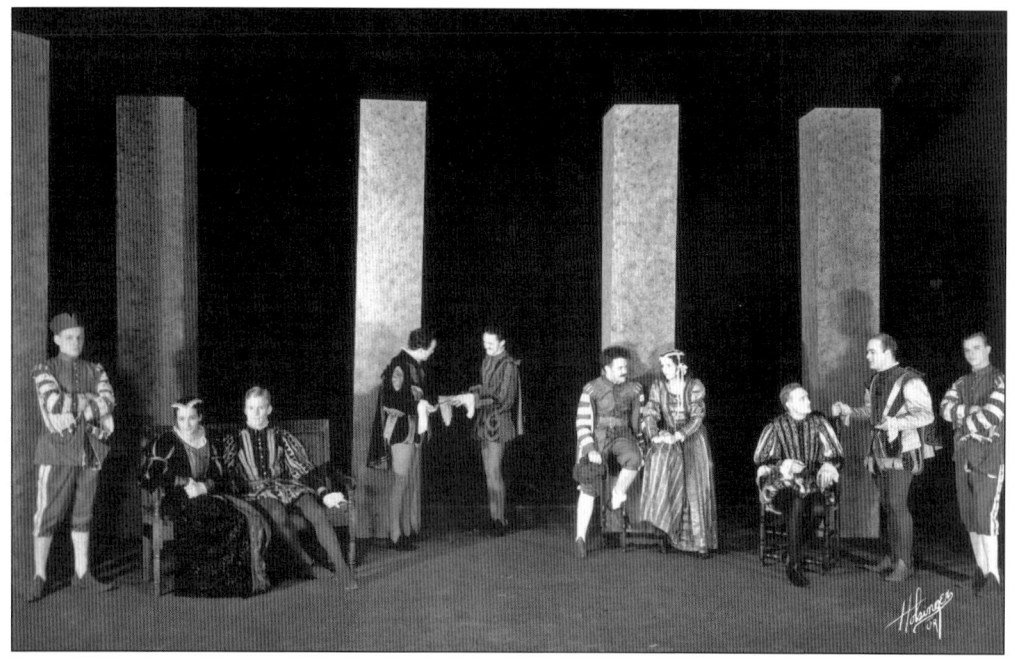

The University Players at the University of Virginia perform Poe's only play, *Politian*, in this 1933 image. Though Poe had written the play almost a century earlier and had published his unfinished text in the *Southern Literary Messenger*, the play received its world premiere on Poe's birthday, January 19, 1933, at the university's Cabell Hall.

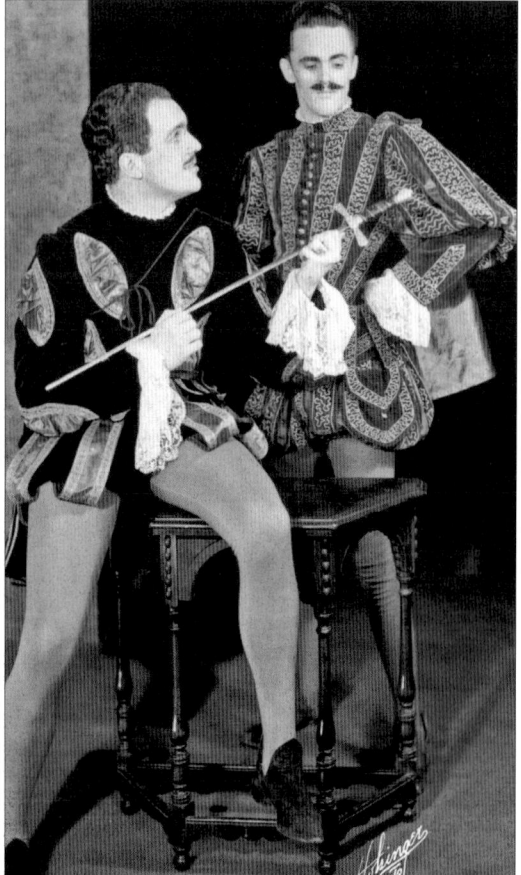

James Young (left) and Everard Meade of the University Players perform in Poe's play, *Politian*, in this 1933 photograph by Holsinger. Meade played Castiglione and Young played Baldazzar in this play of love and murder based on a real-life murder and love triangle that took place in Kentucky in 1825.

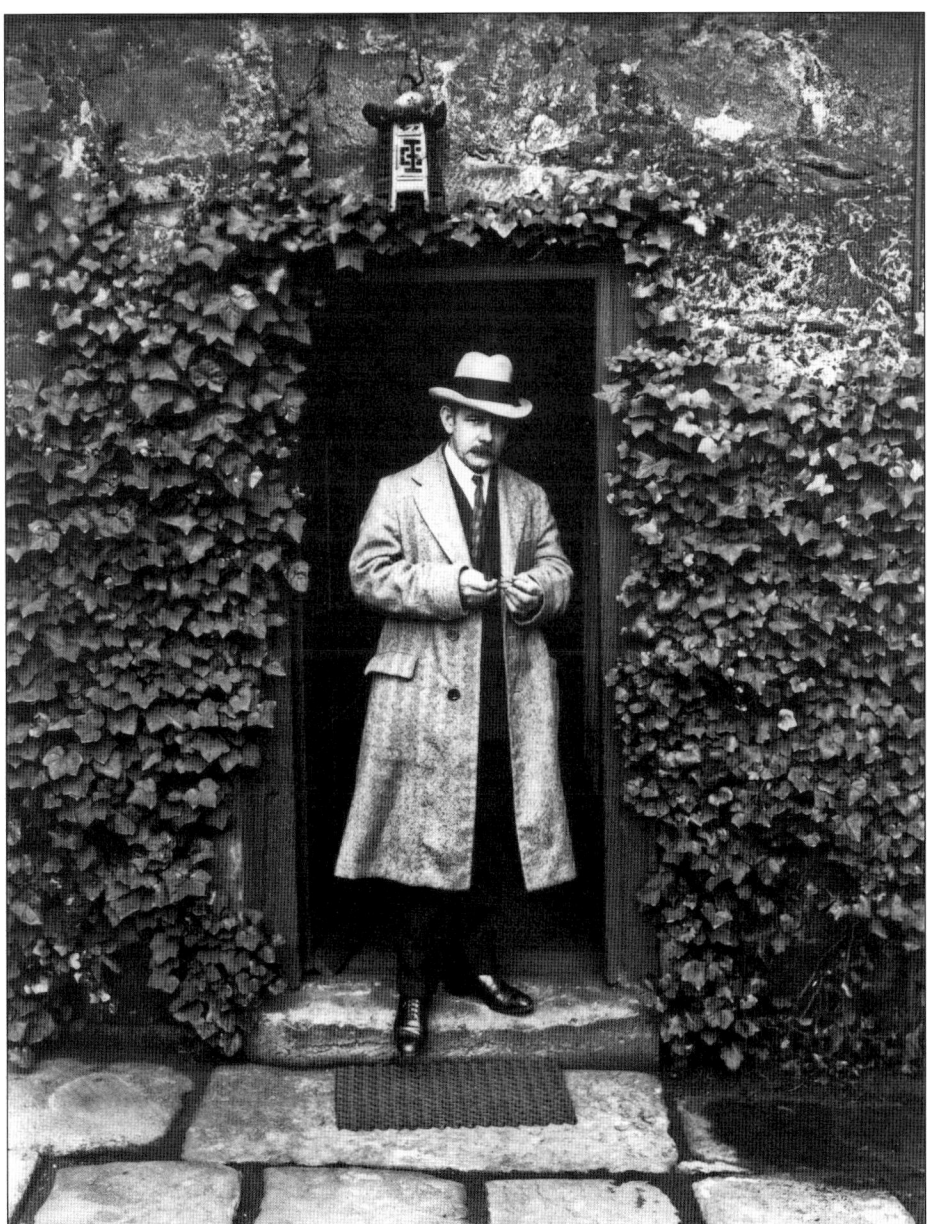

John Gutzon de la Mothe Borglum is best known as the artist who created the president heads at Mount Rushmore in South Dakota as well as the Confederate memorial at Stone Mountain, Georgia. After visiting the Poe Shrine in 1922, he offered to create a Poe sculpture for the garden to embody his ideal of the "great American dreamer." He volunteered his services but asked the Poe Foundation to pay for the bronze he would need. At this time, Borglum was also engaged with the Confederate memorial in Georgia. After a disagreement with his backers there, he destroyed all of his models and fled the state. In 1924, he informed the Poe Foundation that his model for the Poe monument had been lost in Georgia and that he would sculpt a new one. Unfortunately, the second model was never made because Borglum left to begin work on Mount Rushmore. After Borglum's death in 1941, the Poe Foundation lost all hope of acquiring for its shrine a sculpture by this renowned artist.

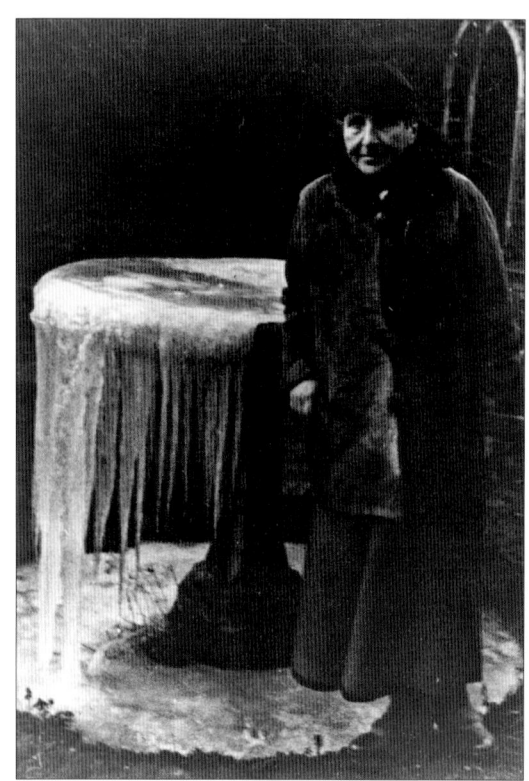

American poet Gertrude Stein visited the Edgar Allan Poe Shrine in 1936 with the photographer Carl Van Vechten, who took a series of photographs of her in the complex. Stein inscribed each of the prints, which were then given to the Poe Shrine. The image of Stein standing by the door reads, "For the Poe Shrine and open." The picture of her next to the fountain is inscribed, "For the Poe foundation naturally in winter." Stein's small stature is especially apparent in the image in which she is posing next to the fountain.

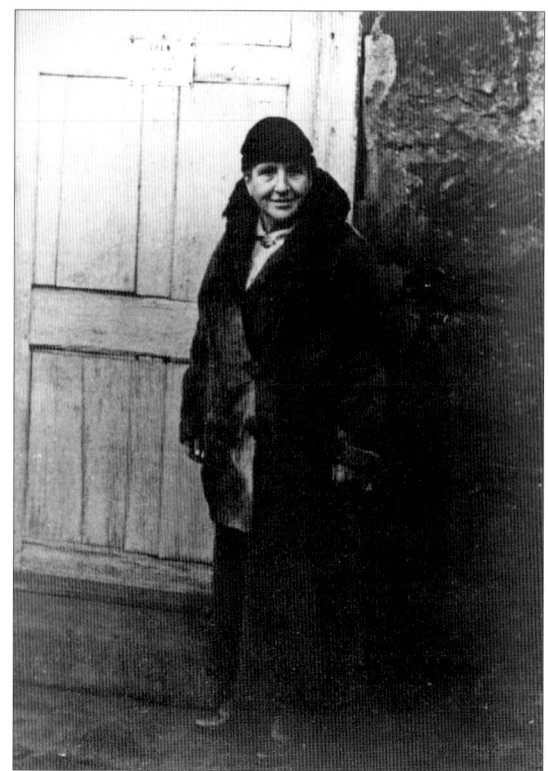

Carl Van Vechten was a writer and photographer who captured the images of many celebrities, including Ella Fitzgerald and Billie Holliday. Van Vechten was greatly involved in the emergence of the Harlem Renaissance. Gertrude Stein made him her literary executor. He inscribed this photograph to Poe Shrine cofounder Annie B. Jones

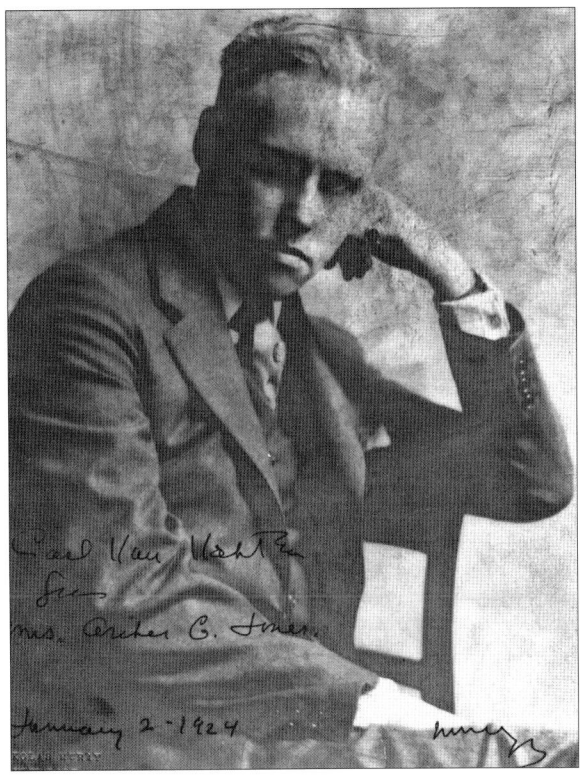

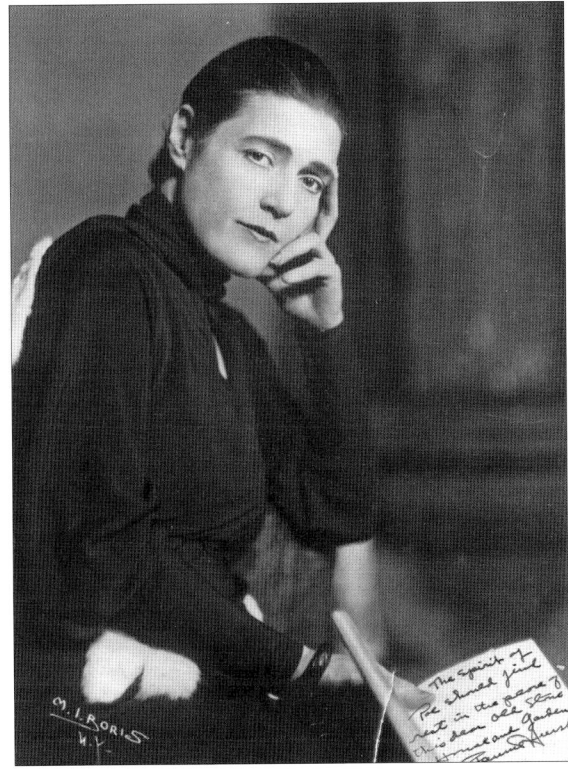

One of many famous visitors in the early days of the Poe Shrine, novelist Fannie Hurst had a prolific career in which she produced 17 novels, 9 volumes of short stories, and 3 plays. Her book *Imitation of Life* was made into a film in 1934. Hurst inscribed this picture, "The spirit of Poe shall find rest in the peace of this dear Old Stone House and garden."

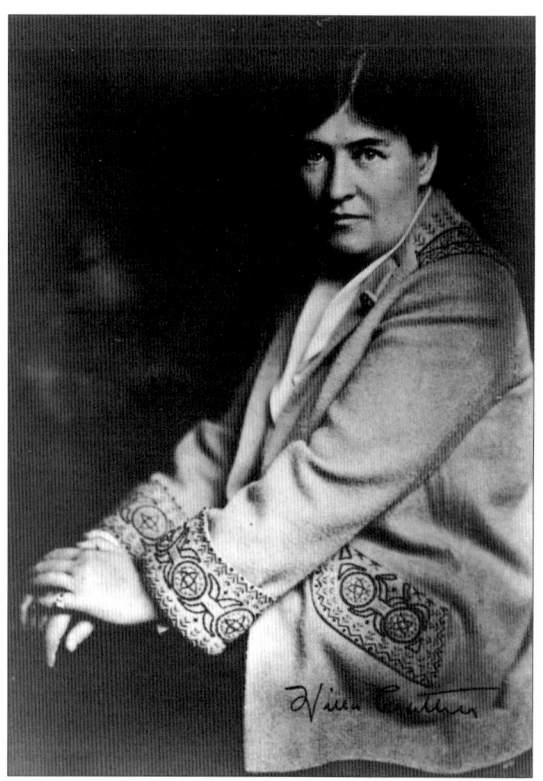

The author Willa Sibert Cather was born in Winchester, Virginia. She won the Pulitzer Prize in 1923 for her novel *One of Ours*. Cather's writing was influenced by reading Poe's work. She left this autographed photograph of herself at the Poe Shrine after her visit.

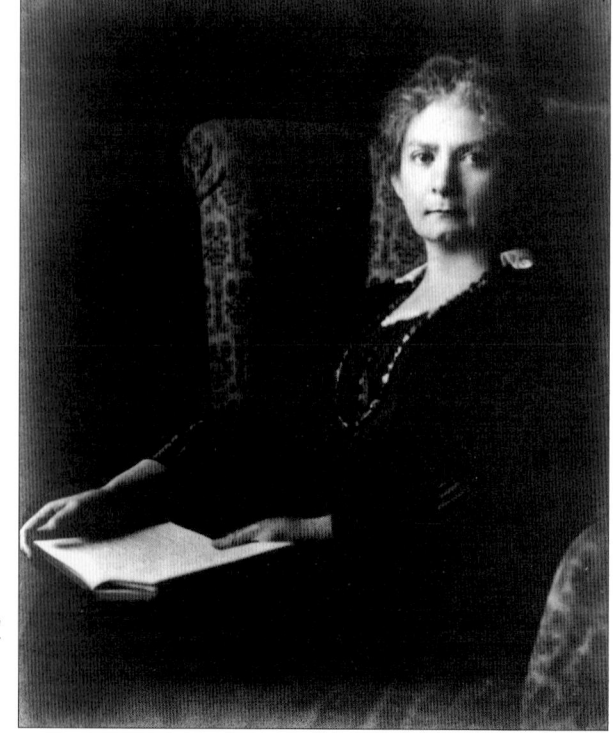

Another famous visitor to the Poe Shrine, Mary Johnston, wrote historical books and romantic novels. According to the *New York Times*, her novel *To Have and to Hold* was the bestselling book of 1900. Johnston is buried in Richmond's Hollywood Cemetery.

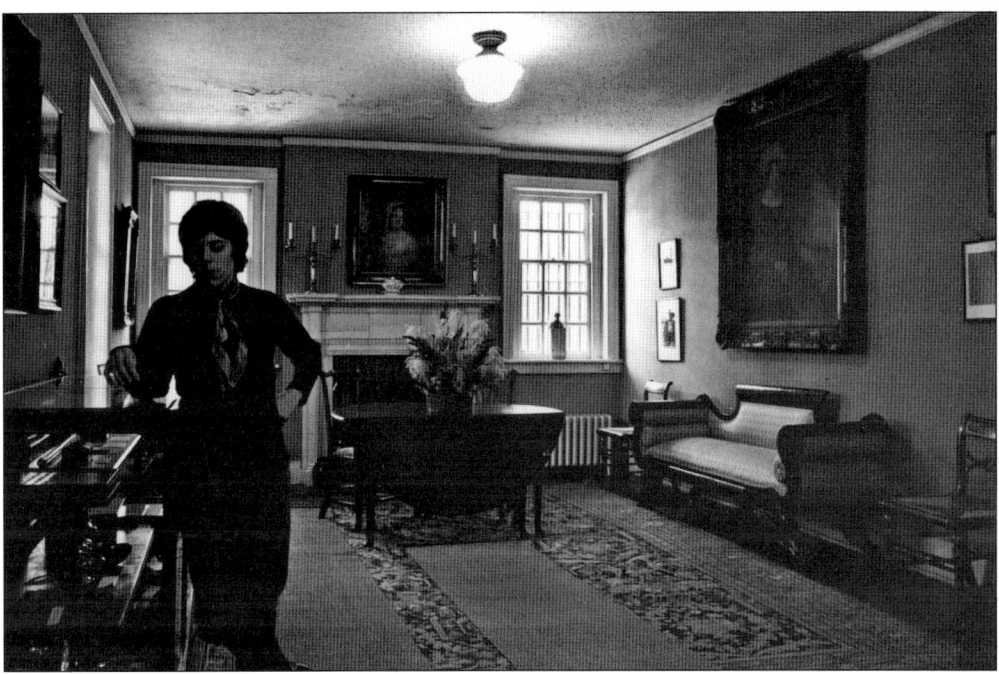

Two unidentified models flagrantly violate museum etiquette by leaning on the exhibit case and sitting on historic furniture in these 1979 photographs of the Elizabeth Arnold Poe Memorial Building by Cyane Lowden. Among the artifacts visible in these images are chairs and a table from the Allan mansion, Moldavia. The candelabra on the mantle belonged to Poe's nurse Marie Louise Shew, who claimed he wrote his poem "The Bells" by their light. The desk came from the offices of the *Southern Literary Messenger* but is not Poe's desk, which is now owned by the Harry Ransom Center at the University of Texas at Austin.

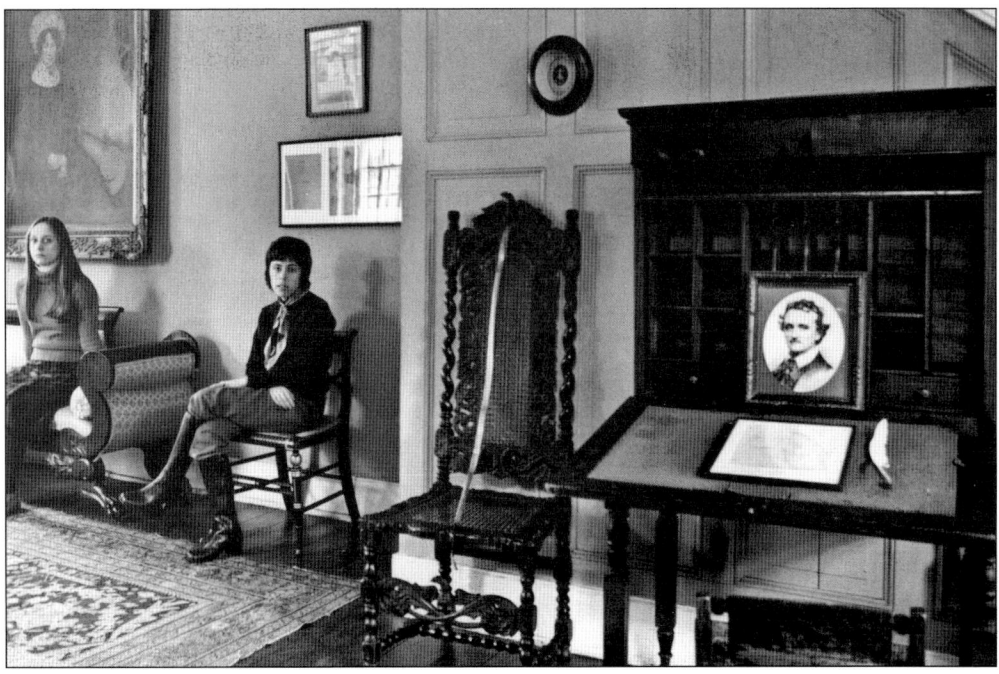

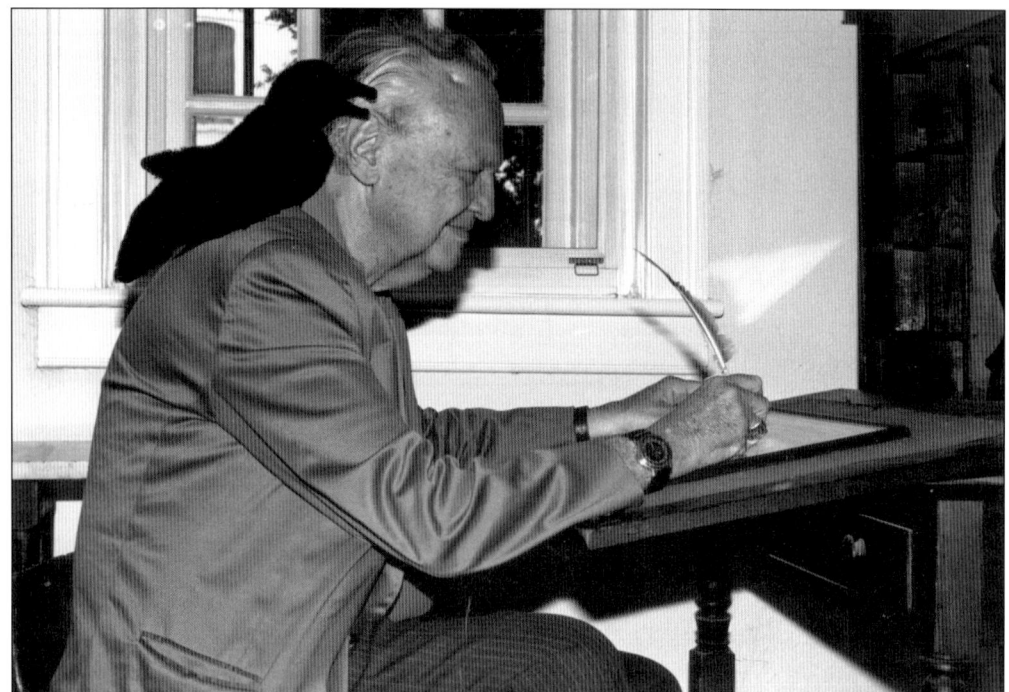

James Dickey was a poet and novelist best known for his novel *Deliverance*. A film version of this novel was released in 1972. In this photograph of the author's visit to the Poe Museum, Dickey is sitting on Poe's chair from the *Southern Literary Messenger* while a raven perches on his shoulder to offer inspiration.

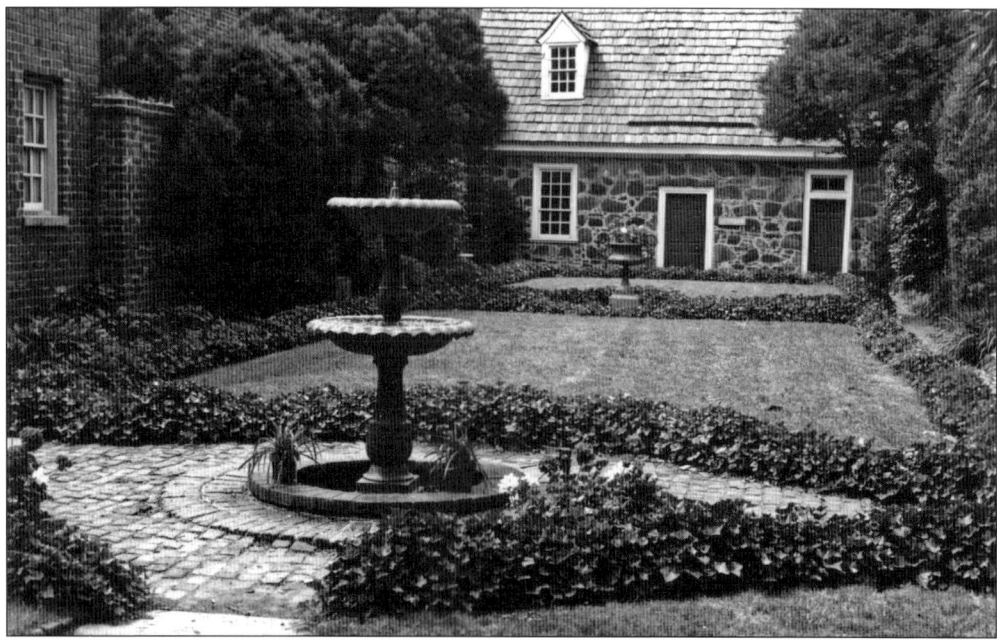

As seen in this image from the 1970s, the Enchanted Garden was revitalized in 1964 with the assistance of renowned landscape architect Charles Gillette, who added a variety of exotic plants and installed a new fountain and sculpture.

Five

POE'S RICHMOND TODAY

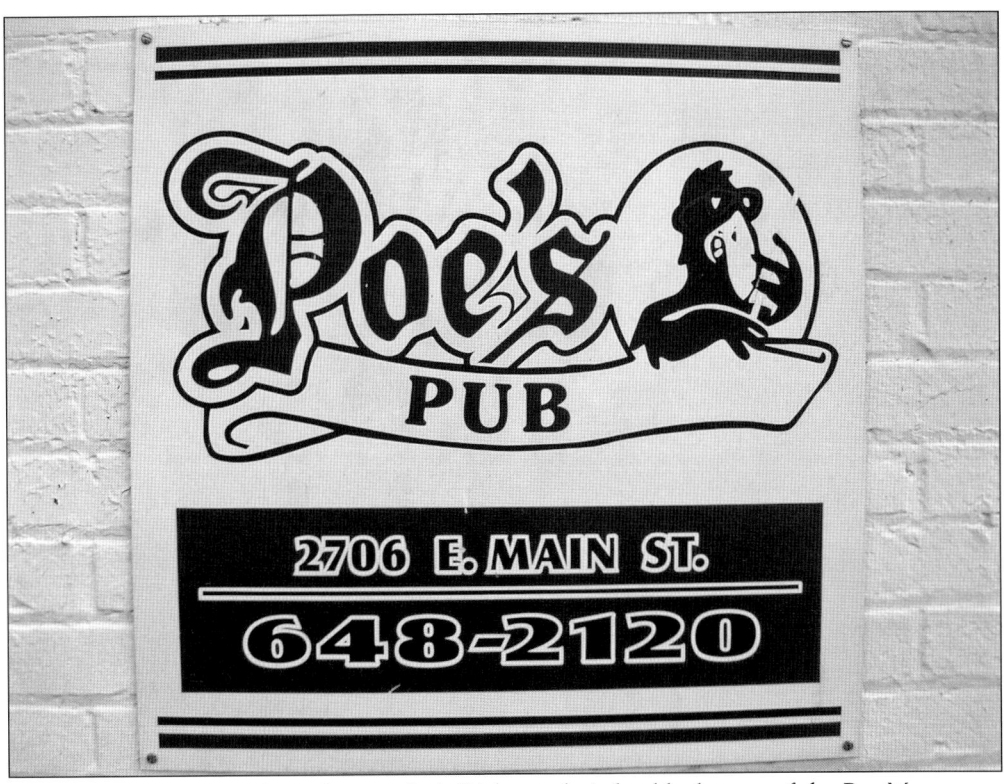

Poe's presence remains throughout today's Richmond. A few blocks east of the Poe Museum at 2706 East Main Street, Poe's Pub bears the name of Richmond's most famous author. Visitors can enjoy raven fries while listening to live music. Although the building did not exist during Poe's time, he would have known the neighborhood, which is within blocks of his mother's grave, his fiancée's house, and his place of employment.

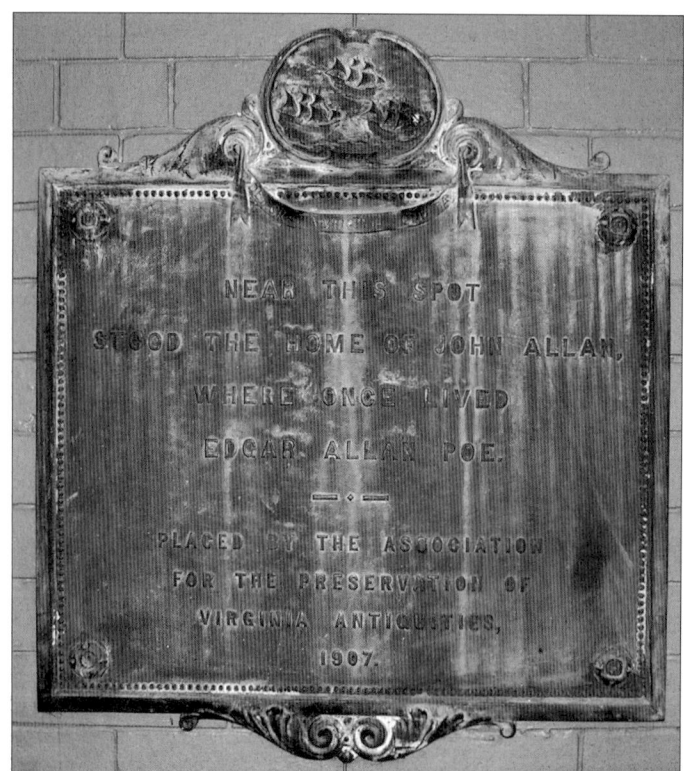

Although none of Poe's Richmond homes have survived to the present day, this plaque marks the site of one of his homes, Moldavia, where he lived with his foster parents before attending the University of Virginia. Moldavia was demolished in 1890. This plaque was placed in 1907 on the Virginian Building (built in 1901) on the southeast corner of Fifth and Main Streets.

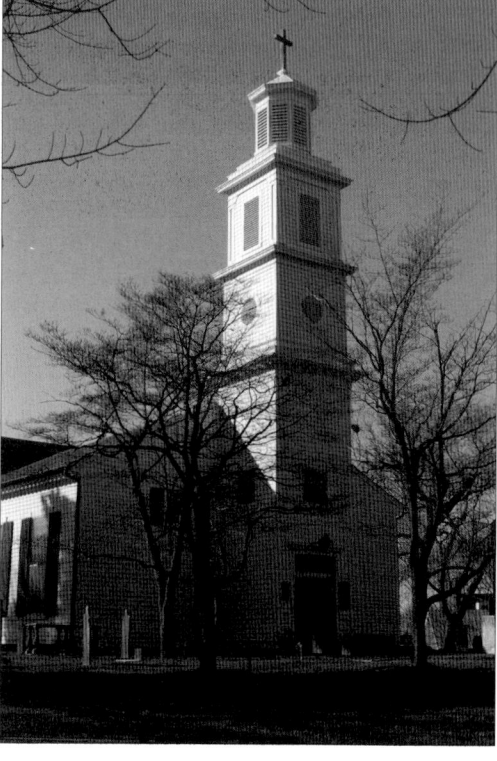

St. John's Church, a National Historic Landmark, is the site of Patrick Henry's infamous "Liberty or Death" speech. The graveyard surrounding the church is where Poe's mother, Elizabeth Arnold Poe, was buried. The church is located in Church Hill, Richmond's oldest residential neighborhood. Services are still held every Sunday, and reenactments of Patrick Henry's speech are performed during the summer.

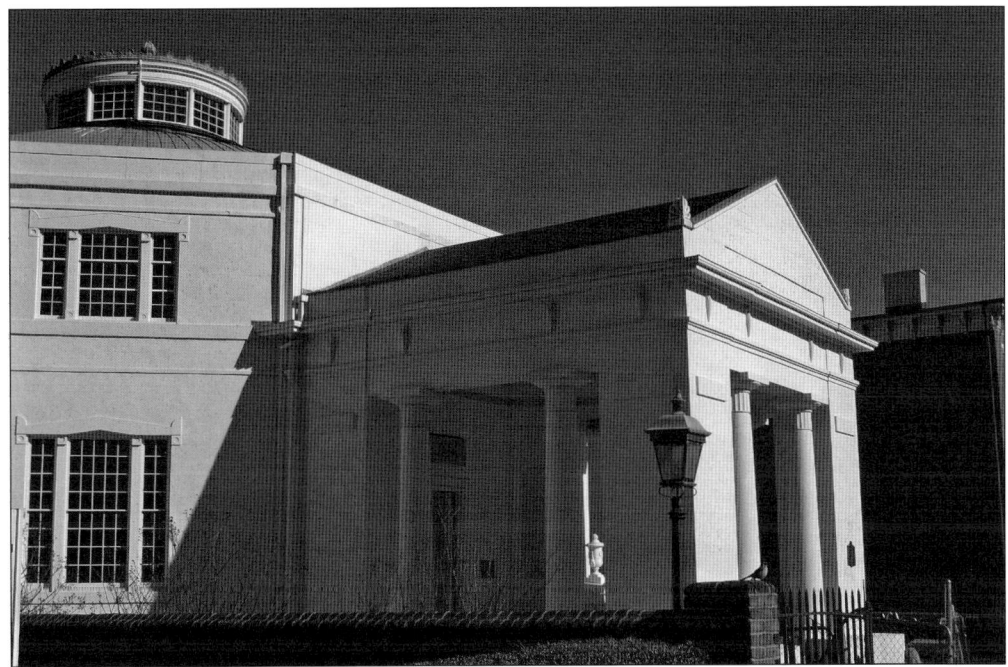

Located at the corner of Broad and College Streets, Monumental Church has recently been restored to much the way it would have appeared when Poe worshipped there as a boy. Built in memory of the 72 victims of the 1811 Richmond Theatre fire, the church still houses the ashes of the victims in its basement. The ceremonial urn in the portico does not contain any of the ashes, but the names of the victims are listed on its base. Without an active congregation, Monumental Church is now maintained by the Historic Richmond Foundation and is open to the public for tours during the summer.

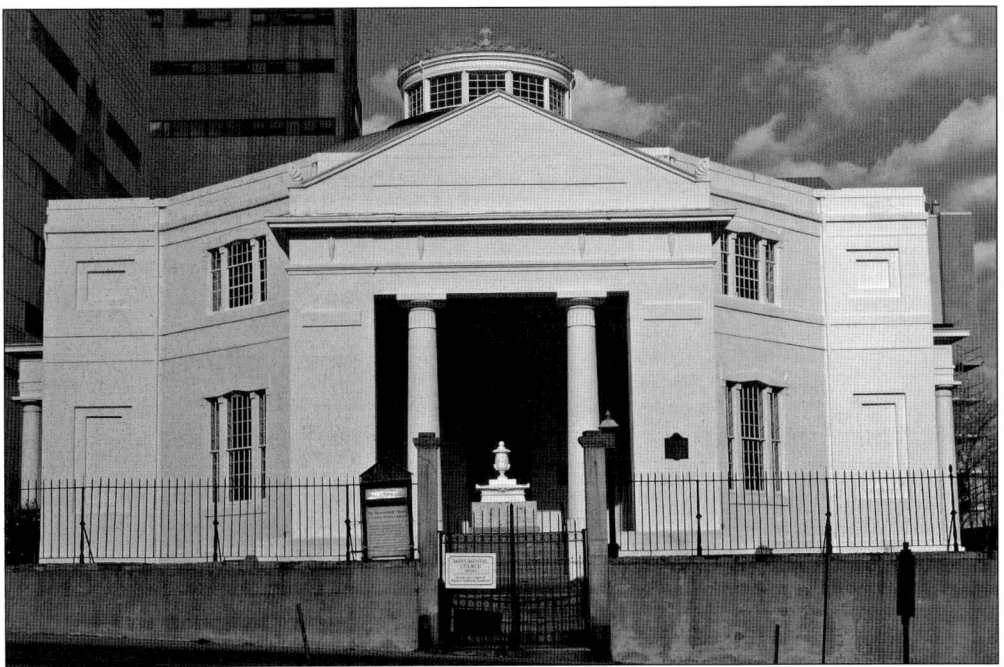

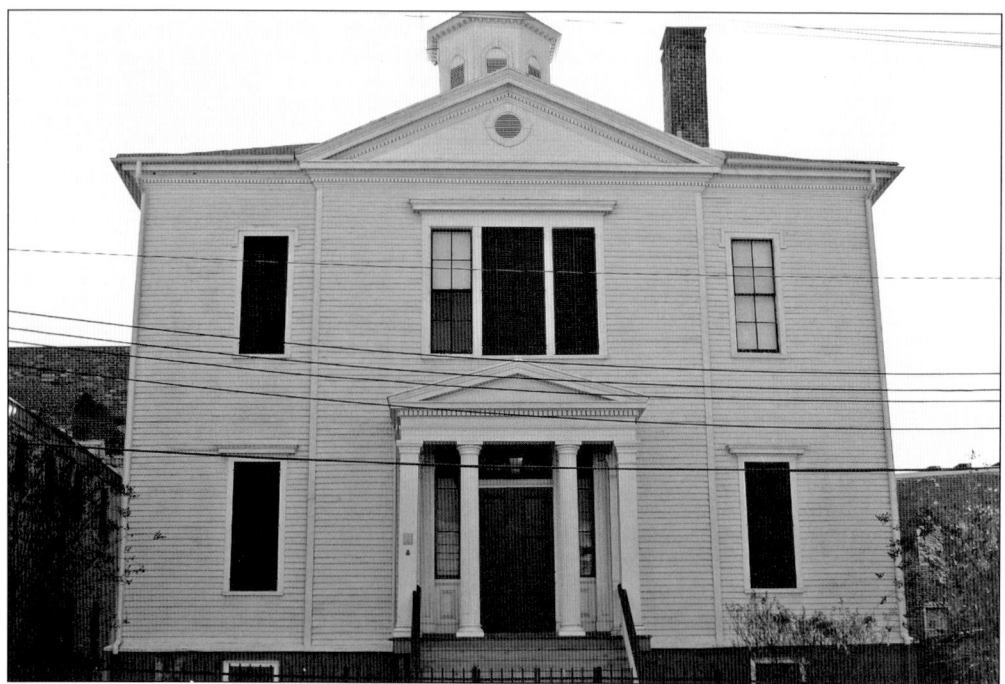

The Masonic lodge to which Poe escorted Lafayette in 1824 still stands at 1805 East Franklin Street. Gen. George Washington was among the many famous visitors to this building. During its illustrious history, the Masonic lodge was also used as a hospital in the War of 1812. The structure is now maintained by the Richmond-Randolph Lodge and is not open to the public.

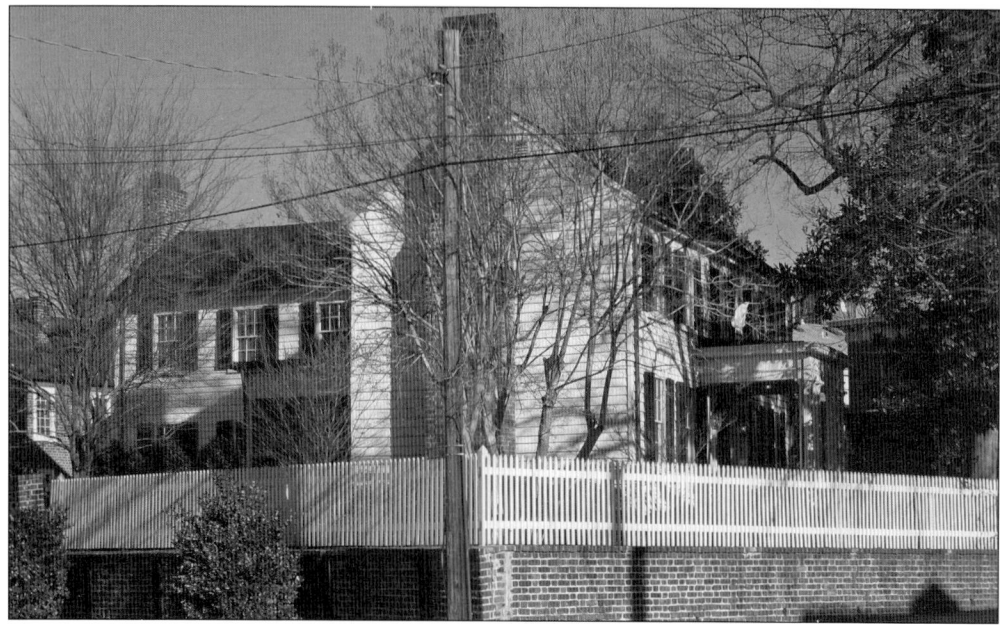

The Craig House, the birthplace of Poe's first love, Jane Stanard, is located at Nineteenth and East Grace Streets. Having undergone extensive restoration, the home is in excellent condition. The home is now privately owned and, therefore, not open to the public. A historic marker on the sidewalk describes the history of the house and its connection with Poe.

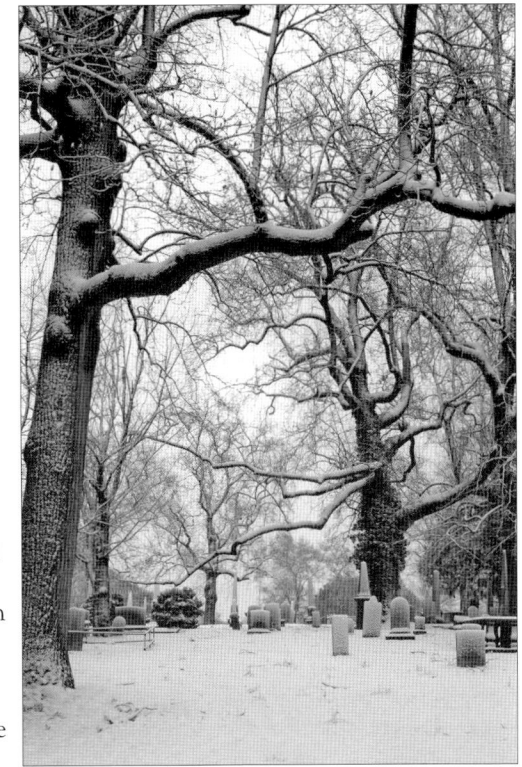

Located at Fifth and Hospital Streets, Shockoe Cemetery is one of Richmond's oldest cemeteries. Among the notables buried here are Chief Justice of the U.S. Supreme Court John Marshall and Union spy Elizabeth Van Lew. Edgar Allan Poe's foster parents, John and Frances Allan; his first love, Jane Stanard; and his fiancée Elmira Shelton were laid to rest here as well. Elmira Shelton's grave is pictured below.

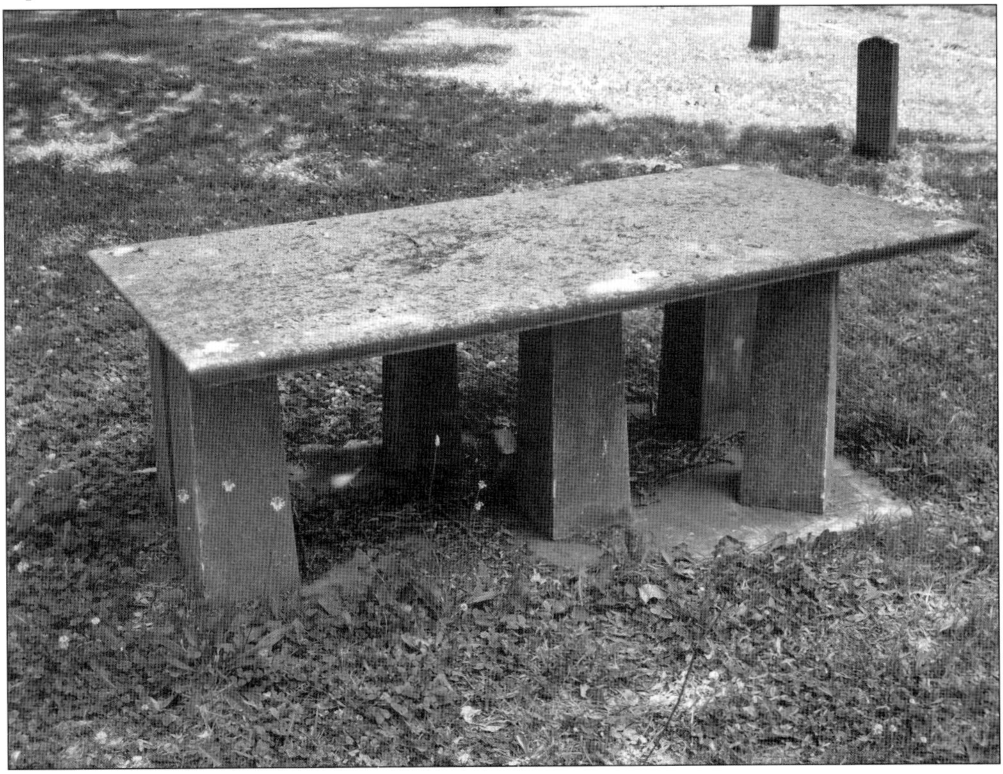

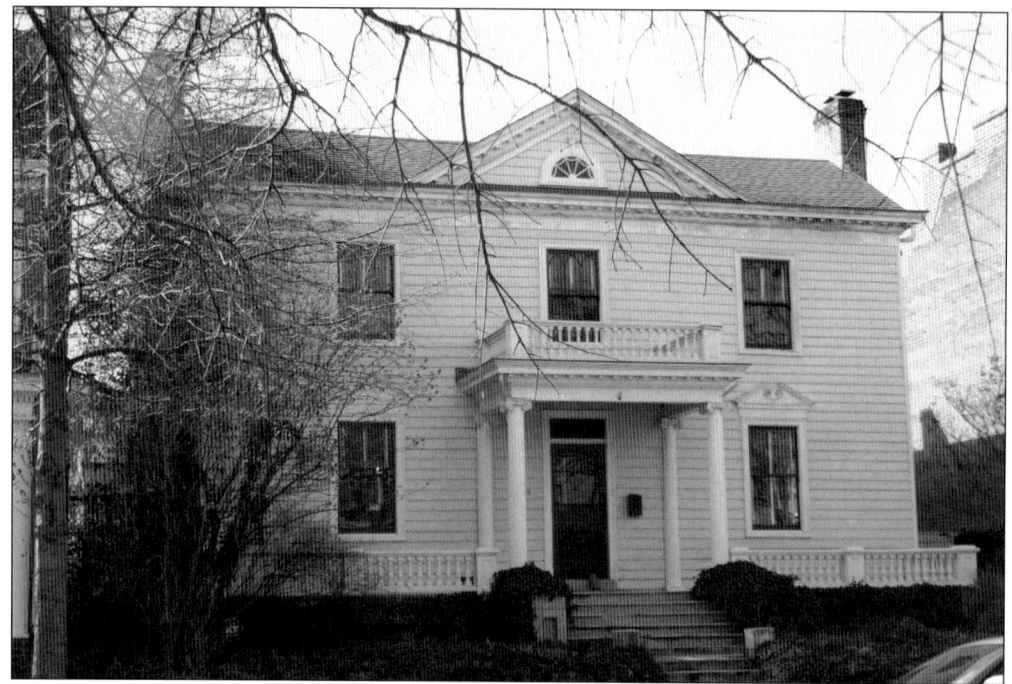

Built in 1835, Talavera was the home of Rosalie Poe's friend Susan Archer Talley Weiss. Since Poe's day, the house has been moved twice to save it from destruction, and it now stands at 2315 West Grace Street in the heart of Richmond's Fan District. Talavera is a private residence and is not open to the public.

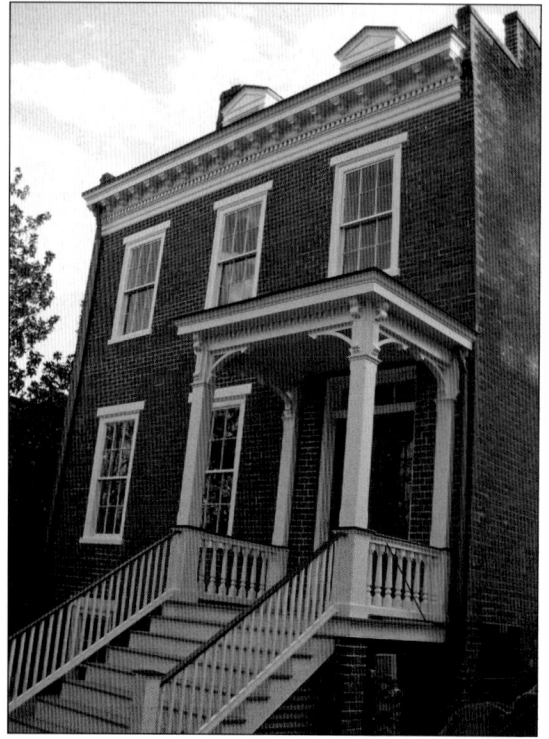

The home of Poe's fiancée, Elmira Royster Shelton, the Shelton House still stands at 2407 East Grace Street on Richmond's historic Church Hill. The home has recently undergone many renovations in anticipation of being returned to private ownership after years in the care of the Historic Richmond Foundation. The house is not open to the public.

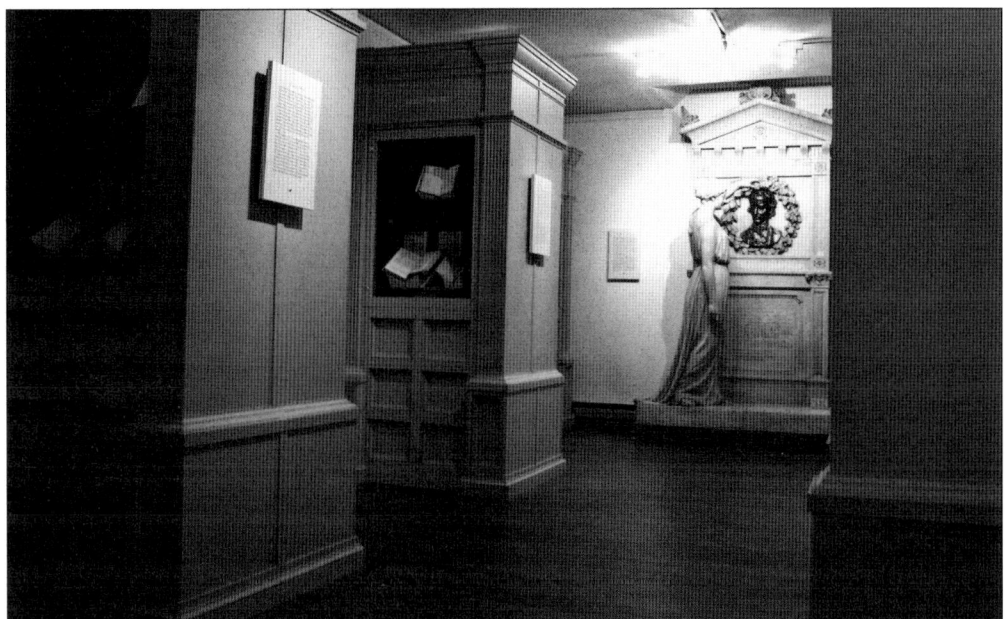

Today the Poe Museum's Elizabeth Arnold Poe Memorial Building contains an exhibit of rare Poe manuscripts and letters. Prominently featured at the end of the gallery is the 1885 monument to Poe commissioned by the Actors' Guild of New York. The president of the guild, Edwin Booth, brother of presidential assassin John Wilkes Booth, officially unveiled the sculpture at the Metropolitan Museum of Art in New York City.

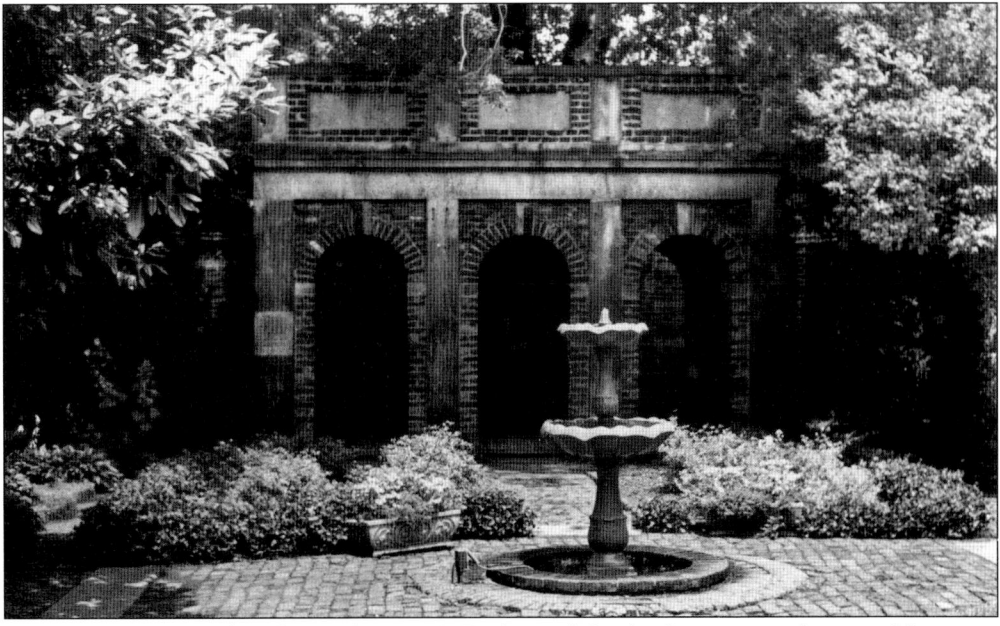

For almost nine decades, the Poe Museum's Enchanted Garden has remained a peaceful oasis in the middle of downtown Richmond. In recent years, it has become a popular site for wedding ceremonies, and Poe's birthday is celebrated there annually. In the warmer months, the garden hosts monthly Unhappy Hours, in which visitors can relax after work while listening to music, poetry, or dramatic readings.

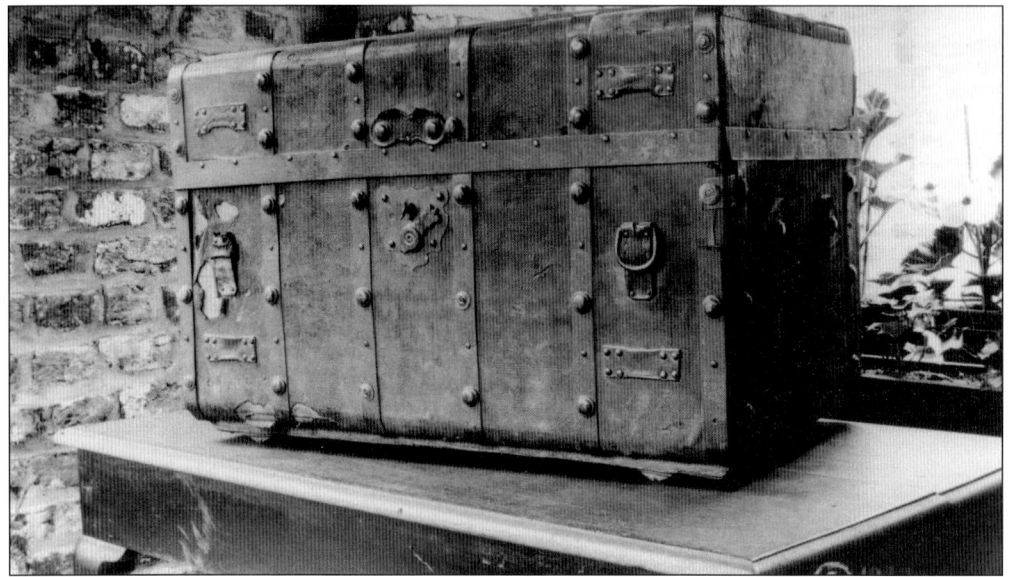

One of the finest pieces in the Poe Museum's collection is the poet's trunk, which came directly from the foster family of Poe's sister Rosalie Mackenzie Poe. The key to the trunk, which was found in Poe's pocket after his death, is also on display at the Poe Museum. This photograph was taken in 1922 in the Poe Shrine.

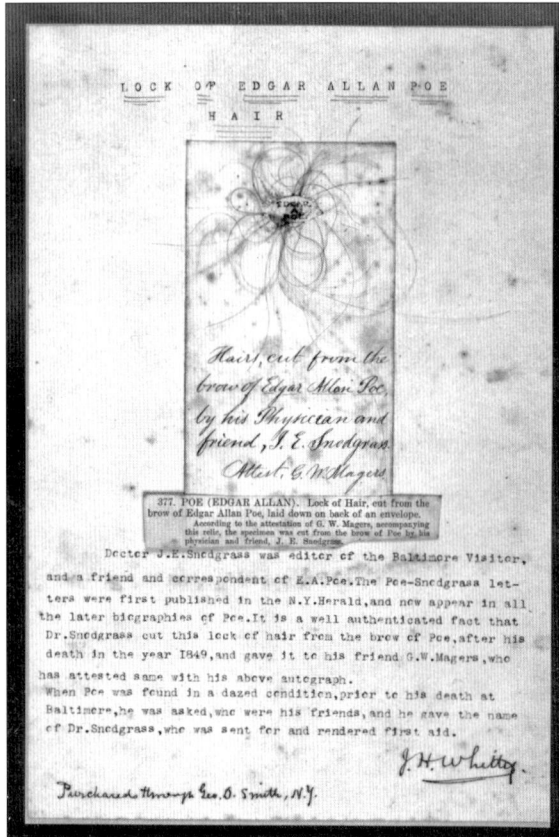

Another treasure of the Poe Museum is this lock of Poe's hair cut from his brow after his death by his friend Joseph Snodgrass, the man who sent Poe to the hospital after finding him semiconscious at a Baltimore polling place. At first glance, many visitors miss seeing the hair, which is glued to the back of an envelope, which, in turn, is glued to a letter by James Whitty.

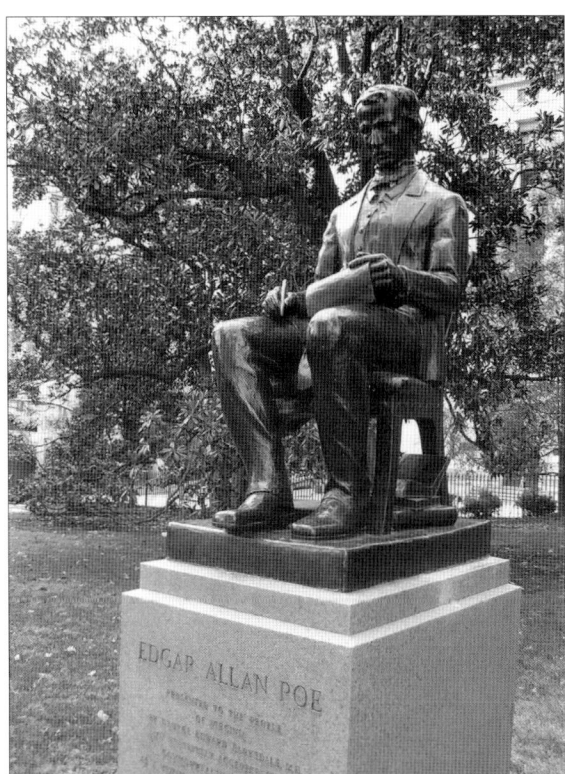

At the top of the page is an image of the first statue of Poe in Richmond. The statue by Charles Rudy was placed on the grounds of the Virginia State Capitol on October 7, 1959, the 110th anniversary of Poe's death. Still a controversial figure in conservative Richmond, Edgar Allan Poe had previously been denied the honor of a statue in the city when the Poe Memorial Association had tried to erect one in 1906. Even when the Philadelphian Poe admirer Dr. George Edward Barksdale sent this statue to Richmond, it sat in storage for three years before it was finally placed on the capitol grounds. The bottom photograph depicts the Virginia State Capitol. Poe knew the building but might not recognize it today, because the appearance was dramatically altered with the 1906 addition of wings.

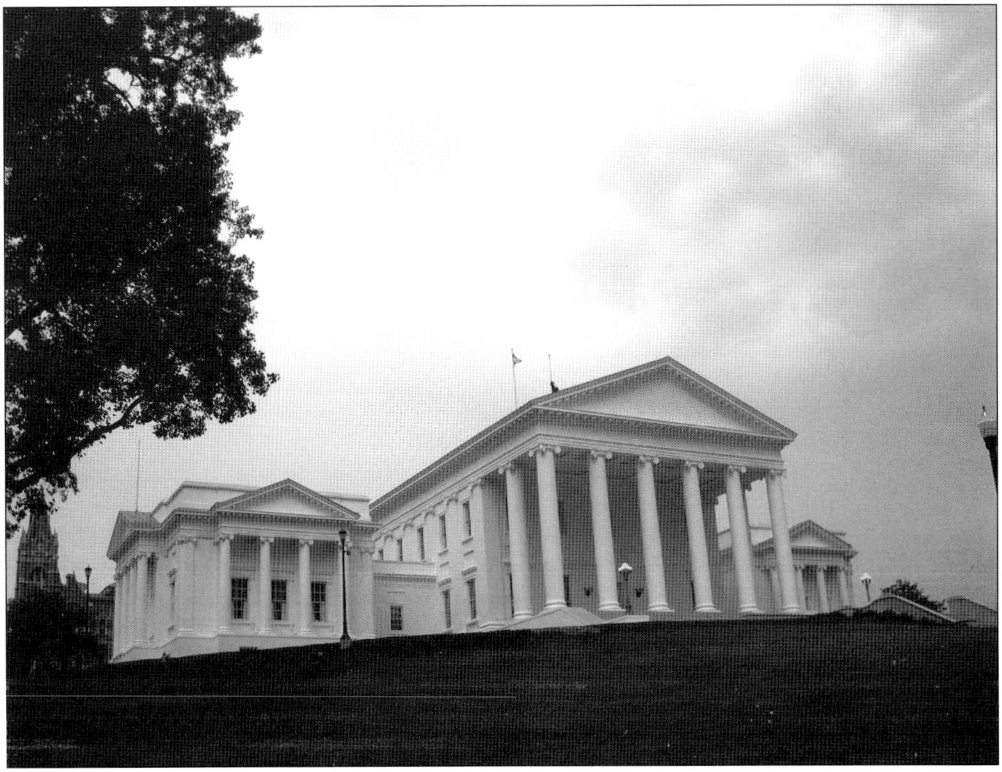

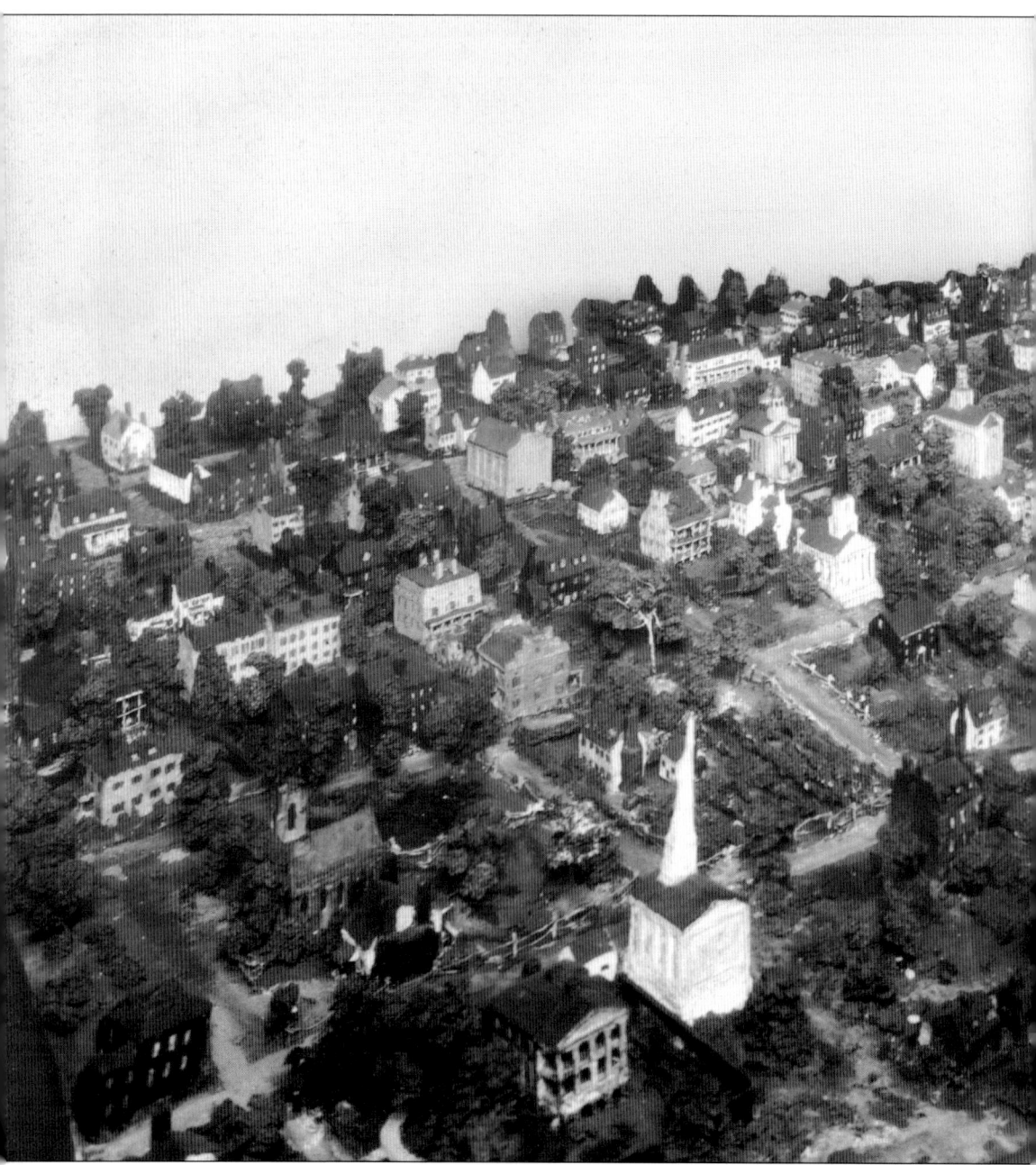

The Poe Museum's model of Poe's Richmond still fascinates visitors of all ages. It contains models of many of the buildings featured in this book, including the Virginia State Capitol, Monumental Church, St. John's Church, and Moldavia. This photograph was taken in 1927, shortly after the

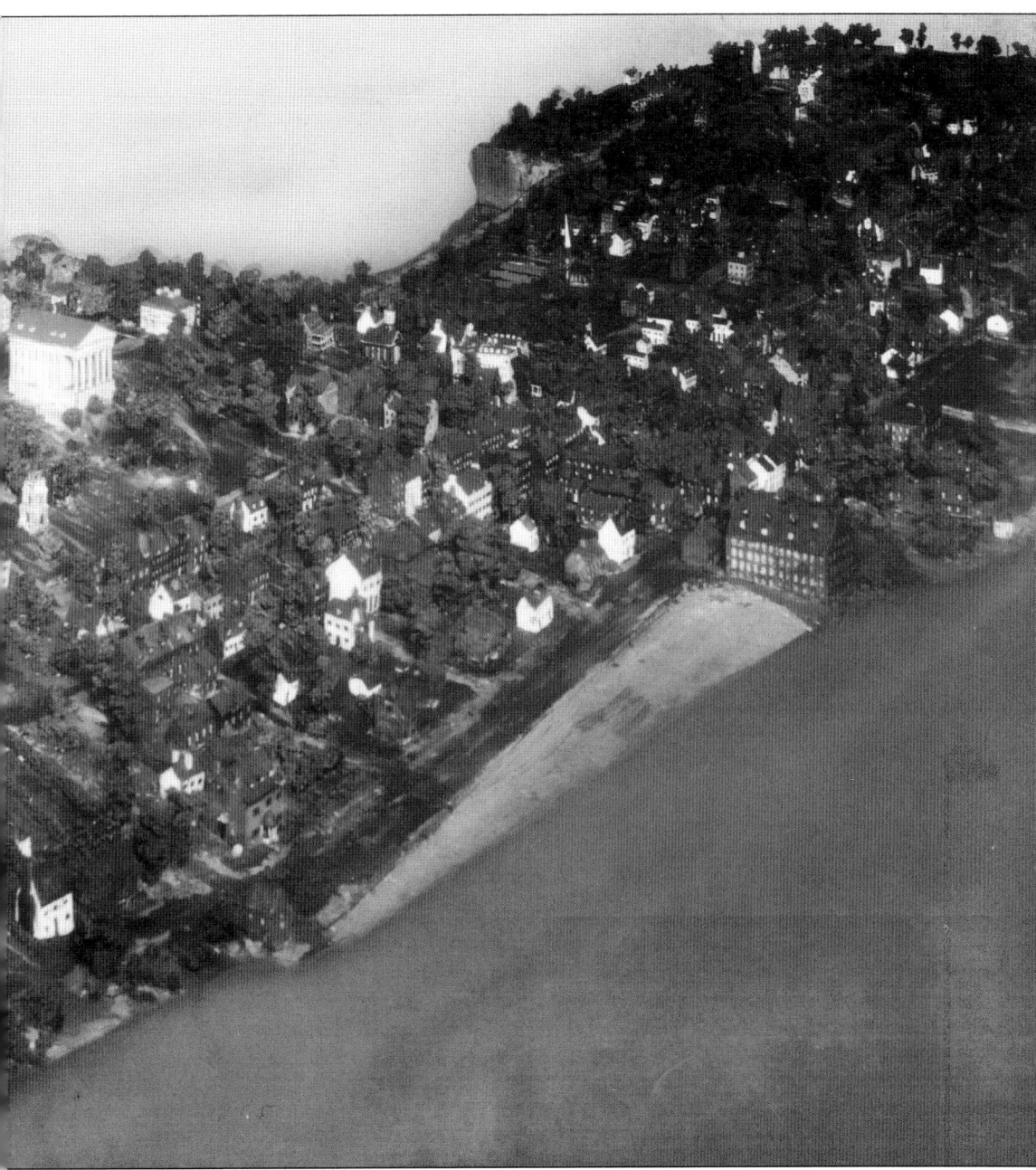

model's completion. It was restored in 1964 and in the 1980s. After the most recent cleaning in 2000, the model was installed in a new case. Now that so much of Poe's Richmond has vanished, this model allows viewers to imagine, if only for a moment, the city he would have seen.

BIBLIOGRAPHY

Bondurant, Agnes M. *Poe's Richmond*. Richmond: Reprinted by the Edgar Allan Poe Museum, 1999.

Dabney, Virginius. *Richmond: The Story of a City*. New York: Doubleday, 1976.

Deas, Michael J. *The Portraits and Daguerreotypes of Edgar Allan Poe*. Charlottesville: University Press of Virginia, 1988.

Jackson, David K. *Poe and the* Southern Literary Messenger. Richmond: The Dietz Press, 1934.

Kennedy, J. Gerald. *A Historical Guide to Edgar Allan Poe*. New York: Oxford University Press, 2001.

Mabbott, Thomas Ollive. *The Collected Works of Edgar Allan Poe*. Cambridge, MA: The Belknap Press of Harvard University Press, 1969.

Mordecai, Samuel F. *Richmond in By-Gone Days: Being Reminiscences of an Old Citizen*. Richmond: G. M. West, 1856.

Phillips, Mary. *Edgar Allan Poe: The Man*. Philadelphia: The John Winston Company, 1926.

Quinn, Arthur Hobson. *Edgar Allan Poe: A Critical Biography*. Baltimore: Johns Hopkins University Press, 1998.

Scott, Mary Wingfield. *Old Richmond Neighborhoods*. Richmond: William Byrd Press, 1950.

———. *Houses of Old Richmond*. New York: Bonanza Books, 1941.

Silverman, Kenneth. *Edgar Allan Poe: A Mournful and Never-Ending Remembrance*. New York: HarperCollins, 1991.

Thomas, Dwight, and David K. Jackson. *The Poe Log: A Documentary Life of Edgar Allan Poe, 1809–1849*. New York: G. K. Hall and Company, 1987.

ABOUT THE ORGANIZATION

Opened in 1922, the Edgar Allan Poe Museum in Richmond, Virginia, interprets the life and influence of Edgar Allan Poe for the education and enjoyment of the public. Located at 1914–1916 East Main Street in the heart of the city's Shockoe Bottom District, the museum possesses the world's finest collection of Poe artifacts and memorabilia, including Poe's boyhood bed and a lock of the poet's hair. In addition to guided and self-guided tours of its four-building complex, the Poe Museum hosts book signings, concerts, and performances in its Enchanted Garden. For more information about the Poe Museum or about joining the Poe Foundation, which supports the museum, please visit the Poe Museum Web site at www.poemuseum.org or call 888-21-EAPOE.

ACROSS AMERICA, PEOPLE ARE DISCOVERING SOMETHING WONDERFUL. THEIR HERITAGE.

Arcadia Publishing is the leading local history publisher in the United States. With more than 4,000 titles in print and hundreds of new titles released every year, Arcadia has extensive specialized experience chronicling the history of communities and celebrating America's hidden stories, bringing to life the people, places, and events from the past. To discover the history of other communities across the nation, please visit:

www.arcadiapublishing.com

Customized search tools allow you to find regional history books about the town where you grew up, the cities where your friends and family live, the town where your parents met, or even that retirement spot you've been dreaming about.

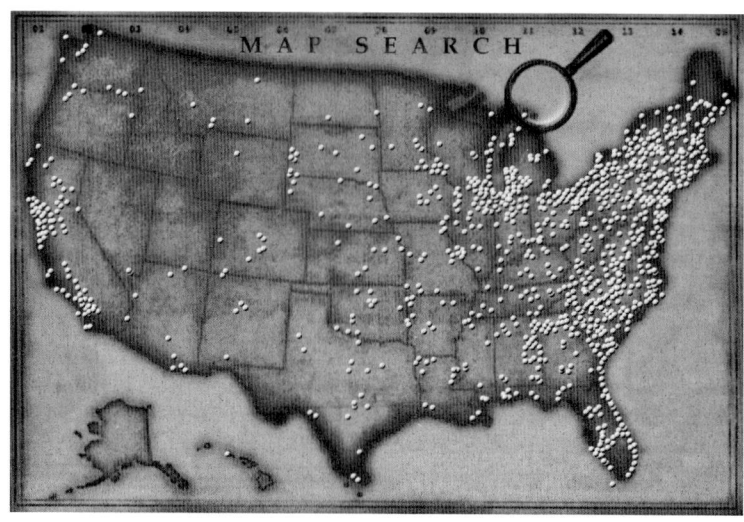